D1645134

The Regional Books Series

GENERAL EDITOR: BRIAN VESEY-FITZGERALD, F.L.S.

THE VALE OF PEWSEY

THE REGIONAL BOOKS SERIES

Edited by BRIAN VESEY-FITZGERALD, F.L.S.

THE Regional Books *deal in the fullest manner with certain highly individual and remarkable areas of Britain. In every instance the Region itself is a clear-cut entity, with a marked individuality of its own.*

The following volumes have been published or are in preparation.

Black Country .	Phil Drabble
Breckland	Olive Cook
The Broads	R. H. Mottram
The Channel Shore .	Aubrey de Selincourt
The Cotswolds	Edith Brill
Dartmoor	Hamlyn Parsons
Exmoor	Laurence Meynell
The Fens	Alan Bloom
Forest of Dean	F. W. Baty
Gower .	Olive Phillips
Holiday Lancashire .	Sydney Moorhouse
The Isle of Wight .	Monica Hutchings
The Mendips .	A. W. Coysh, Edmund J. Mason, and Vincent Waite
The Northern Marches	Cledwyn Hughes
Peakland	Crichton Porteous
Pembrokeshire National Park	R. M. Lockley
The Rhondda Valley	A. Trystan Edwards
Romney Marsh	Walter J. C. Murray
Salisbury Plain	Ralph Whitlock
The Scilly Isles	C. C. Vyvyan
Sedgemoor and Avalon	Desmond Hawkins
Solway Firth .	Brian Blake
The South Hams	Margaret Willy
The Southern Marches	H. J. Massingham
Suburban England	Jean Hadfield
Thames Estuary	William Addison
Torridon Highlands .	Brenda G. Macrow
The Vale of Berkeley	Lewis Wilshire
The Vale of Pewsey	H. W. Timperley
The Weald of Kent and Sussex .	Sheila Kaye-Smith
The Wessex Heathland	Ralph Wightman
The Wirral Peninsula	Norman Ellison

Other titles will be announced later.

PLEASE WRITE TO THE PUBLISHERS
FOR FULL DESCRIPTIVE PROSPECTUS

THE VALE OF PEWSEY

H. W. TIMPERLEY

ROBERT HALE LIMITED
63 Old Brompton Road, London S.W.7

First published 1954

MADE AND PRINTED IN GREAT BRITAIN BY
WILLIAM CLOWES AND SONS, LIMITED
LONDON AND BECCLES

CONTENTS

Chapter		page
I	THE VALE	1
II	ROADS	12
III	SWANBOROUGH TUMP	21
IV	THE CANNINGS VILLAGES	
	Bishop's Cannings	32
	All Cannings	40
V	ONE SOURCE OF THE AVON	49
VI	CURLEW ON CANNINGS MARSH	60
VII	TAN HILL	67
VIII	THREE SMALL CHURCHES	
	Manningford Bruce	79
	Alton Barnes	86
	Chirton	93
IX	MARDEN	101
X	AROUND BEECHINGSTOKE CLUMP	113
XI	WILSFORD	122
XII	THE CANAL	133
XIII	CHARLTON AND STEPHEN DUCK	147
XIV	SHARCOTT	158
XV	PEWSEY AND THE SOUTHEAST CORNER	165
XVI	WHITE HORSES	180
XVII	MARTINSELL	188
XVIII	WOOTTON RIVERS	199
XIX	SOME ANTIQUITIES	209
INDEX		225

TO ROBIN
Who sang on Wansdyke

ILLUSTRATIONS

1   Southward across the Vale of Pewsey   *frontispiece*

facing page

2   Adam's Grave on Walker's Hill   16

3   Harvest-time near Stanton St Bernard   17

4   Cottages at Woodborough   32

5   Picked Hill from Swanborough Tump   33

6   The Salisbury Plain skyline from Swanborough Tump   48

7   Horse-ploughing at All Cannings   49

8   Wansdyke   64

9   Manningford Bruce Church   65

10   Alton Barnes Church   80

11   Chirton Church   81

12   Marden Manor House   96

13   Beechingstoke Clump   97

14   A Corner of Wilsford   112

15   Kennet and Avon Canal above All Cannings   113

16   Kennet and Avon Canal near Bristow Bridge   128

17   Kennet and Avon Canal near Brimslade Farm   129

18   Charlton   144

19   Statue of King Alfred in Pewsey   145

20   In Milton Lilbourne   160

21   Thatch at Easton Royal   161

ILLUSTRATIONS

facing page

22 The Alton Barnes White Horse   176

23 The Pewsey White Horse   177

24 The Vale towards Martinsell   192

25 In Wootton Rivers   193

    Sketch Map of Area   *follows page* 220

*A sketch map is included at the end of the book,
but for more detailed information readers are
referred to the respective Ordnance Survey sheets.*

ACKNOWLEDGMENTS

*All the illustrations listed above are reproduced from photo-
graphs taken by Miss Monica Scott, Yeovil, Somerset.*

CHAPTER I

THE VALE

THE Vale of Pewsey runs from east to west among the downs in the very heart of Wiltshire. When you stand in the middle of the Vale you are about as far from the northern edge of the county as from the southern, which means that you will be approximately midway between Gloucestershire to the north and Hampshire and Dorset to the south. In the opposite directions, though, the symmetry is not quite kept, for the eastward line from the Vale to where Berkshire and Hampshire come together is only about half the length of the westward line to Somerset. To me the Vale of Pewsey is truly the heart of downland Wiltshire not merely because it happens to lie this or that number of miles inward from this or that point on the county border, but because when I am there I feel no separation between the spirit of this valley and the spirit of the downs, for the Vale belongs as much to them in feeling as it does in situation. Reaching away southward are the expanses of Salisbury Plain with more downs beyond, northward are the Marlborough Downs, and eastward more downs still. West is the direction in which the look and feel of downland are soonest left behind. Etchilhampton Hill, a smooth, easy swell of a little over 600 feet, stands isolated in the middle of the valley mouth, and within three miles the last downland skyline is behind, seen as the crest of a steep scarp rising from the clays in the valley of the Bristol Avon. On the other side of this valley are uplands of oolitic limestone—the hills around Bradford on Avon—but no more chalk downs.

The Vale of Pewsey is really a hanging valley, with a step down to the lower chalk between Etchilhampton Hill and Devizes and then the fall to the clay valley. The Kennet and Avon Canal needs a stairway of locks to reach it. The valley was formed by the erosive action of rain, frost and flowing water upon an upfold of chalk layers which were originally continuous with the present edges of the Marlborough Downs and Salisbury Plain and rose to the crown of an arch above what is now the valley. Like the chalk which still remains, this eroded arch lay upon a bed of the sands and sandstones known as Upper Greensand, and that bed upon another of Gault clay. The greensand and gault remain, but the chalk has gone. During the bending the layers of chalk were stretched and loosened in a way that left them with little resistance to the disintegrating action of rainwater and of uncountable freezings and thawings, those destructive alternations of temperature under which rock-held moisture can reduce its rock to fragments, even to powder. Drainage did the rest. The flow of streams in flood, fed by their networks of tributary rills, gradually carried away the friable chalk until none was left, except for that of Etchilhampton Hill in the west end of the valley and of two other little hills, Woodborough Hill and Picked Hill, outliers which stand side by side between Wilcot and the Alton villages. A geological arch became a geographical vale. The floor of the vale is the greensand that lay under the vanished chalk. The line of folding followed by the Pewsey arch or anticline has been traced from the Mendips through the Vale of Pewsey and along past Kingsclere in Hampshire to the Hog's Back in Surrey.

Two of the streams from the lost ridge, one from each end, gathered all the others into the volume of their flow until they came together at the middle of the southern base of the arch, there to scour and deepen an outlet through the chalk of Salisbury Plain, and flow on across the remainder of south Wiltshire and across Hampshire to reach the Channel. To the people of Celtic Britain the river was Avon, which means nothing but "river". The One-Inch Maps of the Ordnance Survey imply that it has a double source, for they give the name "Avon" to both the converging branches of the headwaters that join at Scales Bridge half a mile east of Rushall in the gap through which the main river then leaves the Vale. To reach this confluence the west branch comes winding diagonally across the valley from its source at Bourton under the downs at the northwest corner, with Bishop's Cannings close by and Horton about half a mile downstream, these three making a cluster of small places backed by the downs. The next villages along it are well across the valley towards the

2

Plain, a string of them—Chirton, Patney, Marden, Wilsford, Charlton and Rushall. The east branch winds counter-diagonally from near Wootton Rivers in the northeast corner of the Vale, with no village between Wootton Rivers and Pewsey, but after Pewsey a succession of places—Sharcott, Manningford Abbots, Manningford Bohune, Manningford Bruce and North Newnton.

The chalk from the upfold that was slowly denuded into this break between the Marlborough Downs and Salisbury Plain was river-borne miles away to the sea. Today the slightly undulating floor of the valley, tilted in a not very perceptible fall to the footslopes of the Plain, is still more than 300 feet above sea-level at the lowest part, which is, of course, the area opposite the gap the Avon breached in the Plain. The Vale gives no impression of being overpoweringly shut in by the downs, of being sunk between and overhung by the flanking ridges in any part of its twelve miles from Etchilhampton Hill to Burbage. Indeed, the downs seem to lie back and keep it open, with the curves of great concavities sweeping up and round between correspondingly massive shoulders of down in a sequence of bay and headland along valley-sides rising to ridges that, when seen from the valley or when you walk them, surprise by the levelness of their flow. There are many steeps in the hollows and down the shoulders, but most of them ease into long footslopes that die away gently in merging with the valley bottom. The valley widens gradually from east to west between downland edges that are three miles apart at Wootton Rivers and nearly six at Etchilhampton. It is a natural channel of communication joining east Wiltshire and the Kennet valley east of Hungerford to the regions west of the downs. A deserted waterway, the Kennet and Avon Canal connecting the Kennet at Newbury and the Bristol Avon at Bath, and a railway, a branch of the old Great Western from London to the West Country, follow the length of the Pewsey Vale. Canal and railway enter together at the east end but at Pewsey are half a mile apart, the canal lying nearer to the footslopes of the northern downs. They continue to diverge until, in leaving the Vale, Etchilhampton Hill stands between them, with the canal passing to the north of it and the railway to the south.

At first sight the shape and build of Pewsey Vale suggest that its river should be winding along it from a source at the east end (which seems the natural valley head) and passing between Etchilhampton Hill and the edge of Salisbury Plain to join the Bristol Avon; but, as I have said, the drainage is all inward towards that surprising break in the Plain before which the twin source-branches of this other Avon, usually called the Salisbury Avon, combine their waters and flow south as one stream. The Vale thus became the gathering-ground of the headwaters of the Salisbury Avon, and no stream or brook finds another way out of it. Of the many tributary waters that have come together in the main river before it leaves the valley, only one is from a source under the edge of the Plain—the brook which rises just above Easton Royal, where the foot of the slope below the beeches of Easton Clump, seen high on the crest of the downs, reaches the end of the village. From Easton Clump to Urchfont Hill at the other end of the Vale this is the only one. And though the source-waters of this Avon spring and flow in Pewsey Vale, it is right that the Vale insists on a separate identity by taking its name from the village of Pewsey on the east branch of the stream, instead of obscuring the fact of its separate individuality by taking its name from the river and being known as only a part of the Avon valley. To think of it as that alone is so difficult as to seem unnatural, yet this is what Pewsey Vale was to crusader Cobbett when, on Monday, 28th August, 1826, he came riding "over the downs, in a northwesterly direction, in search of the source of the Avon river, which goes down to Salisbury". Reaching the edge of the Plain at the crest of the steep called Milton Hill, he saw the Vale open before him for the first time, "and a most beautiful sight it was!" But let us feel something of the gust of Cobbett's enthusiasm in the phrases it inspired. It is a well-known passage in *Rural Rides*, yet is still so vivid and true that I cannot resist the temptation to bring it in. Here it is:

"In steering across the down, I came to a large farm, which a shepherd told me was Milton Hill Farm. This was upon the high land, and before I came to the edge of this Valley of Avon. . . . The shepherd showed me the way towards Milton; and at the end of about a mile, from the top of a very high part of the down, with a steep slope towards the valley, I first saw this

4

Valley of Avon; and a most beautiful sight it was! Villages, hamlets, large farms, towers, steeples, fields, meadows, orchards, and very fine timber trees, scattered all over the valley. The shape of the thing is this: on each side downs, very lofty and steep in some places; but each out-side of the valley are downs. From the edge of the downs begin capital arable fields generally of very great dimensions, and, in some places, running a mile or two back into little cross-valleys, formed by hills of downs. After the corn-fields come meadows on each side, down to the brook or river. The farm-houses, mansions, villages, and hamlets are generally situated in that part of the arable land which comes nearest the meadows.

"Great as my expectations have been, they were more than fulfilled. I delight in this sort of country; and I had frequently seen the vale of the Itchen, that of the Bourn, and also that of the Teste in Hampshire; I had seen the vales amongst the South Downs; but I never before saw anything to please me like this valley of the Avon. I sat upon my horse and looked over Milton and Easton and Pewsey for half an hour, though I had not breakfasted. The hill was very steep. A road, going slanting down it, was so steep, and washed so very deep by the rains of ages, that I did not attempt to ride down it, and I did not like to lead my horse, the path was so narrow. So seeing a boy with a drove of pigs going out to the stubbles, I beckoned him to come up to me; and he came and led my horse down for me. . . . Endless is the variety in the shape of the high lands which form this valley. Sometimes the slope is very gentle, and the arable lands go back very far. At others, the downs come out into the valley almost like piers into the sea, being very steep in their sides, as well as their ends towards the valley. They have no slope at their other ends: indeed they have no back ends, but run into the main high land. There is also great variety in the width of the valley; great variety in the width of the meadows; but the land appears to be all of the very best; and it must be so, for the farmers confess it."

There is no doubt about it, the eastern half of Pewsey Vale gave as much pleasure to Cobbett the enjoyer of natural landscape as to

Cobbett the critical farmer on that morning at the end of August a century and a half ago. There is no doubt, too, that his was the right kind of approach for a first view of the Vale. Over the downs is the way, either from the north or south, so that the moment comes when a skyline ahead turns out to be the edge from which the valley is revealed, the more suddenly the better. I have always been sorry that my first view, now more than twenty years in the past, was from just inside the western end after coming by train from a distant county to Devizes and then being taken by car to Coate, near Bishop's Cannings, where I was to stay for a few weeks one summer. I did not begin to find out what the Vale looked like as a whole for several days, not until I walked the three miles or so to Clifford's Hill, a shoulder thrust from the northern edge of the downs, and from the banks of Rybury Camp on the hilltop saw the length and width of the valley all open below me. After that, on days when I came back to Coate over the downs from Avebury and Silbury Hill and East Kennett village and long barrow, there was always the moment to look forward to when, Wansdyke crossed, the downs fell away from the crest overlooking the Vale. The approach from the Kennet valley is always upward, a rise of three miles that begins gently and swings up to its steepest in lifting to Wansdyke and the last crest. Another revealing place was a later discovery, and I have still to find a better. The Ridgeway, coming south from Hackpen Hill and the Kennet crossing to reach Salisbury Plain, leads to it, as does a surfaced byway from Clatford in the Kennet valley after being joined by roads from three other Kennet valley villages— Lockeridge, Overton and East Kennett. The turf track and the metalled road are both heading for the same place on the edge of the downs along Pewsey Vale. They meet and join to go through the airy gap separating Walker's Hill and Knap Hill. This is their gateway to the Vale. Until the road is between the hills the Vale is hidden—and then it is there, more and more of it, as the gap ends and on each hand the two hills fall into line as the nearest slopes in the flowing recession of a long valley-side.

On a day towards the end of March I walked up the road from Lockeridge to the edge of the downs between Knap Hill and Walker's Hill to renew the pleasure of seeing again the sudden

unfolding of Pewsey Vale there, and to refresh my memories of
the approach. The road follows the gradually ascending bottom
of a shallow hollow, and when it has cut the massive bank of
Wansdyke, here not open and turf-covered but overgrown by
beeches, the two hills on the downland skyline are about a mile
ahead. The Wansdyke beeches were noisy with a brisk northwest
breeze and the cawing of rooks about their nests in the treetops,
the clamour of the rooks diminishingly carried away when the
stronger gusts of the fluctuating breeze surged and roared through
the bare boughs. It was a day of lark-song and sunshine as well,
under a sky loosely spread with steadily drifting, linked-up clouds
of all sizes from small, ragged wisps to broad, fleecy-edged expanses, cold grey where the sun did not reach them, but gleam-
ingly white, either all through their fleecy texture or else at their
billowing edges, where it did; and among them were ever-
changing glimpses of blue, deepest in the heights away from the
early afternoon sun, but paler with the lustre of sunlight on it the
nearer the blue was to the sun's part of the sky.

After cutting Wansdyke the road is almost level, its hollow
widening and dying away into other slopes that lift to the sky
above the hidden Vale. This was the direction of the cloud-
shadows, their southeasterly drift taking them a little aslant but
always up to the sky-crest in front. I sat on a sarsen stone at the
roadside to watch the drift of cloud overhead and its dark counter-
part on the ground. On the turf the shadows made a continuous
change from dull olive green to brighter green tinged with the
parched brown of last year's dead growth under which the new
green was springing, and then back again in the endless alternation of sun and shadow. When the shadows rose to the skyline
and vanished it was as though they had gone back to the sky.

I went on and the two hills were soon very near, the gap between them widening. Knap Hill stood against the sky on the left,
a rather flattened dome of down with the very much time-
smoothed traces of its neolithic ditch and bank ringing the hilltop
plateau that curves into view above the earthwork. On the right
of the gap the east slope of Walker's Hill swings down to a bank
along the road's verge. Both hills are about the same height, and
if no prehistoric camp encloses the top of Walker's Hill the

remains of other neolithic handiwork are there all the same. The summit is peaked by the mound of a huge long barrow which, caught sideways, has the look of some bison-like monster crouching head down on the hilltop. Known as Adam's Grave or Adam's Peak, it is a familiar landmark from the Vale, and it was the place I had chosen to be that day's lookout from the edge of the downs.

In its March bareness, which is not the same as midwinter bareness, the valley could not have been more clearly revealed. The slow movement of cloud-shadows, rather smudgily margined, filled the valley bottom with a soft dapple of sunlight and shade from end to end. Just below me, along the footslopes of the downs, were cornfields that had a downland look because of their size and the absence of hedgerows. Field after field, pale brown in the sun, darker and colder in the cloud-shadows, were now thinly misted with the clear green of springing corn-blades, a bare field here and there among them making the drifts of tender green more definite. Beyond this open cornland the middle of the Vale was darkened by the many elms and the small woods and copses that mark the change from chalky soils to those on the greensand. The tree darkness was not that of winter boughs but the brown and red and purple-tinged bloom the sun reveals on bud-scales when the buds they protect are swelling. The richest tones of this bloom were on the elms, for they were flowering; and as there were still no newly-broken bud-points to spangle and mist them with pale green, the elms were tinged deeply with a purplish red no brighter than a dusky flush, even in the sun. I caught glimpses of other cornfields among the trees, but there were more meadows and pastures among them than under the downs. Here, too, just within the fringe of this tree-belt along the middle width of the valley, are some of the Vale's farmhouses and villages, the nearest being the twin Altons—Priors and Barnes— a loose grouping of farmhouses and cottages round their churches among the elms where the last vestiges of the Ridgeway can be traced before the ancient track is lost after descending from the downs to cross the valley. At the other side of the Vale, as on this side, there is open cornland on the footslopes of the downs beyond the elms and the hedged fields. From my lookout on Adam's

Grave I could see, nearly five miles away, these barer fields as a background to the farthest elm-tops, and see the steepening of the slopes lifting from them to the edge of Salisbury Plain. The Vale of Pewsey lay open before me under the sunny cloud-play of this March sky. The only hidden part was the continuation of the valley-side eastward from Martinsell: this great bluff was thrust up too high and out too far to let the edge of the valley from it to the southern end of Savernake Forest be seen. In that direction from Walker's Hill the flow of the scarp, its sweeping hollows and smooth shoulders, led from one high place to another above the Vale—Knap Hill, Golden Ball Hill, Draycott Hill, Huish Hill, Oare Hill, with Martinsell completing the chain; and in the opposite direction Milk Hill, Tan Hill, Clifford's Hill, Easton Hill and then, though outside the Vale, Roundway Hill holding its beech clump above Devizes. On the far side of the Vale the edge of the Plain was only a little less clear, its flow another succession of hill names from Urchfont Hill and beech clump in the west to Wilsford Hill, Cleeve Hill and Rushall Hill above the Avon gap, then Upavon Hill, Pewsey Hill, Milton Hill and, at the east end of the Vale now, the other Easton Hill distinguished by its beech clump, and miles on beyond the Vale a level sky-silhouetted ridge ending at the blunt northward fall of Berkshire's Inkpen Hill.

It was a long sweep to bring the eye back to the other end of the Vale where, opposite Urchfont Hill, the low, smooth tilt of Etchilhampton Hill to its rounded apex was brightening and darkening under the drift of cloud-shadows. In front of me, about a mile from the foot of the downs and a little to the left of the Alton villages, were Woodborough Hill with its even top and Picked Hill that is as pointed as its name implies. I could see clearly how the footslopes of Knap Hill, instead of dying into the valley, gently rise again to the green ridge on which the tops of these two outlying hills are the highest parts. Both are under 700 feet. In going about Pewsey Vale one soon begins to feel like waving to them as old familiars whenever they come into view, especially to Picked Hill.

After this wide visual ranging from Adam's Grave I found myself delighting in the unexpectedly discovered beauty of a flowering plant so miniature that the great mound of the barrow, at the base of which it was growing, seemed a mountain. A turf-covered anthill near my feet drew my attention because of a kind of hoary whiteness on its dark green. I bent down for a closer look and the discovery was made—spring whitlow grass was in flower. In spite of its name it is not a grass, nor is it an uncommon plant, but one whose early flowering on exposed chalk and limestone heights makes the discovery that it is out again a surprise, even when it has been sought. The closer look changed the hoariness into thin drifts of tiny flowers, white and starry, loosely clustered in threes and fours at the tips of fine though sturdily upstanding stems less than an inch tall, each rising from a tight rosette of lance-shaped, dark-green leaves. Leaf, stem and flower were perfectly proportioned to the plant's miniature scale. There must have been about two hundred of the plants crowded together on the anthill: it was their rosettes of root-leaves which made the little mound look so green where most of the new green of the hillside turf surrounding it was yet under the bleached, winter-stricken tangles of last year's herbage. The wind, suddenly freshening, brought steely-blue cloud and a stinging hail-squall from the northwest and gave what was to me a new setting for the March flowering of this tiny plant.

There were three of these flowery anthills at the barrow's eastern base. Having all my attention on them, and with the barrow's curving bulk hiding the northwestern sky, I was slow in noticing that the sun-holding fleeces overhead were being followed by a wide bank of blue-grey cloud which, as it rose, quenched the sunlight on the downs below it in grey obscurity of filmy vapour that seemed to be both hanging and streaming from it. A flurry of hail pellets, some of which clung to my coat as firmly as goose-grass cleavers, caused me to look up and then to the top of the barrow to bring more of the windward sky into view. That was when I saw the storm-cloud. Whilst I stood watching it the scatterings of hail grew into the streaming slant of a squall driving across the downs behind Walker's Hill and just coming to the edge of the Vale. There was cold greyness in it but no gloom. The sunlight dwindled before it, but on each side of it the sky always remained sunny, these parts of the valley still a dapple of sun and cloud-shadow seen dimly through curtains of hail. This outside brightness was reflected by the hail as a subdued greyish-white glow. By the time the front of the squall was greying the edge of the Plain round about Easton Clump its tail had cleared Walker's Hill, and soon the whitlow grass, Adam's Grave and all the Vale of Pewsey were in the sun again.

It is today no less an agricultural valley than it was in Cobbett's time. Corn, cattle, milk and sheep are its chief concern, though there are fewer sheepfolds on its downs than there used to be before the last Tan Hill Fair was held twenty years ago. At Woodborough, in the middle of the valley, the fields of a bulb farm are full of the colour of tulips and irises in early summer. So far the Vale has been left almost undisfigured by the encroachment of military camps. Just outside its west end, along the road between Bishop's Cannings and Devizes Barracks, there is a large camp, but inside the Vale the only thing of this kind is a small establishment of the Ministry of Supply at Alton Barnes. All the same, there are times when we are reminded a little too audibly that this is a valley at the edge of Salisbury Plain.

Chapter II

ROADS

PEWSEY VALE has a network of roads, most of them twisty, angular byways linking the villages by fitting as best they may into another network, that of the two branches of the Avon and their tributary brooks. I shall never attempt to count the little bridges along their windings. There are several cross-valley roads, two coming south from the Kennet valley to the crest of the northern scarp and there finding a way down. One of the latter begins as a delta of lanes leading from the Bath road and the half-dozen riverside villages west of Marlborough and drops into the Vale between Knap Hill and Walker's Hill. As it clears the two hills its open fall to Alton Barnes at the foot of the scarp exposes the valley under it, and beyond the valley the Plain is a wide and far recession of downland waves into southern distances. From Alton Barnes it goes on, more like a wavering lane than a marching highway, to Woodborough, North Newnton and Upavon, where it enters the cleft in the Plain by which it and the Avon leave the Vale.

The second of these two cross-valley roads comes from Marlborough to reach the edge of the Vale at the top of Oare Hill not quite three miles east of the first road's descent to Alton Barnes. Its long fall to Oare at the foot of the hill begins in too deep a chalk-cutting and then continues under the boughs of too many trees to have the valley wide open before it; but its descent follows the lip of Rainscombe, so to hold the eye instead there is the great hollow scooped in the west side of Martinsell, with Rainscombe House and its timbered parkland in the bottom. Going on across the Vale from Oare, it bridges the Avon on the southern outskirts of Pewsey and then turns southwest to run for three level, airy miles between river and Plain and past the riverside cluster of the Manningfords—Abbots, Bohune, Bruce—before joining the other road in following the Avon valley through the Plain to

Salisbury. It is much the busier of these two cross-valley roads—
by traffic a main road, yet by appearance hardly a broad highway
until it has left Pewsey behind.

Another road crosses the Vale's west end, in fact it could not be
much farther west and remain within, which it does by keeping
inside Etchilhampton Hill. It comes over the downs from Calne
and drops into the Vale above Bishop's Cannings where the road
from Devizes to Beckhampton touches the scarp-crest, so that its
fall to the valley begins where it crosses this main road. It is a byway descending a much diminished valley-side: its short, almost
gentle slant to Bishop's Cannings church is very different from
the long, swinging curve of the fall to Alton Barnes under
Walker's Hill, or the shady steep that lips Rainscombe in falling
to Oare. It has an end-of-the-valley look. After Bishop's Cannings
it is a lane that suddenly goes rigid in a left turn to cross the canal's
Horton Bridge and a quick right turn back to its line again, and
then winds and wavers to Coate and Etchilhampton with—
between these two villages—a glimpse of Woodborough and
Picked Hills away back in the Vale as it rises over the inner end of
Etchilhampton Hill; and when, almost half a mile past Etchilhampton village, it sidles into the Devizes road near Stert, I am
always a little surprised at finding myself there and never quite
sure whether it leaves me just within the Vale or just without.

There are two direct roads along the Vale, "shelf" roads under
the escarpments. In calling them shelf roads I mean that they run
within the lower margin of the gently shelving footslopes into
which the steeps of the escarpments subside along the greensand
of the valley floor. This is the drier ground just above the spring
line, a natural shelf giving the two roads a downland openness
between the bare scarps and the elm-fringed, brook-threaded
fields farther within the Vale. Traced from west to east they come
to the Vale divergently from Devizes. One, the quieter, branches
from the Devizes–Beckhampton highway about a mile and a
quarter out of Devizes to follow the foot of the northern scarp
until, drawn away from it by the needs of Pewsey, a southeasterly
slant through Wilcot swings it across the Vale in the direction of
Pewsey and the Plain. East of Pewsey it is the way to Hungerford
in the Kennet valley, its first three miles taking it to Burbage at

the end of the Vale. The other road, the Andover road from Devizes, follows the foot of the Salisbury Plain escarpment eastward from Wedhampton to the Avon gap, which it reaches at Rushall and crosses at Upavon before rising from the river to become a downland road over the eastern part of the Plain. As far as the gap it is mostly a treeless highway shelved in the lower spaciousness of the chalk footslopes that fall gently between the steeper slopes of the scarp and the brookland of the valley bottom. It is a main road, but even under today's burden of traffic often lies empty through long intervals of quietness

> "Hushing the roar of towns
> And their brief multitude,"

though it must be said that there are days when the quietness here in the Vale has for background the concussions and reverberations of gunfire and bombing within the Plain's forbidden solitudes. For the four miles of its course along the Vale the road does not pass through but keeps a little above the evenly spaced succession of villages below the Plain, and the villages—Wedhampton, Chirton, Marden, Wilsford, Charlton—stand between it and the young river, the Avon's west branch which, fringed and overhung by many poplars and willows, winds in secret unobtrusiveness near them, giving them less and less room the closer it comes to the gap through which, after joining the east branch at Scales Bridge, it leaves the Vale.

It is noticeable that the cross-valley roads pass through most of the villages along them, whilst we must turn aside from the scarpfoot roads to come to their villages. Marden and Wilsford, for example, are almost half a mile from the highway under the Plain, Bishop's Cannings about the same distance from the other road, although the rest are not quite as far back as that. These valley-side roads were sited for firm dryness, their villages for wells that were not likely to dry up. West of Pewsey the villages they pass lie a little below them, closer, that is, to the last of the chalk, an exception being Bishop's Cannings; east of Pewsey they lie on the downland side of the Burbage road, for Southcott, Fyfield, Milton Lilbourne and Easton Royal find water between it and the Plain.

The remaining byways thread the Vale's quietest corners as if there were no other world to draw them on beyond. They are the kind along which the span from a village just left behind to the next ahead can seem world enough, especially if the distant thudding and hollow reverberation of gunfire and bombing and the drone of aircraft are sounding from the interior of the Plain. In this they are all alike, but they have their differences as well. Those around Wootton Rivers in the somewhat humpily broken ground below the diminished scarp from the Martinsell heights to the southern edge of Savernake Forest give the impression of having been secreted between the high-banked hedges along their narrow windings. On the other side of Pewsey those among which the Manningford villages lie as if meshed in a cast net have a less secret air, but here the marshy fields through which the Avon winds between the willows, alders and poplars on its banks, and the lesser watercourses and the close succession of wood, and copse, allow them little openness and no directness in reaching bridge and village. Farther west, between Woodborough and All Cannings, the Vale is more broadly undulatory. Here the byways expand into a larger mesh as the villages they link are a little more widely spaced. The fields are larger, copses are infrequent among them, and except about the villages there are fewer trees. Any rise in a road may edge one side of the Vale with a downland skyline, if not both. Here the undulatory northward swell of the valley bottom from the river keeps the roads more open, but they are always quiet byways.

Yet I must not imply that all these byways begin and end in the Vale—many have extensions to and over the downs, tracks which can often be picked out easily enough as white streaks curving and slanting up the scarp and vanishing over the crest opposite the village from which they have climbed. Most of the Vale parishes are long and narrow, with one end in the valley and the other on the downs, thus giving their farms downland as well as valley acres, an arrangement that goes back to the Saxon settlement of the Vale. Their villages lie along the spring-lines below the scarps, and sometimes, as with those under the Plain west of Pewsey, close to river water too. So we often find that a village street becomes another way out of the Vale, one that changes at the scarp-foot to a white-rutted track which may take us not only to the scarp-crest and then, smoother and greener, across a down with the same name as the parish and its village, but on over the downs beyond to a village in another valley.

There is one derelict, scarp-climbing track with a name I first heard at Alton Priors, the village opposite Knap Hill. The road from Pewsey to Wilcot and the two Altons heads northwest towards the escarpment on a line that would, if kept, take it slantingly up the steepening of the slope under Knap Hill to the pass between this hill and Walker's Hill; but when it is about to go between outlying Picked Hill and the downs it forks, the lower branch to the Altons, the upper keeping the original line and changing at once to the track that is Workway Drove. It is hedged across the half-mile or so of cornland to the scarp-foot, its rutted width tangled with herbage and, in some places, with thorns and other bushes springing into thickets between its hedges. At Knap Hill it slants up the slope as a deepening groove in the chalk, narrower there and still rough, but gradually shallowing again towards the brow of its rise. From this it runs almost level in passing beside the mounds of two barrows to cross the Lockeridge road and Ridgeway in going on to meet Wansdyke at Milk Hill.

"Why Workway?" I wondered, and once again found myself turning the pages of *The Place-Names of Wiltshire* in the hope of discovering something in a name. There I went from eighteenth-century *Workway* to fifteenth-century *Warkweye* and finally to thirteenth-century *Warckweye* and *Warckewee*, with a derivation from Saxon *weorc-weg*, the way or road by the stronghold, the stronghold here being the camp on top of Knap Hill. This, from the learned in these matters, seemed convincing enough—until I chanced on a reference to the name of the track in *Wiltshire Notes and Queries*. Here it was mentioned that an old shepherd had been heard to call it Walcway, not Workway, this being used in support of the suggestion that Workway and Walcway were both corruptions of *Weal-a-wege* or Welshway, the Anglo-Saxon name for a British road, for to the Saxon the conquered Britons were, derogatively, the Welsh or serfs. A vivid memory of Workway Drove takes me back to a sunny break between the showers of an

16

afternoon in early spring, when its inner bank under Knap was blue with violets among the sparkle of raindrops, its hedges down in the cornfields glowingly stained with the deep red of the dog-wood's bare twigs, and its valley end filled with a small camp of gypsies—horses, a van and cart, men, women and children and dogs—through which I had to pass on my way home.

Today the footpaths in the Vale, like those everywhere else, are not as they used to be. Ploughing has obliterated some of them, stiles have gone or are wired up, and many a formerly well-trodden path is vanishing or becoming impassably overgrown through disuse. Disuse is, I think, the chief cause of their dis-appearance, for they were, after all, the result of local needs in the days before bicycle, motor-cycle and bus had so greatly dimin-ished the necessity for most countryfolk to be walkers in going about the parish or from village to village. Footpaths are distance-savers in cutting off the corners and windings of roads; it is easier now to cycle or else wait for the next bus. But there are still foot-paths to be followed in the Vale, even one or two with finger-posts to take the place of Edward Thomas's Lob in saying

"Nobody can't stop'ee. It's
A footpath, right enough."

When asking village people about the line of this or that footpath I have usually found them sorry to see their fieldways becoming lost. "Nobody uses them nowadays", is what I am told.

Richard Jefferies was always for getting over a stile—too often today the trouble is that all traces of the footpath beyond have vanished, and those who venture may find themselves pioneering apprehensively through a growing crop. A recent experience in the Vale illustrates what I have in mind. With a friend I stood at a point in a lane where a path across a field should have come to it. Map in hand, we were looking for a stile, or the remains of one, in the hedge. We could find none. The farmer happened to come along the lane and seemed interested in our map-reading. When we explained what we were looking for he said, "I thought so", and added, "The path should run from here in the hedge right across my corn to those red roofs over there, and if anyone likes to walk it I can't stop him." This reminded me of my boyhood in

2* 17

Harvest-time near Stanton St Bernard

another county and—so it seems now—in another world, for the
time was before 1914. I recalled a footpath that was never spared
when its field was ploughed; but very soon, sometimes before
the ploughing was finished, the first line of human footprints
made a diagonal across the furrows from stile to stile. The land
was clay, stickily clarty in a wet season, yet each year, at ploughing
time, the reclaimers of this short cut to a village put up with its
heavy going rather than follow the very roundabout firmness of
the road.

Dotted about within the Vale are short lengths of green tracks
or droves, some of which, as far as can be made out from their
appearance today, seem always to have been cart-ways ending in
the fields, often firm tracks into marshy, brook-threaded land like
that in the Vale's west end. Others, such as the quarter-mile across
the angle of the two roads converging on Pewsey north of Sharcott, are obviously unneeded bits of old roads abandoned to
greenness when the other parts were first macadamised. But the
most puzzling old road in the Vale is the Ridgeway, that main
member of the great trackway system of pre-Roman antiquity
which carries the imagination in spacious sweep along the chalk
ridges from East Anglia to Dorset and on beyond the chalk to the
mouth of the Devonshire Axe, with the banks and ditches of
camp after camp and the mounds of many a barrow on the high
places along it, and the Stones of Avebury in sight below it where,
Chiltern chalk, Thames Gap, White Horse of Uffington, and
Wayland's Smithy miles behind, it follows the long fall from the
Hackpen ridge to the Kennet valley and then lifts to the downs
again and cuts Wansdyke in coming to Walker's Hill at the edge
of Pewsey Vale. From there, with the long barrow called Adam's
Grave on the right and Knap Hill's neolithic camp on the left, it
can be traced leading from today's road as a rough, deeply sunken
groove, tangled with vegetation, down the scarp to Alton Priors,
but after that not at all as a green road until, the Vale crossed, it
mounts the scarp of the Plain where the earthworks of Broadbury
Banks overlook Wilsford and is back in its own downland world
and on its way to the southwest by St Joan à Gores and Imber the
lost.

The name "Walker's Hill", like the name "Workway Drove",

may not be what it seems. It may have little to do with Walker as a surname but much to do with the Ridgeway. *The Place-Names of Wiltshire* traces the name no farther back than 1773, to the Andrews and Dury *Topographical Map of Wiltshire*, and states that the property passed by marriage to a Clement Walker who died in 1801. But calling the hill Walker's Hill may really be another way of naming it Welshway Hill, as, to the Saxons, the green road we call the Ridgeway must have been another *Weal-a-wege* or Welshway.

The hard road that descends to the Vale under Adam's Grave on Walker's Hill touches the west side of Alton Barnes on its way to bridge the canal at Honey Street and then to skirt Woodborough in crossing the Vale. Alton Barnes stands between the road and Alton Priors, though these two little places are so close together as to seem one. The Ridgeway, after grooving the slope below the road, is still faintly traceable through Alton Priors, east of the church, and the older One-Inch Maps of the Ordnance Survey even continue it a short distance beyond the village, cutting it off before it reaches the canal. A line continuing this abrupt ending would join the Woodborough road at the bend after Honey Street Farm about a quarter of a mile south of the canal bridge. According to *The Place-Names of Wiltshire* Honey Street was "a name given to the Ridgeway as it crosses Pewsey Vale. Probably so called because it was a muddy road." Yes, in winter at any rate, an earth road would be muddy enough for that at the Alton villages, the Alton of their names coming from Saxon *æwielletun*, the farm where the springs rise.

For the next mile or so from Honey Street Farm to Broad Street there seems to be no alternative to the line of today's road, but after Broad Street the mile and a half to Wilsford, with the river just in front of this village and the Plain rising behind, brings up the question: where did the Ridgeway in arriving at Broadbury Banks cross the Avon at Wilsford? It could have followed the course of the present road from Broad Street to the cross-road to North Newnton and on beyond this for the further quarter-mile that is aligned on the east end of Wilsford before it swerves away to come to Cuttenham Farm east of the village, the Ridgeway not swinging with this bend but keeping the alignment that would bring it to a ford which still exists beside a bridge near Wilsford church. Or the Ridgeway may have come to the village's name-ford—*Wifel's ford*—which *The Place-Names of Wiltshire* locates "at the northeast corner of the parish where Beechingstoke and North Newnton meet Wilsford". This is opposite the other or west end of the village, where today there is an old bridge between it and Puck Shipton at the north edge of the river's flood-plain. It seems a likely place for the crossing. To reach it the Ridgeway would have diverged from the line of the present road at Broad Street, on the right about two hundred yards before the left-hand turning to Bottlesford, where the One-Inch map shows a footpath along the boundary between North Newnton and Beechingstoke par-ishes leading almost straight to the river and the bridge. The path has the look of a much diminished trackway. In about a quarter of a mile it crosses the lane leading to the Beechingstoke Clump and then tunnels into the shade of tall trees hiding it. I have not been able to recognise the remains of a ford where it comes to the river, but, as I have said, there is an old bridge, and from it a wagon-track runs open across a riverside pasture and enters the west end of Wilsford between hedges. After that the Broadbury Banks earthwork is straight ahead on the skyline of the Plain. Yet there is, of course, always the probability that the Ridgeway divided into several seasonal tracks in crossing the Vale.

CHAPTER III

SWANBOROUGH TUMP

A TUMP is a little hillock or a barrow mound. About two-thirds of the distance along the road from Pewsey to Woodborough the inconspicuous remains of what looks like a round barrow, with three tall ash trees growing on it, are in the wayside corner of a field where it adjoins the coppice called Frith Wood. The mound is Swanborough Tump, the trees are Swanborough Ashes. In monastic records of the tenth century the mound is named *Swanabeorgh*, which means "the barrow of the swains or peasants". There is no village of Swanborough in Pewsey Vale, but in Saxon times the part of the Vale round about the tump was Swanborough Hundred, the Saxon "Hundreds" being originally land divisions, each the area in which a hundred invaders had set up their households during the conquest of Britain. Domesday Book names this one as Swaneberga Hundred. In each there was a recognised place at which the "Hundred-moot" or council of the district assembled when called together. For Swanborough Hundred the meeting-place was this mound.

From the road today the three ash trees rising up behind the hedge and just outside the wood are much more noticeable than the mound. Cattle have not only trampled it almost bare of turf, but their hooves have broken and eroded its surface more deeply, until it is now only a slight swell in the corner of the field. And yet it remains a place on which we can stand and look back into the Wessex of Alfred the Great, to a time when the Saxon conquerors of the Roman British were, in their turn, facing the threat of conquest by the Danes. The Vale of Pewsey lay towards the middle of the West Saxon kingdom. Some of Alfred's own lands were in this part of the Vale. Wessex was hard-pressed indeed, the Athelney twilight ahead, when Alfred, writing down his forebodings in his famous will, brought Swanborough Tump into history. I quote a passage from the will as translated by F. E.

21

Harmer in *Select English Historical Documents of the Ninth and Tenth Centuries*. It runs:

"But it came to pass that we were all harassed with the heathen invasion; then we discussed our children's future—how they would need some maintenance, whatever might happen to us through these disasters. When we were assembled at *Swanborough* we agreed, with the cognisance of the West Saxon Council, that whichever of us survived the other was to give to the other's children the lands which we had ourselves acquired and the lands which King Ethelwulf gave us. . . ."

Yet it was not until about 1890 that the meeting-place mentioned in the will was definitely identified—by the Rev. H. G. Tomkins —as the almost obliterated mound called Swanborough Tump.

Before the winter of 850–51 the Danes were summer raiders of the English North Sea and Channel coasts, but in that winter an army remained in the Isle of Thanet in Kent. The raiders were becoming invaders. Ethelwulf, King of Wessex, opposed them. The Anglo-Saxon Chronicle tells us that in 851 "King Ethelwulf, and his son Ethelbald, with the army of the West Saxons, fought against them at Acklea [probably in Surrey] and there made the greatest slaughter among the Heathen host that ever was heard tell of, and there won the day." So were the invaders halted on the eastern fringe of Wessex; and except for a raid on Winchester from the south coast in 860 they got no farther into Wessex until, fifteen years after Acklea, they took East Anglia. The Chronicle records that in 866 "came there into Angle-kin Heathen host and wintered among the East Angles. And there they were horsed. And the East Angles made peace with them." The Danes knew that England would never be theirs until Wessex, its best-defended and best-ruled kingdom, had been mastered. So in the December of 871 they followed the Icknield Way along the chalk from East Anglia to Wessex and occupied Reading, making it into a stronghold from which the heart of Wessex could be assailed. King Ethelwulf, Alfred's father, had been dead fifteen years then, and two of Alfred's elder brothers had also ruled and died. A third elder brother, Ethelred, was now king of the West Saxons, very ably seconded by Alfred. It was these two who agreed at Swanborough Tump "that whichever of us survived the other was to give to the other's children the lands which we had ourselves acquired and the lands which King Ethelwulf gave us".

From their base at Reading the invaders at once began to harry the countryside round about. The men of Berkshire encountered and defeated one band of raiders. A day or two later Ethelred and Alfred brought larger forces to attack the stronghold but lost a fiercely fought day and retired northwestward to the northern edge of the Berkshire downs close to where the turf-cut shape of the Uffington White Horse overlooks the valley to which it has given a name. The Danes came after them, and four days later, early in January, the battle of Ashdown was fought somewhere along that edge, round a "lone thorn tree", the one army "bent upon all mischief, the other to fight for life and land and dear ones". This time the West Saxons won, thus proving that the Danes, however successful as marauders, were not invincible in a pitched battle. They needed this proof afterwards, the memory of it to keep them tenaciously at the invader when, in "the year of battles" as the year 871 was called, they were losing fight after fight in their efforts to keep the Danes from thrusting farther and farther into Wessex. A fortnight after their victory at Ashdown the Saxons were defeated at Basing, near Basingstoke, and again in March at Meretune, a battle-site the historians have found very troublesome to identify. At one time it was thought to have been Marden, the Vale village three miles to the southwest of Swanborough Tump. A later identification made it Marten on the east side of Savernake Forest; but now it looks as if Marten will have to give way to Martin, a border village that was transferred from Wiltshire to Hampshire in 1895 and lies on the downs to the southwest of Salisbury. Such were the events during which the meeting of the West Saxon Council took place at Swanborough for the melancholy business mentioned in Alfred's will, though its exact date has not yet been determined. An April Easter followed, and with it came the news that Ethelred had died at Wimborne, probably of wounds suffered at Meretune. He left two young sons, but this was too dark a time for setting a child upon the throne of Wessex so Alfred was chosen to succeed his brother. King at twenty-two, Alfred found himself carrying the whole burden of leadership in scheming to save Wessex and Saxon England from the Danes.

Swanborough Tump is marked and named on recent editions of the Ordnance Survey maps but not on earlier editions. Not so long ago it was known to the older people in the Vale as Swanborough Ash or Swanborough Ashes, which suggests that at one time a tree stood alone where three stand today. It was "Ash" in 1764 when (to quote from a document printed in *Wiltshire Notes and Queries*, Vol. 2, 1896–98) the "Tithingman of Cheverell Parva in the said Hundred of Swanborough" was "required to be and appear before the said Steward at a Court Leet to be holden at Swanborough Ash . . . in and for the said Hundred on Monday the 15th day of this instant October by ten oclock in the forenoon of the same day. And pay to the said Steward your Law-day Silver for the said Tithing being £0 10s. 6d." Here is evidence that the spot was still used as a Hundred meeting-place in the eighteenth century, whilst its name in this document indicates that it had been known by its ash tree or trees for a long time.

As the Swanborough meeting of the West Saxon Council took place in spring I shall try to picture the Tump and its setting in the Vale as I have found them at this season, though not because of that alone. For even if the mound and its ash trees had been obliterated long before our time and its historical associations forgotten completely, the place would still be one that I should be sorry not to see in spring, whether in its earliest days of winterlike bareness when the hazels are hung with pollen-yellow catkins, the sallows spangled with silvery catkins, and, high above these, the elm-tops stained with the dusky crimson of their tufted flowers, or later, in the days which soon follow, when elm, hawthorn and hazel are misted with the first definite green of bud-crinkled leaves. In some years the latter are Easter days, too, as they were in the year that is freshest in my memory now. It was an almost mid-April Easter, with primrose clusters dotting the floor of the copse against which the ashes rise, and people gathering the flowers, the few handfuls they carried away seeming no loss where so many were growing.

I am remembering two spring days—one at the middle of March, the other in April, nearly a month later. I had not been there since the previous autumn and the first thing I noticed was that the pasture in the corner of which the Tump stands had been ploughed: in the heats of the coming summer I should see no cows bunched in the shade of the ash trees or enjoying the easing pleasure of rubbing their necks against the knobby boles. No doubt the field has changed from grass to corn and back again to grass a number of times since the oldest of the Tump's three ashes grew from a seedling into sapling height and slenderness. Today they are all old, but one is much more of an ancient than the other two, which, though past the smooth grace of the ash in its prime, are nearly as tall as the full-grown elms lining the roadside close by. The great trunk and limbs of one of them slightly overtop the thinner, less branched trunk and lighter limbs of the other. The third tree, now coming to a weather-battered decay, though far, yet, from being totteringly decrepit, has lost the upper height of its trunk and several limbs, its bark is rougher and much more deeply fissured than that of the others, and it also differs from them in broadening out at the base into a radiating tangle of exposed roots. Above this tangle the bole is knobbed with protuberances that give it the look of being covered with old and very rough hide. All three are hoary with lichen. Just above the mound the hollows and wrinkles in each bole are green with an encrustment of velvety moss. On that March day the ash twigs still held a few tattered remnants of bunched key-stems against the sky and it still seemed to be winter with their black buds; for the ash is always spring's laggard in breaking out first its flowers, with their dark-purple clustered stamens, and then its long, pinnate leaves. Seen from the open field they were a very coldly grey trio in contrast with the tones of the wood behind them and those of the elms ranged along the lane on their right, not smooth and silvery like the young boughs rising from ash-stools in the wood, but with a rough, lichened hoariness in which the sunshine, even the most reluctant, seemed to light an incandescent glow.

This was to be one of March's gentler days, with mild westerly breezes that were always stirring the laneside elm-tops into movement but were hardly felt under the trees. Two kinds of cloud were passing across the sky, one a fairly high, irregular drift of rounded, often ragged and overlapping forms, rainy-looking in greyness but with sunshine behind and among them shaping their darker grey against a very different spread of brighter cloud. This was all sunny, a layer of smoothed-out streamers of vapoury whiteness fading into narrow glimpses of the indefinite blue separating them but sometimes broadening into blue-dappled expanses. These higher clouds were fluctuatingly revealed by the ever-changing gaps in the lower. Now and again an expanding gap overhead in each layer would coincide and uncover the sun, and for a few moments all the Vale in sight would be sunny until the clouds closed in again and the widespread radiance broke up into its former scattering of gleams among the cloud-shadows.

Tump and copse are about halfway along the Vale and about midway between its downland flanks—they cannot, in fact, be far from the Vale's centre. From the Tump my glimpses of the Vale were north, east and south, as the copse—in length more than a quarter of a mile, in width about a furlong—screens all the Vale west of it from Bottlesford to Etchilhampton Hill; and in these directions, but particularly eastward, the many hedgerow elms and the other copses and small woods make the floor of the Vale seem much more wooded than it is. This impression is deepened by the full leafage of summer, but even when every leaf is folded in its bud-scales such a deceptive press of boughs massing only a field or two away, with hardly a roof or a chimney and no church tower to be picked out, makes it map-work to see that Swanborough Tump is ringed by a circle of hamlets and villages all within a radius of two miles. The three Manningford villages, North Newnton, Sharcott, Wilcot, West Stowell, the two Altons, Woodborough, Hilcott and Bottlesford, might not have been there for all I could glimpse of them from the Tump. But the foreground and nearer middle-distances keep the trees open in their true hedgerow lines—the wooded look is always the length of a field away at least. These March fields lying around the Tump were beginning to be green with the cool, sun-holding clearness of tone that marks the quickening of grass and winter corn into spring growth. Cornfield tones were the richer and the more uniform, those of the turf in the pastures still remaining tinged in places with sere vestiges of last summer's herbage not yet submerged in the new green. The green came to life the most radiantly when, lying beyond the dark trunks of elms, it slowly brightened in the sunlight following the drift of a cloud-shadow.

Neither the margins of the lane past the Tump nor the level floor of the copse behind it were quite as green as the open fields. Not for lack of new growth along them but because, under the elms on the farther side of the lane and the thorn hedge on the nearer side, the multitudes of plants that would grow into the green jungles from which, in May, whitethroats will scold us had still to rise above the tangles of dead growth, ragged, bent and awry, which would be keeping autumn and winter visible there until the tide of spring green covered them. Chervil, cow-parsnip, dock, goose-grass, campion, stitchwort, Jack-by-the-hedge, dead-nettle were so crowded together in their emergent stages as to seem to be jostling each other in thrusting up, unfolding and spraying out to the sunlight. The winter's hedgeside wrack was not yet what it would soon become—unseen debris sunk in green shade. By then these plants would be ribboning the waysides with the second wave of flowering that leads the spring into the earliest moments of summer, a white wave in which the out-numbering chervil umbels—old ladies' lace, one countrywoman called them, though perhaps the name had once been Our Lady's Lace—and stitchwort chalices that become stars, each with its own sublety of whiteness, are the most delicately formed shapes. But just now the first wave of spring flowering was spreading its colour before the second arose and shut out the sun. The snow-drops that grow along the lane had faded, leaving no white among the yellow, the yellowish-green and the blue of celandine, mos-chatel, dog's mercury and violet.

The copse today is chiefly hazel-stools with here and there a few of ash which, like the hazels, are cut almost to ground-level and in March sunshine hold the silver-grey slenderness of their young boughs vividly in contrast with the dark, greyish-brown bareness and the more dense clustering of the hazel wands, all under a few oaks and free-growing ashes which are too widely spaced to form a canopy of boughs. I picked my way between hazels hung with loosely dangling catkins, ripe now and yellowed by pollen, whilst a different kind of catkin spangled silver points on male sallows towards the edge of the copse. The copse floor was less continuously verdant than the wayside margins and hedgerow banks, but the new green was springing up there as well. The brown of its winter covering of dead leaves and shrivelled bracken was not only patched with the emerald moss—it was everywhere a colour in eclipse among expanding tufts of bluebell leaves, clusters of primrose leaves, drifts of dog's mercury, moschatel, sanicle and the root leaves of woodland campion. Spring only seemed reluctant where bramble trailers had arched themselves into entangled, bracken-choked thickets that still had their March look of being too winter-stricken ever to bear leaf again.

The copse was noisy enough with bird-voices if not with birdsong, continuously so with the cawing and other rook-talk in a small rookery at its Woodborough margin, and sometimes with the chatter of jay and magpie. The quieter voices of the ring-doves sounded like the murmuring of confidences amid the other very public vociferation. A robin's cascades reminded me of sun-glint on a pebbly brook. Thrush and blackbird were spasmodic singers, the one not yet come to full self-confidence in his bold reiterations or the other in the phrasing of his mellow sequences. Willow-warbler and blackcap had either not returned to the copse or were silently unseen. I knew the chiff-chaff was there because one bird revealed its presence in an unexpected way by coming down to bathe in a wheel-rut puddle only three or four paces from where I sat by the Tump. It crouched in the shallowness of the puddle, relaxing its plumage, drooping its wings, and with quick, quivering shakes splashed itself with water. It was as unafraid as if there were no human being on earth, let alone within a pace or two, and it did not flit back to the copse until it had finished its bathe and had given me ample time to be certain it was my first chiff-chaff of the year. It was also the first chiff-chaff I had ever seen bathing.

Slender elm-suckers have grown up seven or eight feet in the gaps between the full-grown trunks lining the north side of the lane past the tump-field and the copse, forming a thin screen from trunk to trunk. On this March day they were an open screen hiding little of the Vale and the crest of its downland escarpment eastward from Knap Hill to Martinsell, a loose network of twigs just passing from bareness into the stage when elm-buds are tipped with green points emerging from pinkish-brown bud-scales. This

28

first green was hardly noticeable unless low down and caught in the sun, as I saw it there, and was lost at the height where the mature elm-tops seemed stained with the dusky red of their flowers. So it was through an unconcealing screen of elm twiggery that I watched the interchange of sunlight and cloud-shadow in the Vale between the copse and the sky-crest of the scarp about two miles away to the north, with the two outlying bits of downland, Woodborough Hill and Picked Hill, standing together at just the right distance for seeing them in a setting that might have been designed to reveal how oddly, even strangely, and always rather surprisingly they make themselves at home in the Vale.

A level pasture extended towards them for a quarter of a mile to a dark line of trees and the banks of the Kennet and Avon Canal, beyond which there was about the same width of corn making a greener band of the gentle tilt of ground that is the common base which steepens into the separate shapes of these little hills. Caught at this angle they lie side by side, their inward slopes forming the saddle that parts them, Picked Hill on the right, a smooth cone with a silhouetted tuft of beech boughs on the outer slope a little short of the summit, Woodborough Hill longer, its level ridge half-crested with a silhouette of beeches in line. The lynchets into which the latter hillside is stepped, and the thorn bushes dotted about them, make it look a rougher hill. This side of Picked is bare except for a thorn or two along the edge of the corn at its base. In sunny moments the sharp transition from corn-blade green to the brownish green of old turf gave both hills an almost golden tinge. They hid the Vale's downland edge westward from Knap Hill, but the face of Picked's east side exposed Knap Hill itself and the four-mile flow of skyline and the uppermost steeps of the escarpment eastward as far as the Martinsell bluff, though in many places glimpsed only through the tops of the highest trees in woods darkening the Vale about Stowell and Wilcot. The slow drift of the cloud-shadows dulled and brightened the olive-green downland turf above and behind elm-tops that were the more deeply reddened in their flowering by contrast with the smoky sombreness of the woods as a whole. In one sunny moment the white under-plumage of a solitary bird, a peewit flying low over the woods nearest the downs, was like a flickering gleam as the beat of seemingly black wings carried it into the breeze.

When I turned to look south and southeast across the Vale towards the edge of Salisbury Plain the press of elms and other hedgerow trees beyond the tump-field made a far from drab darkness of their March greys and browns broken here and there by the green of pasture and cornfield. The Plain's north-facing escarpment, which is not as close to Swanborough Tump as the other downland edge facing it across the Vale and is neither as steep nor as deeply hollowed by coombs, rose beyond the trees to a crestline reaching from Easton Clump, its farthest visible landmark, inward to Upavon Down. Here again, but less fretted by the intervening tree-tops, the openness of downs edged the Vale. On this side the flow of skyline carried a wide spacing of beech clumps as if they were buoyantly afloat. I could pick out the Pewsey Horse below the clump on Pewsey Hill but distance reduced it to a small white scar in the turf. Sometimes the valley floor was sunny when the Plain's edge was shadowed and hazily darkened almost to the simplicity of a silhouette behind the glow of colour on the brown earth of the tump-field and the flower-reddened elms. Then the sunshine would brighten the downs again, and by the shadows it made along turf-covered mound, ridge and depression would reveal how these hillsides had long ago been mounded into the barrows, banked into the enclosures, stepped into the lynchets, and grooved and ridged with the boundary ditches and banks that took shape there in the sun. West of Upavon Down the continuation of the scarp and all the Vale under it were hidden by the copse.

The next time I came to Swanborough Tump was towards the middle of April nearly a month later, when, as I have said, there were people in the copse gathering Easter primroses. I wondered how many of them knew anything at all about the happenings that took place so long ago here in the Vale of Pewsey. In our own times, only twelve years earlier, we in Britain had feared and prepared for Hitler's invasion which, if it had come, would once again have carried slaughter and destruction across the downs to the Vale, this time with much more terrible effect than when the Danish invaders drove our West Saxon forefathers to desperation but never to defeated despair. The kind of human peace in which I and the primrose-gatherers stooping under the hazel wands were enjoying nature's springtime resurgence at Swanborough Tump seemed so very frail that I found myself remembering A. E. Housman's line "The tree of man was never quiet", and then putting it out of mind again because another spring had brought chiff-chaff and willow-warbler back to this budding copse in the Vale. Spring had done this more than eleven hundred times since King Ethelred and his brother Alfred called the West Saxon Council together at Swanborough Tump. Perhaps, as countrymen, there were some among the assembly who were even not too "harassed with the heathen invasion" to give an ear to the springtime bird-song.

CHAPTER IV

THE CANNINGS VILLAGES

BISHOP'S CANNINGS

ONE morning in the last week of October I came towards Devizes along the road that is both a highway and a high way over the downs from Beckhampton; and when Shepherds' Shore—the gap it makes in Wansdyke—was a mile behind me, Devizes less than three miles ahead, and, on my left, the western half of the Vale of Pewsey was revealed below the road, I stayed for a while at the upper turning to Bishop's Cannings before following the byway to the village. Bishop's Cannings is the last village westward along the foot of the Vale's northern chalk-scarp. It lies about half a mile south of the turning, the byway to it descending the scarp, here much diminished, and then going on through Bishop's Cannings to Coate and on over the out-thrust east end of Etchilhampton Hill to skirt Etchilhampton village, finally joining the Devizes to Andover road that passes Wedhampton under the northwest corner of Salisbury Plain. These four villages are spaced across the extreme west end of the Vale—Wedhampton under the Plain, Etchilhampton and Coate separated by the long tongue of Etchilhampton Hill, Bishop's Cannings under the Vale's northern flank of downs. From the turning I could see something of Bishop's Cannings but nothing of the farther places among elms and beeches with many autumn leaves still to fall and with the morning's sunshine glowing among them like a bright mist.

It was during the half-hour or so spent at the brow of the rise overlooking Bishop's Cannings and the Vale that I began to notice how many skylarks were up and singing in a westerly breeze just lacking the briskness that would have made it chilly. The singing of a bird overhead set me looking about to discover how many more were helping to weave the web of notes pulsating in the air above the treeless downland rising behind me to the summits of Roundway Hill and Morgan's Hill and falling

32

before me to the press of valley trees about the village. I counted three or four I could hear as separate singers and saw others too far away for their notes to be caught except as part of the general voice. These larks were not soaring to springtime heights, nor were they cascading their notes with the springtime fervour that fills the air with a shimmering mixture of silver-toned sound which, to me, seems almost as if it should be seen as well as heard. Then it is an ecstasy that takes possession of the birds and drives them skywards; now the birds were moved by a less compelling impulse, for they could break off their soaring and singing at any moment when the play of chasing each other down to and over the stubble seemed the whim to follow. Yet these October sky-larks were not half-hearted singers when, head to wind, their quick-fanning wings lifted them.

At this mid-morning hour of what was, by the manipulated clock, the year's last day of summer time, the sun was still as far east of his meridian as the Plain's Avon gap and therefore not yet directly facing me across the Vale behind Bishop's Cannings. The sky was changingly spread with an airy ceiling of cloud in two distinct layers, a darker though far from gloomy grey against a lighter, the higher layer a slow drift of soft-edged oyster-grey shapes smooth in texture and with a pearly lustre where sunny. Narrow lakes of clear blue, palest towards the sun, opened and closed among them. The under layer was dove-grey, a less con-tinuous but quicker drift of looser, more ragged shapes that some-times dropped a brief sprinkle of rain into the wind. There were moments when, southward above the Plain, the drift of lower clouds obscured the sun and reduced his radiance to a shafting of far-off beams, leaving the Vale shadowed until the wider radiance flooded back across it to the downs where I stood. On this, the Vale's sun-facing scarp, the cloud-shadowed moments dulled the pastures to the greyness of olive green whilst darkening the newly ploughed cornfields to a richer tone of brown; but when the sun-shine again flooded the slopes it brightened the turf to a luminous clarity of green and paled the brown of the ploughed fields with a chalky greyness revealed in their downland earth.

This open sunniness extended no farther below me than the scarp-foot and Bishop's Cannings. The village lies just within the

3   33

Picked Hill from Swanborough Tump

margin of what, summer or winter, looks rather like an expanse
of glady woodland, or, perhaps, of closely timbered parkland,
where the flat-crowned towering of elms greatly outnumbers the
more broadly rounded contours of the other tree-shapes. To many
a traveller passing along the highway Bishop's Cannings must be
no more than a name on the guide-post at the turning and a grey,
slender spire tapering above the tree-tops. From where I stood I
could pick out little more than a partly seen roof and chimney
here, a house-wall and gable there, to suggest the size of the village
and how it was grouped about the church. The shadow sides of
the trees being towards me I caught but dimly, and only at the
village, the ambered foliage of the elms and the coppery smoulder
of the beeches in the mist of sunshine glowing behind them. Beyond this shadowy warmth of autumn colour the width of the
Vale was greyed to monochrome in which the glow of sunlight
among the trees took the place of the colour it enriched in the clear
air on the open scarp. In this different radiance the elms appeared
as if ranged along the Vale in dark, irregular lines close behind
each other, very dark just behind the village, paler in succession
to where the last had the long, silver-grey silhouette of the Plain
rising behind it. The church spire would have tapered less clearly
against the Vale if, on its east side, the slant of its shadowed grey
had not been outlined by a narrow edging of sunlight.

The clouds had already begun to open out and leave wider gaps
of blue for the sun when I descended to this village that shows so
little of itself from the outside. Neither does it give itself willingly
to the eye from the inside. It is a small place, dispersed loosely
rather than clustered about its centrepiece the church. Ida Gandy,
in her charming book *A Wiltshire Childhood*, published in 1929,
caught the look of it very deftly:

"All round the church was scattered the village. There was
no concentration of houses in any particular place; they just
gathered in little groups along the roads and by-lanes like
friendly neighbours met for a gossip. Some, of a less sociable
nature, had set themselves right in the heart of the fields."

Bishop's Cannings is just the same today—half concealed among
the trees, hedges, gardens and fields round a church that still leaves

me wondering, as it did the first time I saw it years ago, why such a large church should be gracing so small a village; for it is not only surprisingly large but in its balanced unity and lightness of poise is the finest church in the Vale.

The most likely explanation is suggested by the name: the place is called Bishop's Cannings to distinguish it from All Cannings two and a half miles to the southeast, the "All" coming from an earlier "Alde", meaning "old". They were separate places long before the Domesday Survey, the manor of Bishop's Cannings having been a Royal gift to the See of Sarum at an unrecorded date, perhaps a grant from the Crown of Wessex. At first the bishop's lands extended far enough westward from the actual Vale to include the castle, park and borough of Devizes; but in 1139 King Stephen, fearing the power of bishops whose lands made them overlords of castles, reclaimed the manor of Bishop's Cannings for the Crown. By a deed of 1159 Henry II restored it to the See of Sarum—all but the castle of Devizes, the park and the borough. The name "Bishop's Cannings" means, then, the Bishop of Sarum's Cannings, and A. G. Bradley, in *Round about Wiltshire*, states that the bishops once had a palace there. They certainly gave the village a church that proclaimed the place to be their Cannings.

It is a cruciform building. A central place under spire and tower has chancel to the east, nave and aisles to the west, transepts to north and south. The east side of the south transept opens into a chantry that became the Ernle chapel in 1563 but was originally dedicated to "Our Lady of the Bower". A porch shelters the south door of the church. Like the majority of old churches this one has been altered from time to time, each piece of new work reflecting the changes in architectural style from Norman Romanesque to Perpendicular Gothic. The lofty nave is separated from the aisles by Transitional Norman arcading in which the piers keep their Norman strength and severity whilst the arches have lost their semicircular camber in a Gothic point. Above these arcades the walls rise to the Perpendicular tracery of three-light clerestory windows that help to brighten the nave under its timbered roof, in which, between the window arches, the principals are strutted upon stone corbels, each a head of bishop or king. The plain simplicity of Early English lancets, symmetrical triplets in which the

35

middle light makes the point, gives just the right balance of wall and window in the high west end of the nave, as well as in the end walls of chancel, transepts and Ernle chapel. Central place and chancel are stone-vaulted. The tower is Early English, the spire fifteenth-century. The south or main door is very plain Norman within a porch with Decorated doorway and stone-vaulted roof. That is a bare catalogue of the parts which come together in the grace and unity of this church: but who is to say how much of the result was foreseen and how much was accidental rightness? From end to end of the interior, along the nave with its high-beamed roof and smooth-columned arcades, on through the span of the arch beyond which there is the first lowering of height in the groined vaulting of the central place and then another lowering in the longer recession of chancel vaulting, as if gradually to lead the eye down to the altar with the trio of lancets shaped in colour-transfused daylight behind it, is a vista that proves the rightness, whether accidental or not.

In the south transept is a movable piece of furniture, a wooden, box-like pew that, when its nature is perceived, seems to me to gloom in its own little cloud of pessimism amid the clearer light of day everywhere else around it. Fashioned in oak, it has a heavy-handed, novice-made look. It is perhaps a yard square and about the same in the height of three sides, the fourth side being from two to three feet taller. The door is opposite the taller side, whilst the left side has a plank seat and the top of the right side a slightly tilted desk. Anyone sitting in this pew would always be aware of a pallid, gigantic open hand, a left hand with palm outward, painted to fill the surface of the upper half of the taller side within a carved border, crudely picked out in colour, which frames the hand. On thumb, fingers, palm and wrist is a succession of moral maxims. Sitting there, the occupant would only have to turn his head to be faced with warning after warning, some of them cynical in bluntness, that the world of men is all wickedness and ingratitude. The maxims, inscribed in what may be fifteenth-century lettering, are in Latin and are headed "Manus Medita-cionis"—Hand of Meditation. For those of us, including myself, who have little or no Latin, a card in the pew gives them trans-lated. As a sample I quote the four from the little finger: Thou shalt quickly be forgotten by thy friends—Thy heir will seldom do anything for thee—He to whom thou leavest thy goods will seldom do anything for thee—Thy end is miserable.

Very little appears to be known about the pew—where it was made, who made it, when it was made and for what purpose. It has been called a pre-Reformation shriving pew, a confessional chair, a church shrine-keeper's chair, and a carrel or stall. The best attempt at explaining its existence that I have come across is in Archdeacon Macdonald's "Memoirs of the Parish of Bishop's Cannings", printed in Vol. VI of the *Wiltshire Archæological Magazine*. The Archdeacon quotes a correspondent who wrote:

"For myself I conjecture that this so-called Confessional chair is a valuable, and perhaps unique, example of the ancient 'Carrel', or stall, usually fixed in the cloister of monastic buildings, and which probably occurred as frequently with large parochial churches, such as Bishop's Cannings, in immediate dependence on the Cathedral. These carrels were used by the monks or clergy for daily private study and meditation."

It is pleasant to turn away from this gloomy stall and in the open air remember John Aubrey's account of certain activities of "Mr Ferraby, the minister of Bishop's Cannings", a talented man who, when James I was King, served God, enjoyed his days and lived in the sun. But for Aubrey's seventeenth-century account we perhaps might never have known that George Ferraby, as well as being the parson at Bishop's Cannings, was also a musician and one who loved poetry, pageantry, open-air games and the sound of a steepleful of bells, pleasures he wished his parishioners to share. The situation of Bishop's Cannings close to the Bath road twice gave him the chance to entertain royalty, on which occasions he displayed his own talents and those he had discovered and trained in his rural flock, thereby putting—as we say nowadays—his village on the map. But let Aubrey do the telling. Of one of these occasions he wrote:

"Mr Ferraby, the minister of Bishop's Cannings, was an ingenious man, and an excellent musician, and made severall of his parishioners good musicians, both for vocall and instrumental musick; they sang the Psalmes in consort to the organ, which Mr Ferraby procured to be erected.

When King James the First was in these parts he lay at Sir Edw. Baynton's at Bromham. Mr Ferraby then entertained his Majesty at the Bush in Cotefield, with bucoliques of his own making, of four parts, which were sung by his parishioners, who wore frocks and whippes like carters. Whilst his Majesty was thus diverted, the eight bells (of which he was the cause) did ring, and the organ was played on for state; and after this musical entertainment he entertained his Majesty with a foot-ball match of his own parishioners. This parish in those days would have challenged all England for musique, foot-ball, and ringing. For this entertainment his Majesty made him one of his chaplains in ordinary."

The other occasion was when Anne of Denmark, wife of James I, travelled along the road over the downs above the village on 11th June, 1613. On this day, Aubrey tells us, "when Queen Anne returned from Bathe", Ferraby "made an entertainment for her Majesty on Cannings-down, at Shepherd's-shard at Wensditch, with a pastoral performed by himself and his parishioners in shepherds' weeds". It was "voyc't in four parts completely musicall", and "was by her Majesty not only graciously accepted and approved, but also bounteously rewarded; and by the right honourable, worshipfull, and the rest of the generall hearers and beholders, worthily applauded". Aubrey does not say what the weather was like, but could there have been a better setting for a pastoral than these green and flowery downs in the sunshine, cloud-shadows and lark-song of a June day? No doubt the "generall hearers and beholders" included an authentic if something less than Arcadian shepherd-boy or two whose flocks had slowly drifted near enough for the boys to be able to listen and gaze.

A large, grassy graveyard surrounds the church and makes a comparatively open space in the middle of the village. To look across its width in any direction is to find the stone-grey unity of the church clear against a low background of trees among which are glimpses of even-toned red brick and blue-grey slate, or the darker and less even tone of older brick under thatch, or—but less frequently—whitewashed, timber-framed walls under more thatch, and in one direction the whitish-grey walls and dark-red tiles of a small group of very new council houses. The village is dispersed on level ground, and the houses and cottages seem too earth-held among trees and hedgerows, orchards and gardens to weaken the impression of levelness given by this corner of the Vale. The church strengthens the impression, for though it is earth-borne it never seems earth-bound, especially when seen from the south side and, as on that October day, with its masonry taking the sunlight between cloud-shadows, as if the stone were incandescent. I had come to the southward side of the village then. My viewpoint was the gate where a path leaves the southeast corner of the churchyard and becomes a narrow byway between cottages. Here I could see the chancel-end, all the south side and the full rise of tower and spire, including the dumpy turret-spire on the northeast angle of the tower, and in the fusion of parts appreciate the niceties of balance in the contrast between horizontals—roof-ridges, parapets, window-bases and tower-stages— repeating the levels of the Vale, and verticals—wall-angles, lancet parallels, the buttresses, pinnacles and crenellation of the nave— culminating in the tower and soaring spire. The gable-points of chancel and nave, transept, porch and chapel, at their different heights, terminate or else cut the horizontals, whilst from them the roof-ridges lead inward to the base of the tower. The tapering gables prepare the eye for the spire's crowning slenderness, the final touch that gives the bloom of grace to a dignified tower and thereby to the whole building. Afterwards I followed a footpath through level, rushy pastures to a wooden swing-bridge over the canal a quarter of a mile farther to the south. Here I stayed for a last backward look at the village before going on across the Vale. The Bishop's Cannings elms were golden amber in the sun, the church tower and spire rising against the green downs beyond the elms, the slenderest part of the spire above their skyline.

ALL CANNINGS

The village of All Cannings lies about two and a half miles southeast of Bishop's Cannings. It is not as close as the latter place to the foot of the downs along their side of the Vale, All Cannings being two or three fields from the south or inward bank of the canal, whilst Bishop's Cannings is between the canal and the downs. Opposite All Cannings the downland scarp has risen to the height and massiveness of Tan Hill, from which Milk Hill, a few feet higher, carries on the eastward boldness of steeps that become in succession Walker's, Knap, Golden Ball, Huish and Oare Hills, and end on the great bluff of Martinsell. Tan Hill stands far enough from the village for the long and high spur of down called Clifford's Hill to come to its dying fall at All Cannings Cross Farm by the scarp-foot road from the Alton villages to Devizes, and still to leave almost half a mile of nearly level ploughland between road and canal, and another two or three hundred yards from the canal to the first houses in the village. A little to the west of Clifford's Hill, between road and canal, is Allington, the nearest village to All Cannings. Like Bishop's Cannings, All Cannings stands on level ground at the edge of what was the Canning's Marsh of ancient times, the site of the marsh a brook-threaded region of damp fields stretching eastward below the village as far as Beechingstoke.

All Cannings is grouped a little away from the cross-valley road —the only metalled road to it—that passes its east side and sends out a couple of byways to make a loop through the village, an interesting piece of road behaviour. For this road across the Vale's width, linking the one under the edge of Salisbury Plain to the parallel one under the Tan Hill downs, and passing through Chirton and Patney but by-passing All Cannings in doing so, looks as though it may originally have been not only a way over Cannings Marsh but part of a cross-route connecting the downland Ridgeway at points south and north of the Vale. It can be followed southward from Chirton until, at the scarp-foot highway, it changes to a track up the side of the Plain to the Ridgeway on Chirton Down, and northward from All Cannings to the road beyond which it is a track rising between Clifford's Hill and Milk Hill to the heights where the east end of Tan Hill looks into the hollow of Milk Hill's great coomb, and then, after cutting Wansdyke and heading for Thorn Hill and the East Kennett long barrow, seems to have continued to the Ridgeway at East Kennett in the river valley near Avebury. I write "seems to have continued" because I have only once attempted to follow it through, and on that day lost it completely on Thorn Hill, a surprising thing with a track that set off so purposefully across the downs. But inside All Cannings the long village street leads northward to a second trackway up the scarp, this one to the west of Clifford's Hill. It climbs to the west end of the Tan Hill plateau, makes another gap in Wansdyke and goes on, much less indefinitely, over the downs to Beckhampton two miles away on the Bath road. In 1809 it was mapped as one of Wiltshire's second-class roads. At All Cannings its beginning is a fenced green road bridging the canal opposite the end of the village and leading straight to the highway between All Cannings Cross Farm and Allington. It does not now continue beyond this road, although I imagine it did in earlier times: today we must go left along the quarter-mile of highway to Allington and there turn right to be on the track it would join if it continued along its line from the village. These tracks up the scarp on the side of Clifford's Hill can be seen from All Cannings as chalk-streaks curving up the green steeps of turf, and from the other side of the Vale, too, particularly when their whiteness gleams in the sun.

Before coming to the village itself I should like to say something about the farm of All Cannings Cross and its cornfields at the foot of the downs; not, in this chapter, about the Early Iron Age farmstead that was discovered and excavated in one of its fields and made the name "All Cannings Cross" familiar to archæologists, but about the horse-ploughing I see going on there in these days of tractor-drawn ploughs. As recently as the September of 1952 I was watching three two-horse teams furrowing the year's stubble below the end of Clifford's Hill, and wondering where else in and around the Vale of Pewsey horse-ploughing was still going on. It was like being put back twenty-five years in time, to the Vale as I first knew it, when towards the end of harvest at the foot of these same downs there was corn in stook, corn being carried and stacked, fields of stubble, fields ploughed and being ploughed, and never the sound or the smell of tractor. I know, of course, why these machines have taken the place of horses and how they lighten the ploughman's labour. Time is antiquating the imagery of poet Gray's line, though it cannot touch its effect in the poem.

The three plough-teams I watched on a mid-September afternoon were working in a roadside field that swells towards the canal with just enough lift to bring its edges against distant tree-tops backed by the scarp-crest of Salisbury Plain. In clear air and an easterly breeze too gentle to be chilly the Vale was under a sky in which the drift of gleaming, cumulus-topped clouds across cold blue made a slow alternation of sunlight and cloud-shadow brightening and darkening the buff fallow of the stubbles, the browns of the new ploughing and the greens of the downland steeps. Sunlit, the stubbles were paler in a sheen of brightness, the ploughed earth chalkier. Here under the downs the great fields are fenced, not hedged, though some of the fences have a thorn or two dotted widely along them. Except for a long line of conifers beside the scarp-track leaving Allington and the elms about Allington village, these were the only trees I could see between the canal and the downland skyline. No stooks remained on the stubble: all the corn was in rick after rick along the downland side of the road and at the farm. I counted twenty-four of them, golden-yellow shapes in their newness, some capped with thatch already; and away up the field beyond the road in front of the ricks the three ploughmen followed their pairs to and fro and seemed small in the scale of spaciousness surrounding them. Separated by pale bands of stubble that slowly narrowed as the dark-brown bands of ploughed earth widened, the teams began each furrow together but did not often finish together. Sometimes one drew a little ahead, sometimes another, and sometimes one lost ground when a man halted his horses for a moment or two and went forward to bend over the plough. After swinging round at the turn and all were in line again they moved off, the horses drawing easily, the two farther teams half-silhouetted against the southern sky for part of their crossing. Except for the occasional sound of a man's voice raised in controlling his team, and the fluctuating swish of the breeze in the autumn stems of roadside herbage, the afternoon was very quiet there.

All Cannings is a larger, more compact village than Bishop's Cannings and very different in shape. It is a long and narrow place on each side of a street that begins about a furlong south of the canal and ends a little more than half a mile farther within the Vale. The church, instead of being the centre-piece, as at the other Cannings, is at the south end among a few trees between the airy openness of the village green and a farm at the edge of the fields. Here again is no small church, yet it is not the church but the green, with its sky-exposing width and its feeling of being broadly shelved between the inner parts of the Vale and the downs, and with the village reaching away from it towards the downs, that always stands out more clearly in my impression of All Cannings. Its four-square expanse of turf has the school and a house or two along the south side, with the church tower rising above the trees behind them. There are houses along the north side. The west side is open to the village street, the east side to the Vale beyond a line of half a dozen elms. The green is large enough for the houses and the six elms to fringe or outline it rather than to enclose it in a way that makes it feel shut in. There is no lack of elms and other trees in the rest of the village, particularly round the outskirts. Approached along the Vale, or overlooked from the downs, All Cannings appears almost as tree-beset as Bishop's Cannings, though within the village this impression changes to one of open sky and light, even, when the green is underfoot, to a sense of being wide open to the surrounding Vale. From the green's east margin all the range of downs from Milk Hill to Martinsell is in view, as well as Woodborough Hill and Picked Hill together in the valley, and the skyline of the Plain disclosed by gaps among the press of tree-tops towards the south.

In the Vale villages there is always variety in building materials and the way in which they are combined. At All Cannings there is as much variety as anywhere else. In its close but not congested grouping along the street and the byways and paths on each side the village has one or two farmhouses and their buildings, a few houses of the larger kind, more that are entirely cottage in size and appearance, and, in contrast with all these, a little group of six new council houses. Except for boarded barns and sheds the usual walling is either brick or brick-filled timber framing which may be under thatch, tile or slate, though one house is stone-slated, an uncommon roof for houses in the Vale. Here and there the brickwork is whitewashed or creamwashed. So as well as the differences in shape and fabric between house and house, cottage and cottage, and the differences in pitch, depth to eaves, and overhang between thatched, tiled and slated roofs, there are also the differences in texture and weather-toned colour between one material and another. The new houses, semi-detached and set in three blocks round a horseshoe of green open to the street, make a bright, though not—even in their newness—discordant contrast with the more sober tones of the older walls and roofs around them. Their wall-colour is the whitish grey of cement, the surface being saved from hard blankness by a darker speckling in the grey and by being coursed to give shadow lines that suggest but do not definitely imitate the overlap of weather-boarding. More than a suggestion would have been a saddening and wryly comic sight. The light grey is a foil to the warm red of brick chimneys and the pantiles covering the hip-ended roofs. Time will prove whether their first brightness can mellow into closer harmony with the older walls and roofs or only tarnish to weather-stained drabness.

The church, originally Norman, is large, but through the centuries its parts have been so altered by rebuilding—the chancel as lately as 1867—that scarcely any Norman work remains. It has the full form of nave, aisles, chancel and transepts unified into solid dignity by a square central tower rising in massive plainness unrelieved by battlements or pinnacles, though a square turret at the northeast corner holds the javelin-headed and spiny-tailed arrow of a weathervane and a surmounting orb against the sky. Seen from the approach to the north door the tower appears barer in its simplicity by contrast with the ornamentation of the Perpendicular transept at its base, the plain masonry shaping the tower above the transept's double band of carved patterning that is like a crenellated frieze with a crocketed pinnacle on each outward corner of the walls. Within the church are two pieces of carving that to me are notable. They are very different, one being the white alabaster reredos, the other, on the west wall of the south aisle, a sixteenth-century freestone memorial of William Ernle and his wife Joan. The reredos is small and pictures the Last Supper in bold relief with a vivid realism not only of every detail but of pervading atmosphere that makes the scene dramatically alive. The calm figure of Jesus, His right hand reaching towards a bunch of grapes on the table in front of Him, His left hand towards a loaf of bread, sits in the centre place of the table's long side, with the disciples to right and left, most listening to Him but one or two turning to each other in wondering, excited discussion. This grouping and movement about Jesus, who, though in their midst, seems set apart in trancelike serenity, the momentary attitude in which each is caught, the facial expressions, the play of hands in gesture, trick one into listening to as well as looking at what is going on.

The Ernle memorial, a much larger piece of work, is a stone panel under a cornice with three eagles perched on its rounded top. The inscription opens with the prelude

1587
ANNO : DNI
ONELI : HONORE : AND
PREISE : BE : GIVEN : TO : GOD
WHERE : SO : EVER : A : DEAD
CARKAS : IS : EVEN : THITHER
WILL : THE : E : GLES : RESORTE

and continues

I : BELEVE : THAT : MI : REDEMER : LIVETH : AND : THAT
I : SHALL : RISE : OWTE : OF : THE : EARTH
IN : THE : LAST : DAI : AND : SHALL : BE : COVEREDE :
AGAINE : WITE : MI : SKINNE : AND : SHALL : SE
GOD : IN : MI : FLESE : JEA : AND : I : MI : SELFE :
SHALL : BEHOLDE : HIM : NOT : WITH : OTHER
BUT : WITHE : THESE : SAME : EIES
DEATHE : IN : JESUS : CHRISTE : ONLI : IS : ETERNALL :
SALVACION :
: WILLIAM : ERNELE :
: AND : IONE : HIS : WIF :

an affirmation of faith and of belief in the immortality of both body and soul that could hardly have been more clearly phrased.

In the west end of the churchyard there is what I think must be the finest full-grown ash tree I have ever seen. Any ash that is not too closely hemmed in by other trees, and is allowed to grow up undistorted by lopping, will shape itself into a tall tree, massive when at its prime, in which strength and grace are blended as in no other tree. Left alone the ash will branch and spread with a smoothly wavy upwardness that gives the whole tree the appearance of being the most buoyantly earth-held tree of all. Some of the willows and poplars come closest to the ash in this—such as, for example, those alongside the Avon at the Manningford villages; but they often look too rigidly slender in airy height and not so stably rooted, whilst the ash carries itself with just the curving flexibility to give its buoyancy the bloom of grace. The great and ivied bole of this one in All Cannings churchyard rises seven or eight feet from a root-mound to its branching into an upward spread of stout limbs girthed in proportion to the bole, these branching and re-branching from height to height with that smoothness of articulation which gives any naturally grown ash its graceful poise, and for me, at any rate, makes this lofty tree the queen of them all. It is taller by several feet than a large horse-chestnut near the churchyard gate. The season was late summer when I last saw them: the chestnut was then a sombrely green, airless dome by comparison with the ash's pale green and lightly hung spread of leafage.

The ash tree can be well seen from the farmyard beyond the church, best, perhaps, from the outer edge of the great pond that fills the middle of it. In its own way the pond is no less interesting than the tree, for the yard is a very large enclosure and the pond takes up much of its area whilst leaving a broad margin of ground between its bank and the surrounding buildings. It was almost dry in the late summer I have mentioned in connection with the churchyard ash and horse-chestnut, about half of its bottom a bare expanse of grey, sun-cracked mud and most of the remainder covered with the green leaves and pink flowers of persicaria around two or three small willows. The lack of water revealed how firmly the bank-face on one side is strengthened with a revetment of whole tree-trunks and on the other side with blocks of sarsen stone. All Cannings is one of the several places that have been claimed as the setting of the Wiltshire Moonraker legend, the others being, as far as I can discover, Bourton by Bishop's Cannings, Devizes just outside the west end of the Vale, and Collingbourne Ducis among the downs a mile or so south of the Vale's east end; yet it is rather surprising that when the place is All Cannings it was not in this large and deep old pond that the kegs of smuggled spirits are said to have been hidden, but in All Cannings Water, a ford formerly on the road to Etchilhampton and about half a mile south of the pond.

In the sixteenth century the manor of All Cannings became the property of a family named Nicholas. How a son, born in 1597, was in later life reminded of his schooldays, and with what result, is told in the following quotation from the *Spectator* (No. 313):

"Everyone who is acquainted with Westminster School knows that there is a curtain which used to be drawn across the room to separate the upper school from the lower. A youth happened, by some mischance, to tear the above mentioned curtain. The severity of the master was too well known for the criminal to expect any pardon for such a fault; so that the boy, who was of a meek temper, was terrified to death at the thought of his appearance, when his friend who sat near him bade him be of good cheer, for he would take the fault upon himself. He kept his word accordingly.

"As soon as they were grown up to be men the Civil War broke out, in which our two friends took opposite sides; one of them following Parliament, the other the Royal party. As their tempers were different, the youth who had torn the curtain endeavoured to raise himself on the civil list; and the other, who had borne the blame for it, on the military. The first succeeded so well that he was in a short time made a Judge under the Protector: the other was engaged in the unhappy enterprise of Penruddocke and Grove, in the West. Everybody knows that the Royal party was routed, and all the heads of them, among whom was the curtain-champion, imprisoned at Exeter. It happened to be his friend's lot at that time to go to the Western Circuit. The trial of the rebels, as they were then called, was very short, and nothing now remained but to pass sentence

47

on them; when the Judge, hearing the name of his old friend, and observing his face more attentively, which he had not seen for many years, asked him whether he was not formerly a Westminster scholar. By the answer he was soon convinced that it was his former generous friend; and without saying more at the time, made the best of his way to London where, employing all his power and interest with the Protector, he saved his friend from the fate of his unhappy associates."

The reprieved Royalist was William Wake, who was afterwards the father of a son who became Archbishop of Canterbury; the Roundhead judge was Robert Nicholas, of All Cannings in the Vale of Pewsey.

The Salisbury Plain skyline from Swanborough Tump

Happy Christmas
with love
from Hix

SEASONS GREETINGS

CHAPTER V

ONE SOURCE OF THE AVON

GREAT or small, a river, a stridable brook even, puts a spell on those of us who see it often. We watch it at this place and that, and whether its waters go past deep or shallow, singing or burbling, there is always fascination in its flow, in the coming, the momentary passing and then the going away. It is this which reveals to us—usually through a child's urgent desire—that a part of us is still not too grown-up to find a sort of shamefaced pleasure in a paper-boat, or the inner half of a match-box, or a tin-lid, in fact anything that will ride away for a while on the stream. It is all the better, too, if our craft can be launched near the upstream mouth of a tunnel-like bridge or a dark culvert, so that, after watching it disappear, we may be first at the other end and wait hopefully for it to sail into daylight again from the fearful hazards of whirlpool and shoal we imagine it will have to weather. Then there is the magic of being at a source, of knowing that beyond this point the stream belongs to the darkness of waters under the earth. Few of us can have stood on the bank of a favourite river and not thought, "I should like to follow every yard of it back to the source: perhaps I shall—one day", and in the end be happy enough to come there—as I was in coming to the source of the west branch of the Avon in Pewsey Vale—without having traced every reach of the stream between its narrowing banks.

The place is a small, steep-sided hollow at the foot of the downs where the strip-lynchets step the slopes below Wansdyke and Shepherd's Shore. It is by the side of a pair of brick cottages at Bourton, a hamlet about halfway along the threequarter-mile of byroad leading from Bishop's Cannings to Easton Farm, with the shoulder of Easton Hill thrusting out from the scarp above the farm. One of the old tracks that in Saxon charters are named Herepath, meaning "army way", and are named Harepath on today's maps, here dips into Pewsey Vale. It comes (with a made

4*   49

Horse-ploughing at All Cannings

surface now) across the downs from the direction of Calne, rising
to the *col* separating King's Play Hill and Morgan's Hill, and then,
after being cut by the Devizes road, goes green on its slant past
Easton Hill, Easton Farm and Harepath Farm to the valley bottom
at Allington about two miles east of Bishop's Cannings. Inward
along the Vale from Easton Hill and under the flow of a gradually
rising crestline, the northern escarpment is hollowed into the
steep of a bay curving to the next shoulder of down, Kitchen
Barrow Hill, beyond which the scarp is embayed by two more
downland hollows that let the remotely sky-caught tree-tuft on
Tan Hill come into view, with Clifford's Hill holding the embankment of Rybury Camp forward between Tan Hill and the
width of the Vale. In the opposite direction from Easton Hill the
escarpment at first falls away into shallower slopes, but it soon
begins to steepen again as the flank of Roundway Hill under
the long levels of the hilltop reaching out to the west past a beech
clump to a precipitously blunt end that has looked desolately bare
since its hanging woods were so scarifyingly felled.

Against such a background this hollow in which the west
branch of the Avon rises is small indeed. Its width cannot be more
than thirty or forty yards. It is a little longer than it is wide, with
a steeply banked inner end and parallel sides which diminish to
their lowest where the road passes its open end. When I came to it
from Bishop's Cannings on a mid-June morning the enclosing
banks were shaggy with tussocky tangles of grass-blades under
tall, flowering stems, and in some places were covered by nettles
taller than the grass. The flat bottom of the hollow is a withy-bed
in which several small streams, branching from the source at the
foot of the inner bank, thread the pollarded boles before joining
again and flowing away under the road. If I had come a day or
two earlier I should, in exploring the place, have had to push my
way through a more than head-high jungle of stout, upright
stems, a pale, glaucous green in colour, with long leaves droop-
ingly spread whilst branching into a triangular arrangement of
darker and glossily green leaflets. The dampness of the ground and
the shelter given by the banks make the withy-bed a place where
this very handsome umbelliferous plant we call angelica could
grow into perfection if left alone. Here it had not been left alone,

but had been cut down, or most of it, before the purple began to
tinge tall stems that even then had not grown enough to be dis-
playing their sometimes white, sometimes pale purple umbels.
The angelica that had sprung up in the waters of the little streams
was still erect, but the walkable ground between the withy-boles
was thickly strewn with prostrate hollow stems and their wilting
leaves; which was a disappointing way of seeing the plant, although it did make easier my unsuccessful attempt to reach the
place at the foot of the steep end-bank where I could have watched
this beginning of the Avon welling up at my feet. The wands of
the withy-boles standing near the bank had not been cut recently.
They had grown long and were shading a luxuriant undergrowth
of brook and brookside herbage, including angelica, that concealed the running water and the waterlogged ground under
them. This and my not being shod for venturing into such overgrown sogginess turned me away from trying to find the exact
place.

I went back to the firmer ground in the outer part of the hollow.
It was more open there, brighter and warmer after the damp
shade, and I could feel the morning's breeze again and see the sky.
The cleared angelica stems made a green mat of litter between
pollard withy-boles that were shorter than those in the damper
part and had only this year's green shoots thinly tufting shorn
heads which were seldom higher than my waist. One of them was
just high enough to support me comfortably in a half-sitting, half-
leaning attitude whilst looking about and writing a few notes. A
whitethroat began to sing, then a goldfinch. One moment I was
listening to them, and the next, almost as soon as I heard the crack
of dry wood, was lying on my back with pencil in one hand, notebook in the other, and the broken-off bole between my legs. I
made sure the next I chose for seat should be strong enough.

As this suggests, all these short willows were hoary and decrepit
under their crowns of scanty green shoots. Some had ivy twining
round their deeply fissured bark; most had mossy heads on which
ones and twos of various plants were growing in company. I
noticed herb-Robert, forget-me-not, meadow-sweet, goosegrass
and nettle, though not always together on the same tree. Rooted
only in cracks and crannies, they were thriving but small. There was

no overcrowding, each plant having room to be itself with an air of live-and-let-live ease. The little companies graced these pollarded tops with the charm of natural rightness, especially the one in which the reddish purple, the milky blue and the creamy white of herb-Robert, forget-me-not and meadow-sweet flowers were caught together. The brook under the angelica fringing this open part of the withy-bed was flowing quietly below the green succulence of water cress and water speedwell, the speedwell stems reaching up in a straggling way to hold their pairs of long leaf-lances and slender racemes of lilac flowers above the denser leafage and white flowers of the cress. Though numerous, the flower of this speedwell is too small and usually too much among the leaves for its beauty to be obvious. Here it was only about an eighth of an inch across, formed, like the other kinds of speedwell, into an arrangement of four finely curved lobes, all pointed, with the largest broadening its curves to a heart shape before which the others were expanded rather like a three-pointed lip. Proportioned to the small scale of the flower, the greenish-white rim of the corolla tube made a centre to pale lilac which, on the heart-shaped lobe, was faintly lined with thin parallels of purplish-red. From only a few feet away the perfection of these small flowers gave hardly more than a dim impression of grey-blue points among dark-green leaves.

I left the stream-source to the seclusion of its hollow and its water vegetation and returned to the wider world that is neither downland nor valley but the openness of the footslopes dividing them. Less than half a mile southward into the valley the Kennet and Avon Canal lay among the trees between Bourton and Horton, thence winding with the lower edge of the footslopes which take the canal between Allington and All Cannings on its way east along the Vale. As a metalled byway the road led no farther than the farm three or four hundred yards on at the foot of Easton Hill. This hill was a shoulder of downland I had not set foot upon for more than twenty years, and on this June day I was looking forward to renewing the often remembered delights the slopes of its very flowery turf had once given me. I was hoping that the afternoon would be much sunnier than the morning and that the morning's gently westerly breezes would still hold to temper an unclouded sun's heat. The sky so far had been full of a press of high dove-grey clouds that moved very slowly and seldom broke to reveal the sunny blue behind them. The gaps closed almost as soon as they opened. All the sunshine seemed caught in the clouds, transfusing and brightening their soft grey and sometimes filtering through to the ground without casting a definite shadow anywhere. Such a sky brings out all the cool depth in the varied tones of June green, both in the Vale's elmy pastures and cornfields and on the downs overlooking them. A countryside in early summer never looks greener than it does when there are no contrasts between the radiance of direct sunshine and heavy shadows and only the even softness of cloud-filtered sunlight comes down to it. The morning had been like that, but now, at midday, I hoped for a clearing sky and an afternoon aglow with full sunlight to give the last touch of beauty to the hosts of down and flowers I knew I should see on Easton Hill. By the time I set foot among them it had all happened—even the breeze held.

But the hill was half a mile away yet, and I was in no hurry. A track from the farm led up a gentle rise to the foot of its rather steep, smoothly rounded shoulder that is really the south end of Easton Down projecting towards the Vale. At the beginning of the track I began to realise that though the spring in the hollow I had just left behind is the permanent source of the Avon's west branch, there might also be a slightly higher and very intermittent spring to supplement it—in fact the source of a winterbourne, one of those downland streams that dry up in summer, when the underground water-level falls, and sometimes fails to flow in winter or a succession of winters. There is a shallow depression beside the first hundred yards or so of the track's west margin with a line of pollard willows along the outer edge. The grass and other growth in the bottom had the appearance of being rooted in damp ground, and because of this and the willows I walked it to see if I could find damp ground and perhaps water there. For most of the length the ground was very dry, but in the last twenty yards of the higher end I came to puddles of standing water, as if the flow of a spring were dwindling away. This place is about as much above the 450-feet contour as the other is below it, and would be the true source of the stream if it were not the head of a very erratic winterbourne that only flows during such an exceptionally wet autumn and winter and waterlogged springtime as had preceded this dry summer. In her book *A Wiltshire Childhood* Ida Gandy describes how she and her sisters were surprised one February day to hear and then see it flowing along this hollow at the foot of Easton Hill. To them it was the first time—and the last: "when we went to find it a few days later, behold, it had vanished". An old man who noticed their disappointment at finding it gone, and asked them what they were looking for, said, "'Tis seven years since he last came slipping down the hill, and maybe 'twill be seven years or more afore he comes again. It do take a terrible hard winter to bring *him*."

By the time the track brought me to the foot of Easton Hill the morning's press of cloud was breaking up, loosening into an eastward drift under which the evenness of diffused sunlight changed slowly, first to a definite brightness in widely separated places along Vale and downs, then to a glowing dapple of sun and cloud-shadow everywhere, with the shadows leaving more and more of the land to the sun as the clouds loosened and the blue intervals among them expanded in becoming an open sky across which the clouds were drifting. The turf on the hill was wonderfully green under its hosts of flowers. This is the greenest season for downland turf, a mat of sweet herbage in which the grasses are greatly outnumbered by the other plants growing in it; for how, otherwise, could it cover itself with such an array of flower-colour from spring to autumn, from the yellow, blue and white of cowslip, milkwort and meadow saxifrage to the white, mauve and purple of burnet saxifrage, small scabious and autumnal gentian? As I began to walk up the hillside, with skylarks filling the air above it with the silvery pulsation of their singing, and the cadences of a blackbird's calm phrases sounding distantly from trees in the valley beyond the farm, and the glow of sunshine increasing, with the sun's heat pleasantly tempered by the breeze, and the green hill with its multitudes of chalkland flowers rising against the sky, I thought there was no other place to which I could have come more happily on this June day.

My first impression was that the hillside, seen from its foot, appeared drifted with the colour of yellow flowers only—rock-roses in uncountable numbers, and here and there bird's-foot lotus, horseshoe vetch and mouse-ear hawkweed showing among them. None was raised more than an inch or two above the turf. Each kind, with its differences in form and the characteristic tone and bloom of its yellow, seemed brightened in freshness and beauty not only by the unclouded sun but by the deep contrasting green to which they were all so close. To both the sweeping and the narrowly confined view these rock-roses were making the hillside their own, as those on many another slope of down must have been doing on that day. For by mid-June their first scattered opening on stems which straggle among the other herbage springing from the turf-mat has grown into such multitudes as I saw on the valley-facing side of Easton Hill. It is the daylong sunward side as well, just the place for these fragile-looking flowers that open their crinkled, clear-yellow petals so widely round a tuft of deeper yellow stamens at the sun's touch, and never—until they naturally fade and fall—lose the cool, dewy quality of their colour in the heat of the sun. "Fear no more the heat of the sun" is a line I find myself remembering when I see them as they were flowering then; also I remember that the first word in the rock-rose's botanical name is *helianthemum*.

But it needed only a few minutes on the hillside to discover that a different flower, a white one, outnumbered all the others. Though lifted a little above the turf, it was too small and too airily spaced to take the sun in the glowing way that made even a little cluster of the yellow flowers attract the eye. This was the purging flax, a star-like shape, or perhaps not quite so much a star as a cup with its rim cut into five pointed scallops; and if we were to see rock-roses as suns, then these little flowers would be like stars in size as well as shape. The plant's thin reddish stems were so fine and its pairs of pointed leaves so inconspicuous that the flowers seemed unsupported an inch or two above the turf. Yet their quivering in the breeze proved them earth-caught. Only those around my feet were seen clearly—a few yards of distance and they were lost among the other flowers: but as I walked the hill it was soon plain that galaxies of these white stars were spangling the turf everywhere.

For other flower colour, this year's downland orchids were late in making their contrasts with the yellow of rock-rose and bird's-foot lotus, horseshoe vetch and mouse-ear hawkweed. One or two fragrant orchids were showing the pink of their sweetly scented spikes here and there, and, much more numerously but not the more easily seen because of it, the lesser butterfly orchid was dotted singly among the turf herbage on some parts of the hill and stragglingly drifted among it on others. Their spikes of about a dozen loosely held, greenish-white flowers seldom overtopped the flowers, blades and leafy stems around them, so that in following one of their drifts it was as if more had sprung up as I walked the few paces towards what had seemed the last in that direction. On many spikes the two or three flowers at the top were still in bud. Here, in these slenderly formed shapes of hood, lip and poised wings, cold in their whiteness yet softly lucent in texture, another beauty was quietly taking life from the sun. In scattered places along the turf milkwort had spread a deep blue and thyme a pinky red under the taller flowers. The rather dull reddish-purple of a little gentian, with stems that hardly lifted their flowers from the turf, gave the pleasure of discovery. It was the summer or early gentian, a plant I had never before seen growing, though I had often looked for it on the chalk hills. When I came to the crest of the hill and looked back down the slope I was surprised at the change in colour the high viewpoint caused. It revealed that the tallest flower-stems on that part of the hill were those of the salad burnet. They were thinly but continuously spaced along the turf, and they and the flowers they bore were tinged or stained with a redness under and among which the turf-green and the flower-colour were almost lost to sight. Perhaps the fall of sunlight was coming to the slope at just the angle for brightening the salad burnet into tinging the hillside like that. To find out how much of the plant had this red I examined one or two and saw that not only were the stems tinged with the stain, but that the small green flowers, gathered into pom-pom clusters, were edged with it and each flower-centre had a cluster of reddish stamens as well.

Eastward from its projecting shoulder the hill is hollowed into a green, steep-sided bay facing the valley. On the bay's innermost steeps, reaching up from the foot to more than halfway to the crest, a great colony of the musk or nodding thistle was thriving on the very much broken turf of a rabbit warren. Three or four feet tall, these very spiny thistles formed a dark, greyish-green hanger, broken by gleams of white where the sun caught the cascaded chalk scooped out by the rabbits. Most of their flowers were still rounded in prickly bud, only one or two showing the rich, empurpled red of closely packed florets pushing out and expanding as the flower-head drooped in becoming the nodding thistle of its name. The bare ground under the thistles was far from barren. Forget-me-not and the small-flowered cranesbill made a kind of sparse undergrowth there with the blue and pink of their little flowers sometimes clear in the sun, sometimes dim in the shadows. The foliage of two thorns at the foot of the slope not far from the thistles had grown pale with a yellow-green that seemed unhappily out of tune with the rest of their summer world. The slope immediately behind them was a chalk scar completely denuded of turf, so perhaps their sickly look indicated that too much moisture was draining and evaporating from the porous ground at their roots. Downland thorns usually look toughly green even when, in gnarled decrepitude, their scraggy remains of boughs have only a few twigs left to bud into leaf and, maybe, a tuft or two of fragrant blossom as well.

Turning my back to these pallid hawthorn bushes, I sat down in the sun to look out across the valley. The gentle dip of open cornland and pasture at the foot of the scarp led to the elms crowding the remainder of the distance to Etchilhampton Hill three miles to the south. From where I sat Etchilhampton Hill appeared beyond the elm-tops as a long shape green with corn and the last of its unploughed turf, a low ridge rising gradually from the east to end in a quicker fall to the west, the outward sweep of the hollow on each side of me cutting off the view to right and left of the hill. The higher end of its ridge came against the sky as a smoothly curving interruption to the almost level flow of the scarp-crest of Salisbury Plain, which lay behind it and made a skyline reaching from Urchfont Clump to Upavon Down. The day, now, was completely the sun's. Above the Vale and away southward to the Salisbury Plain skyline the sun and breeze had thinned the morning's press of cloud into a drift of widely spaced, billowing fleeces shining against a blue almost lost in the lustre of sunlight on it. At long intervals a slow cloud-shadow darkened the already dark-toned green of the elms in its path, or quenched the brightness but not the freshness of the green in cornfields which were often glossy with sunlight where the wind rippled them. The sounds made by rooks when the wind excites them into playing the soaring and circling and diving sky-game they appear to enjoy so much came from the air over the downs behind me. I turned away from the valley to watch the birds and was surprised to find that their sky, well north of the sun, was not the sky from which I had just turned. The wing-play went on under a limpid blue that seemed the colour of space made visible in heights far above a dapple of smooth cloud very different from the billowing fleeces in the south.

At last, though reluctantly, I had to leave Easton Hill and go back to the valley. My intention was to follow the Harepath Way on its slant past Harepath Farm to Allington a mile or so eastward along the road under the downs to Pewsey; but the deeply sunken part of the old road at the foot of the hill was so very overgrown by entanglements of herbage, and the sun so warm without the hilltop breeze, that I shirked the effort of pushing through it. Instead, I went down to Easton Farm to a lower track which looked as if it might be an easier way in the right direction. At the farm the cows were in for milking, and to make sure about the track's direction I went into a range of milking-sheds and asked a white-robed dairyman for guidance. (Here I found once again the kindness and the impulse to be helpful I have always found in Pewsey Vale when, needing direction or information, I have had to look about for someone to ask.) Coming with me to the track, he sent me along after pointing out a landmark to make for and two or three intermediate features that would keep me to the line. He knew, I realised later on, that the track ended in an uncultivated marshy place alongside the canal and only about halfway to the road I wanted to reach. This small, hedged-in corner of land was the lowest ground in fields sloping down from the foot of the chalk escarpment to a high bank, bushy and brambly, containing the canal. The embankment and the elms beyond the canal screened it from the breeze. With the sun blazing above it, moist warmth radiating from it, and sunshine glowing in it, the growth of plants springing from its cattle-trodden roughness, now drying and walkable, was like that of lush jungle in contrast to the flowery mat of turf covering the hill. Rushes were almost everywhere, and docks and tall thistles; but the tallest plants were the head-high teazels and cow-parsnips along the ditches. Figwort, brooklime, meadow-sweet and the willow herb called codlins-and-cream were there, all in flower, as well as drifts of moon daisies with larger flowers than any seen on the downs, especially those in front of the open margin of a willow-bordered pool. I felt that this was the edge of the Cannings Marsh mentioned in Saxon documents, the marshland which, to quote *The Place-Names of Wiltshire*, "has commonly been identified with the well-watered land through which the Kennet and Avon Canal now runs, in which All Cannings and Bishop's Cannings lie, some three miles apart, with Allington between them and with Beechingstoke still farther to the southeast".

CHAPTER VI

CURLEW ON CANNINGS MARSH

THE west end of the Vale of Pewsey was once a named marsh. The Saxons called it *Caningan Mærse*, and it was still *Canyngmershe* in the fourteenth century. Today there are the villages of All Cannings and Bishop's Cannings. Whatever it was like as land in Saxon times, it is now farmland, some of it arable but many of its fields marshy pastures. It is as tree-crowded as any other part of this leafy valley—elms and some ash and oak stand in the hedgerows, willows line the streams and ditches, and there are one or two small mixed woods. By the disposition of its villages it seems to have been roughly diamond-shaped, its length extending across the Vale about four miles from Bishop's Cannings to Patney, with about a mile and a half of width between Etchilhampton and All Cannings. From a spring at Bourton, near Bishop's Cannings, the west branch of the Avon threads it from end to end, and with the tributary watercourses from other springs makes this part the Vale's "western brookland". It is crossed by few roads. The canal keeps to the northern margin, the railway cuts it towards the south, and between them the only surfaced roads into it converge from All Cannings, Etchilhampton and Patney to meet not far from where, within the triangle of these three villages, the road from Etchilhampton originally forded a reach of the river named Etchilhampton Water. It is named so on the map, but some of the local folk will tell you it is Cannings Water.

About three miles to the northeast, in the high, bare solitude of downs above the Vale where Wansdyke crosses Tan Hill, a spring and summer bird-call I listen for is the one which has given the stone-curlew, that strange plover-like bird, the "curlew" part of its English name. Every spring a few pairs return to nest on these downs above the Vale, but it is an elusive bird whose presence is more likely to be revealed by a sudden and brief outbreak of calling than by its flying shape. Though I have occasionally man-

60

aged to pick out a stone-curlew on the ground and watch it for a minute or two, I have still to find a nest. Its twilight and night-time flighting and calling—for by day, unless walked up, it is usually a ground-keeper—must have been very familiar to the ancient downlanders whose mounded sepulchres are everywhere about us on the hills. That was long before the waterlogged wilderness at the west end of the Vale had become the Saxon marsh of the Cannings folk; and the barrow-builders, when they ventured below, must have been used to hearing and seeing another strange but larger bird, the true curlew, which still comes to nest in the marshy fields when the stone-curlew returns to the dry downs.

In the latter half of a very sunny May I went to the fields between Etchilhampton and Patney to enjoy again the experience of being among nesting curlew, and in everything the day was most fortunate. It had been preceded by a cloudless week that ended oppressively in heat, thunder and deluges of rain. A grey, drippingly showery and cooler day had followed the thunderstorms, and then came this perfect day with its gentle southwest breezes, its pale blue sky-space filmed with banded drifts and curling flecks of cloud too tenuous to be more than an insubstantial whiteness on the blue, and its bright clarity of sunshine that gave the May countryside the glow and lustre of its greenest freshness. I could not decide whether the day belonged to spring or had become the very first of summer.

The least green tree was the ash, only just breaking into leaf and looking bare by the contrast it made among the others. The oak was so far ahead of the ash as to be almost past the golden-green stage of its leafing, with—as it turned out—a summer to follow that for once did not belie the old rhyme

> "Oak before ash,
>   There'll be a splash;
> Ash before oak,
>   There'll be a soak."

Elm, sycamore, poplar and willow were nearly full-leafed. Horse-chestnut was the candle tree already—broad green domes spangled with white cones of close-tiered flowers. May-blossom was out as well. The hawthorns had snowed their new green with so much of its whiteness that I had to look searchingly to find the leaves, and when I came to the few places to which the breeze did not carry its fragrance I felt that something was missing. It would have been the same with bird-song, but I cannot recall a moment when blackbird and cuckoo were both out of hearing.

To reach the curlew fields I left the road between Etchilhampton and All Cannings and followed a lane that is the beginning of what must originally have been one of the few comparatively firm ways across the ancient marsh. It keeps to a very slight swell of ground which levels almost imperceptibly into the surrounding damp fields. Until it passes the end of a narrow wood and becomes a much more open track it is densely hedged with thorn and hazel and shady under the oaks, elms and sycamores which stand in the hedges. Its cartway has wide borders that the new spring growth of plants had then covered with jungles of goose-grass clingers, slender-stemmed stitchwort in flower, thick cow-parsnip tall enough for its tightly closed umbels to be breaking from their broad sheaths, the green laciness of chervil leaves under the white laciness of chervil umbels, and drift after drift of campion spreading its first flowers in numbers that found a perfect setting for their reddish pink just overtopping the green jungles in the sun-dappled shade along the wayside. Campion stems always spread their flowers airily. Full open, these five-petalled shapes, each petal deeply cleft into two parts, were flat rounds with a whitish frill at the centre and a red-tinged tubular calyx underneath. This was one of the campion places where, from plant to plant, the flowers vary in colour from the depth of normal pink through paler gradations to pink-tinged white, though in this place the deeper tones were predominant. A garden-warbler sang there, cascading his hurrying fall of note-bubbles into the lane. When I came back hours later he was still singing.

The track's lane-like beginning comes to a gated end where it passes the wood. After the gate a line of widely-set oaks interspersed with pines, hawthorns and one or two willows leads on from the wood and gives no feeling of shady enclosure. In May the dark tone of the pines shows how freshly green the other trees are and brightens the glow of buttercup yellow that lets hardly any green be visible in the meadows and pastures which now open out on each side. Here the slight swell of ground under the track is clearest. Slight though the swell is, it sharpens the impression of openness felt when the hedges and overhanging trees are left behind, and seems also to add width and height to the span of sky reaching away to a more distant press of valley trees with glimpses of the downs behind them. I could see the upper slopes of Etchilhampton Hill against the sky above the tree-tops to the west, a treeless shape green with corn above a pale, chalkily brown band of newly rolled arable. Southward the flow of the Plain's crestline was only revealed in gaps among the trees crowding the valley under it. The Vale's northern scarp-crest from Tan Hill to Walker's Hill overtopped the trees in that direction, with a gap in the trees framing one of those unexpected mid-valley glimpses of the Alton Barnes white horse which make it a presence in the western part of the Vale. In the eastward distances there were massed trees and the sky, and except for a grouping of two cottages and a farmhouse by the track ahead of me not another roof or chimney visible in any direction.

The curlew ground was the marshy fields on each side and in front of me. For the quarter-mile or so from the cottages to the railway the track was no longer traceable, even as a footpath, through the silvery green of tall grasses and the buttercup yellow in the next field, though beyond a brook and a level-crossing over the railway it appears again as a rough, almost impassably bush-thicketed drove between ragged hedges and ditches tangled with herbage. Had I been going on it would have taken me to a branching and the choice of either turning left to reach Wedhampton near the foot of the Plain or right to join the road that passes Foxley Corner, the meeting-place of the former Studfold Hundred, and then rises to the Plain up the steep of Redhorn Hill. But I had set out to spend an hour or two where I hoped to hear and see curlew, and so did not wish to go on; neither did my companion, a Wiltshire botanist revisiting these fields to look for sedges and marsh orchids.

Until we left the drier fields alongside the track and crossed a brook to reach damper ground no curlew call broke into the day's mellow leisureliness of blackbird song, and then, distantly, curlew notes were in the air—one brief outbreak of calling that was dying

63

away almost as soon as I recognised it. The day's other bird-song seemed like part of the silence which followed. Waiting for it to sound again I wondered whether a too intent listening had made me imagine it; but a few minutes later, from the same direction and no nearer, I heard it again and did not doubt my ears, though I was to walk the fields for another half-hour with divided attention—eyes seeking orchid colour on the ground, ears alert for curlew notes in the air—before discovering that a silent pair had all the time been much closer than the distant bird. We found the orchids first, and it happened that they were growing in the field which this pair had made their nesting-place. From the middle of one field the botanist caught sight of the sun-enriched crimson of the marsh orchids in the green of an adjoining one, a much damper field that was not only hedged but deeply and widely ditched along all its four sides. The ditches were something of a barrier, for they had precipitous banks and plenty of water bottomed by silted mud and we had to go halfway round the field before coming to a crossable place. At last we were bending over the flowers, the botanist with undistracted interest, whilst I was doing my best to divide myself, as it were, between the beauty of orchids new to me and a renewal of the experience of having curlew flying and calling close enough for their size, the curve of their long bills, and the streaked and barred harmony of dark brown, buff and grey on their plumage to take shape clearly as the birds whose notes have such a wild and melancholy beauty that they need a far more desolate landscape than the vestiges of this ancient marsh in the Vale of Pewsey to match the haunting strangeness of their cadences.

These fields have too many elms round them for flying curlew to remain in sight longer than a few moments at a time unless they are well above the trees or else very close, and even when close the circling birds vanish behind the trees in one place and reappear between others or perhaps skimming over the tops, their calling gaining resonance and the suggestion of an echo among the trees. In fact the elms give some of the fields the look of woodland clearings. The field we were in now was waterlogged under its very green turf, yet not so wet and soft as to be oozy underfoot. Besides the orchids its other Maytime flowers were buttercup,

64

bugle, water-avens, marsh valerian and, along a drier margin, a sprinkling of meadow saxifrage, a white flower I am more used to seeing in downland turf at altitudes where the stone-curlew nests. So, with the curlew we had disturbed flying about us and calling spasmodically, sometimes breaking into "Cur-lee-e-e, Cur-lee-e-e", and often into the long-drawn note that ends with a bubbling trill, we walked here and there, discovering more and more marsh orchids until I think we must have seen all the field contained. They grew in thin scatterings and closer companies and were of three varieties. The flower-spikes of one, the common marsh orchid, were those with the glowing magenta tone which, by its lustre in the sun, had drawn us from the next field. The much paler colour of another variety, the early marsh orchid, did not come to the eye so vividly, yet was no less beautiful with its delicate flush of rose-pink that seemed to give the flower-spikes a dewy bloom where the others were richly lustrous. Both these kinds had unspotted leaves, but the leaves of a third, being spotted with ring-shapes, revealed the presence of the leopard marsh orchid. Its spikes of flowers were almost as rich and deep a red as those we saw first.

As I have told, a pair of curlew remained unseen and silent until we entered the orchid field, and then were seldom out of sight or hearing until we moved away into other fields. From their behaviour I knew that their nest could not be far from us, most likely somewhere among the orchids. That is where it was, and nothing but chance led me to it. Whilst the botanist followed the orchid trail in one part of the field I wandered off to a group I saw in another part, and as I stood among them found myself looking down at two large, brown-mottled eggs lying on, rather than in, a shallow nest of roughly interwoven grass-stems which were becoming the sere colour of the old growth in the tussocks round about. It seemed impossible for a nest to be more exposed. Yet, after looking up from it to call my companion and wave him across to see what I had found, I had to scan the place carefully for a few moments before I could pick out the mottled eggs again, though they were only about a yard from my feet. Soon afterwards the botanist went off into other fields, leaving me to follow when I had watched the birds for a

Manningford Bruce Church

last few minutes from behind a pollard willow at the edge of the field. But it was early evening then, and I felt we had intruded too long into the birds' Maytime affairs, so when one of the pair, just clearing the elm-tops near my hiding-place, arched her wings, dangled her legs under her, and floated down to alight between the elms and the nest, I got across the ditch as unobtrusively as I could and left her in peace.

CHAPTER VII

TAN HILL

TAN HILL is in the middle and highest part of the eleven miles of downland escarpment which flank the north side of Pewsey Vale from the east end of Martinsell Hill to the west end of Roundway Hill. It is not quite the highest part, for Milk Hill, adjoining it to the east, has one or two more than the 962 feet of Tan Hill. The only other part which rises above 900 feet is the Martinsell bluff with 947 feet, and these three hilltops are the highest places overlooking the Vale. The opposite escarpment, the rise to the edge of Salisbury Plain, has no part of its crest higher than 800 feet, nor is this southern flank of the Vale so steeply elevated and so boldly modelled into sweeping hollow and thrusting spur and shoulder as the other. Tan Hill and the high places to right and left of it therefore reach altitudes that do not confine the eye within the southern limits of the valley below them. From these downland lookouts the eye can range southward across the smooth undulations of the Plain to where, on the Plain's edge twenty miles away, Old Sarum's unmistakable mound stands, a massive shape even at that distance and on such a wide horizon; and when the air is clearest, especially in the slant of evening sunlight, the slenderness of Salisbury spire will taper into the sky near the squat form of the mound.

Discovered from within the Vale, Tan Hill does not stand out by being a clearly separate summit or an out-thrust shoulder in the general flow of the scarp. Its top, with a small cluster of weather-worn conifers at the west end, is a narrow, mile-long plateau between a steep fall to the Vale and a rather gentler and shorter fall to the downs which lie between it and the beginning of the Kennet valley about two miles to the north, with Avebury another mile beyond. The great bank and outer ditch of Wansdyke sweep up to and follow this inward edge of the top, rising to it from Shepherd's Shore—the name of the gap made in the dyke for the

Avebury–Devizes road—and going on with it to where it is no longer the north-facing crest of Tan Hill but begins to cross the back of Milk Hill and lift in a green swell that carries Wansdyke eastward behind this broad buttress of the downs. Seen from the valley the shape of Tan Hill is partially masked by the prominent spur of down called Clifford's Hill reaching out from it towards All Cannings village. This hill has two rounded summits, one behind the other, the inner and higher one ringed with the age-smoothed earthwork of Rybury Camp which can be overlooked across the gap separating it from the Tan Hill plateau. The inward end of Clifford's Hill rises from the bottom of the gap to the camp-summit beyond which the hilltop dips gently and rises again to the outer summit and then falls away in a long tapering slope to the roadside at All Cannings Cross Farm. Lying back thus behind the smoothly curving bulk of Clifford's Hill, Tan Hill, whether seen as a downland skyline from below or as a hilltop underfoot, always looks and feels withdrawn from everyday life in the Vale. Westward from it the escarpment diminishes gradually to a less remote skyline carried along to Shepherd's Shore and the Devizes road by the shoulders of Kitchen Barrow Hill, Easton Hill, Roughridge Hill and the crest curves of bay-like coombs hollowing the valley-side between them.

There is a succession of these coombs along the escarpment. They differ in size but have the same kind of shape, which is more or less that of an immense half-bowl green with turf that covers steep sides falling to the margins of bottoms in which their steepness is flattened into an easy tilt towards the open Vale. The bottoms are usually cultivated: with their insweeping margins where the plough comes to the turf, they make the coombs look like bays of cornland along a bluff coast of downs. The largest of these hollows is the one enclosed by Milk Hill, Tan Hill and Clifford's Hill, its entrance the wide gap between the steeps under the straggle of bushes on Milk Hill and a bulge in the flank of Clifford's Hill under Rybury Camp. It goes so far back into the scarp that its inner slope leaves only a narrow ridge between the Vale of Kennet and the Vale of Pewsey to link Tan Hill and Milk Hill like an isthmus and carry Wansdyke past the coomb. Not as simply bowl-shaped as some of the smaller coombs, this one is great

enough in scale to give the surprise of discovering an almost
secret extension, a perfect coomb in itself, that is rounded in the
side of Milk Hill which faces Rybury Camp and is therefore hidden from the Vale. Hidden from the Vale, too, is an opposite
extension leading back to the saddle joining Tan Hill and Clifford's
Hill, though it is shallower and less typically hollowed than the
other. The whole coomb, with no angular form anywhere to
break the smooth sweep of its lines, is great only because the hills
that shape it are greater.

One September morning I stood on Tan Hill looking from
Wansdyke across Pewsey Vale in the direction of Coate, a little
place close to Etchilhampton Hill. Its roofs were among the elms
about three miles away, but I was looking back across the years as
well as across those three miles of distance. I was remembering
that twenty-three years had gone by since I first set foot on Tan
Hill, and this only a week after I came to Coate and the Vale for
the first time. To me, then, the Vale of Pewsey and the downs
north of it were new country to which I came the more eagerly
because a morning's walk would take me to the crest of the escarpment and Wansdyke and on across the downs to the West Kennett
long barrow, Silbury mound and the stones of Avebury. At last,
after reading and hearing much about these famous relics of the
beginnings of civilised life in our land, I should be able to see them
in their own downland world. I recalled that first walk along the
path through the fields from Coate to All Cannings, and on from
there by way of the chalk track that passes under Rybury Camp
to reach the level summit of Tan Hill and the Wansdyke bank;
and how, going on northward across the downs, I climbed the
bank to try to catch my first glimpse of Silbury, the bare, conical,
flat-topped and obviously man-raised hill so often seen in photo-
graph and drawing but never life-size in the physical round. And
there it was, less than three miles in front. I went on to find the
stones of the West Kennett long barrow exposed in their broken
mound, and afterwards the stones that remained standing from
Avebury's avenue and circles. These were the things I remembered
on Tan Hill twenty-three years later.

It would be interesting, I thought, to read again a few impressions written down in a farmhouse at Coate on the evening of

that day; enlightening, as well, to discover which of the things, all seen for the first time, had been put into words and which left for memory to hold fast. I found the notes, and what surprised me as I read them again after so long an interval was that they were almost entirely about the natural scene—the weather, the Tan Hill downs, the colour of downland grass, a bird or two and a flock of sheep. Rybury Camp, Wansdyke and Avebury are mentioned merely to indicate place and direction, Silbury and the West Kennett long barrow not at all. The date was 6th August, the day of Tan Hill sheep fair, and Tan Hill was put down as St Ann's Hill—but more about sheep fair and name later. Here are the day's notes:

"6th August, 1928. A hot sunny morning developed from a misty sunrise, the grass wet with dew. I reached Rybury Camp, then the Wansdyke on St Ann's Hill about noon. On the plateau a strong southwest breeze was blowing, making the tall, brown grasses on the gentler slopes beyond the Wansdyke towards Avebury rustle with a dry sound. Many of the slopes are covered with this grass which varies from very pale brown to a shade that is almost ruddy; but the steeper slopes where the sheep graze are cropped short, and their colour is a deep olive green which varies as the light changes. This green is the only colour on the steeps of the shoulders thrust out into the Vale of Pewsey. In places it is broken by vivid patches of white where the turf has been removed. Birds: corn-buntings on the way up, linnets in flocks, rooks and daws, one or two kestrels, some carrion crows, plenty of larks, several wheatears in one place, whinchats in another. I watched a shepherd and dog gather a scattered flock of sheep together and drive it across the downs. In movement it is like a light grey mass creeping slowly across the green slopes. The sheep must have moved almost touching each other. In the afternoon clouds filled the sky and obscured the sun, and then the olive green of the close-cropped slopes darkened noticeably."

Looking back now, I feel that Tan Hill, so strangely aloof from the Vale, yet not to be imagined apart from it, cast the more potent spell on that day.

I went up to the hilltop again and again in the last weeks of that bygone summer, and have been there occasionally since, at longer or shorter intervals, until the September day which sent me, with the writing of this book in mind, back in memory across the years. As on that first time, I followed the track which skirts the east flank of Clifford's Hill and curves round the edge of the coomb on its rise to Wansdyke. Long use, helped by the scouring hurry of rainwater down its ruts, have scored the track deeply in the chalk and made it a white streak, gleaming in sunlight, that can be seen from the other side of the Vale. The day's wind was a warm southwesterly breeze which kept within gentleness, even on the open hilltop. There was no direct sunshine, only its diminished glow caught in the layer of dove-grey cloud covering the sky everywhere. It was a smooth, not a hanging sky, reaching away airily from grey heights overhead to long downland horizons; and though it looked rainy in a gentle, shower-sprinkling way, and there was always moisture in the wind, the few definite rain-drops it scattered now and again hardly damped the turf. Such a sky's muted sunlight rested too faintly upon downland turf to brighten its tones. Rainy weather which had delayed the harvest had also given to the turf-mat the moisture which kept it green at a time when a dry summer can tinge it with the pallor of sere stems and spent flowers. In darkening the slopes the softness of the day's light made them the more richly green.

Where the track comes to the mouth of the coomb, with the fall from Rybury Camp reaching to its west bank, and the shoulder of Milk Hill balancing the camp about threequarters of a mile away on the east side of the gap, there is an old dewpond. Its sides are now under a tangled jungle of grasses and other herb-age, its water hidden among rushes and sedges that almost fill its bottom. This must formerly have been a much used drinking-place for the sheep and cattle pastured on these downs as well as for those being driven on long journeys across the waterless downs to and from the fairs, including, of course, the annual sheep fair once held on Tan Hill itself. For the botanist this dewpond sets the question of how the glaucous bulrush (*Scirpus tabernæmontani*), usually found in lowland pools near the sea, came to be growing in this downland pond at an altitude of 600 feet and at least fifty miles from the sea. Part of the same question is also suggested by the slender-flowered thistle (*Carduus tenuiflorus*) which grows by the track above the pond. It, too, is usually found near the sea, and on sandy soil, not on the chalk. Probably the answer is that they began to grow here from seeds carried by sheep coming in from coastal pastures in the south, in times when flocks, dogs and drovers had to foot it every inch of the way no matter how distant their destination. J. D. Grose, the Wiltshire botanist, was the first to notice that the bulrush was established in the pond. He has also seen it in four lowland places in the county.

Below the dewpond the track is sunk between steep, head-high banks. When I walked that way in July the grasses there, grown tall, had broken out their varied plumes, panicles and tails of seed-heads, and among them and often above them, in clusters, drifts and a kind of spangled looseness that is neither the one nor the other, were the flowers of knapweed, scabious, moon daisy, yellow bedstraw, bird's-foot lotus and yellow rattle, making colour accents of their purple, blue, white and yellow among green stems and blades, or up among the grey-green, blue-green and lavender of the grass-heads. A whitethroat sang there, in one of the few hawthorn bushes on the banks. But that was in the first half of July, when grasses were pliant and had the bloom of summer on them—on this early-September day they were stiffening and parching into rigid straws, often awry, the flowers dwindling to autumnal fewness. The many spikes of common spotted orchid which, in one place, had opened their pale purple above the turf-mat at the foot of Clifford's Hill had now darkened into the brown of seed-cases.

The most spectacular difference I saw here between a flowering plant's July and its September was that which had taken the green from the leaves and the yellow from the flowers of a great up-springing, almost a forest of ragwort covering the rise from the track to the Tan Hill plateau. For some reason or other this year's ragwort had not been infested with the usual hordes of cinnabar moth caterpillars, those alternately black- and orange-ringed crawlers that often strip the plants of leaf and flower completely. Ragwort may be a detested weed, but it is also a very handsome plant; and this summer—on the North Wiltshire Downs at any rate—

the strange absence of the caterpillars permitted it to show how handsome it can be rising to its full height of about three feet and expanding its decoratively cut, clear green leaves under a broad spread of yellow-rayed flowers.

This patch of ragwort was one of those which, seen from the other side of the Vale after they had begun to flower, were like golden stains on the turf-slopes under the northern scarp-crest. Spared by the caterpillars, it was at its best when I came to it in July. It covered so much of the slope above the track, and the plants were so crowded together, that its stems and leafage under their canopy of yellow seemed truly forest-like. The turf on the hillside was the sheep-smoothed downland mat, but where the ragwort grew it had become an example of what happens when it is too much broken by burrowing rabbits and cascaded with white debris from their tunnels. Seeds had been able to lodge on many a break in the turf and grow into flourishing plants. Forming an undergrowth was a sprinkling of the field thistle, clusters of hound's tongue and, carpeting the bare ground, much silverweed. By September the ragwort colour had changed from clear green under bright yellow to a dark, reddish brown of bedraggled stems topped by the pale, silvery brown of pappus in clusters of flower-heads all gone to seed.

The innermost bay of the great coomb was now on my right. Its bottom, half encircled by vertically grooved sides, is an extension of the cornfields in the outer part of the coomb, and these an extension of the broad undulations of treeless cornland in view eastward between the downs and the road to the Alton villages and Pewsey. The road is near enough to the elmy width of the Vale to run like a division between it and the footslope cornland. It is from this outer spaciousness that the coomb's inner bay is secluded. As I stood to watch two or three wheatears flitting about the tracksides ahead the leaders in a flock of sheep appeared on the skyline of the part of the coomb nearest Wansdyke and began to move down and disperse along the steep of the hollow. With the gradual leisureliness of grazing sheep, which, at a distance, seems more like drifting than walking, a loosely bunched flock of perhaps two hundred and fifty became grey dots spread about the steep turf. To see this number of sheep drift over the rim of the coomb and change into a scattering of small grey dots on the green slope was one way of being helped to realise the scale of the coomb and the stature of the downs enclosing it.

With the wheatears still flitting about in front of me, and a noisy congregation of rooks at their soaring and circling wing-play above Tan Hill, I went on up the track, now nearing the gap in the Wansdyke bank through which it leads to the downs beyond. A stone-curlew called once or twice in the coomb bottom but remained unseen. Wheatear and stone-curlew are not down-land birds in winter, but from their coming in spring to their going in autumn these two birds, each in its own way, seem completely in harmony with the ancient solitude of Tan Hill and the adjoining uplands. For it is not simply that this lonely edge of the downs gives the feeling of being outside today's homeliness and intimacy of the Vale's peopled places: these downs were already a solitude when people first came to them, and finding them habitable when the Vale must have been a waterlogged wilderness, left the Vale empty. The solitude remains, whilst earthwork and burial mound and all the other man-made banks and grooves have become a ghostly part of it. So, too—after how many thousand spring arrivals and autumn departures—have wheatear and stone-curlew. Or that is how I see and hear them. Both have quietly yet beautifully coloured plumage. The wheatear, much the smaller bird, has gradations of grey, cream and buff softening the effect of black and white; the stone-curlew, "a long-legged, large plover", has a streaking of dark brown on sandy brown, and paler brown shading into white. Distance or cloud-subdued light sobers their colouring.

The wheatear is an approachable bird, and yet its habit of short, quick flights a few inches above the turf, ending in what seems at first a sudden vanishing but is only the concealing stillness of its pose after it has settled on anthill or molehill or some such resting-place, gives the impression that wheatears flitting about only a few yards away are haunting this down rather than living on it. In the daytime the stone-curlew—only curlew by its call—is an elusive, ground-keeping bird that is more likely to be heard than to be seen in the air. If seen it will probably be going away fast and not high, and will vanish as it settles. Its call, startlingly like that of the true curlew when you are not expecting it, comes over the downs as if the solitude had found a voice. When the last sound of it has died away, there seems to be a strange emptiness above the downs, especially if the bird has called unseen. After hearing the stone-curlew it was curious that I should see two dead stoats tied by their necks to the top strand of a wire fence along the lip of the Wansdyke ditch. Their heads were close together. One stoat hung limp, its head drooping, the other with face up and teeth bared angrily in an open mouth. Its expression was one of defiant ferocity. Catching sight of this grinning mask that seemed more passionately alive than it could have looked when living, I had the odd feeling that its expression was the creature's final act of protest, the obverse of the stone-curlew's passive call, against man's intrusion into their world.

I left the stoats and came back to the Wansdyke bank and the hilltop. By then it was mid-afternoon. A brief sprinkle of rain, the day's last, was unheeded by the butterflies at September play along the bank. They were never dancingly active and were frequently at rest. One or two were the wall butterfly, some the small copper, but most of them were the chalkhill blue, their reds, browns and blues the brightest colours of the day when the small wings they patterned were caught open on stem or blade in the turf. I found no September flower-colour on the banks to rival the bloom of these butterfly hues—the colours of autumnal gentian, an occasional clustered campanula, plenty of eyebright and the dwarf plume-thistle were too subdued by the grey, even light.

Wansdyke is closest to the Vale here. Its line across the downs from Shepherd's Shore and the line of the escarpment from Easton Hill converge gradually until Wansdyke sweeps up to the west end of Tan Hill, and after running east along the inner edge of the hilltop and passing, almost overlooking, the coomb between this hill and Milk Hill, it veers away from the escarpment again. Together with the curve of the hilltop's crest the great embankment isolates the summit plateau whether its makers intended to do this or not. Tan Hill and Milk Hill are the boldest as well as the highest downs it crosses. I stood on top of the bank so that I could look along it and sense again the flexibility with which, in spite of its massive bulk, it conforms so buoyantly to the smooth rhythm of their flow. There was, particularly, the swinging lift that carried it up to and over a skyline behind Milk Hill. And with the bank under me instead of facing me like a green wall, I could also look across the miles of downland opening out northward from the Vale.

In that direction the foreground was the fall of downs reaching to the Kennet in treeless, irregular undulations of shallow hollows and folds, steeper under the Wansdyke ditch but soon easing and at last dying away in riverside fields. Silbury Hill was a bare, olive-green shape against the dark foliage of Avebury's massed trees. To the right of Silbury, with West Kennett village in the middle place between them, the mound of the East Kennett long barrow, or as much of it as could be seen, might have been mistaken for the obscurity of shade under the trees which cover it. The slopes rising to a skyline behind the village were those of Hackpen Hill, the woods on downs a little to the east of Hackpen were those at Old Totterdown, whilst eastward again, showing as a low, remote silhouette just above the farthest ridge of this North Wiltshire downland, the summit of a bluff at the edge of White Horse Vale brought the eye to rest nearly twenty miles away, on Uffington Hill in Berkshire. To balance these northward distances against those to the south meant leaving Wansdyke and going to the hill-top's outer crest where I could look across the Vale of Pewsey again. The steep of the escarpment and the width of the Vale under them were the foreground then, with the near edge of Salisbury Plain the first downland ridge of the many between the Vale and Old Sarum's flat-topped mound and New Sarum spire, the mound and the spire seen as though side by side at the far edge of the Plain and with many another ridge behind them. There is an east-to-west evenness in the general flow of all these crestlines. The few outstanding hill shapes along them emphasise it. Under the grey tranquillity of that September sky the last ridge of downs beyond the Plain seemed as distant as a skyline at the edge of the world.

I have mentioned that my first walks in Pewsey Vale were round about Coate more than twenty years ago. A discovery soon made there was that this hill had one name on the map and another when it was named by a native of the Vale. When I was

asked, "Are you going to Tan Hill Fair tomorrow?" followed by
—with a humorously doubting sort of look—"You'll have to be
up early if you are", I was so puzzled that all I could say was,
"Tan Hill? Where's that?" If my farmer friend had called it St
Ann's Hill Fair I should have known, but this was a name he
would never have thought of using. The hill was St Ann's to the
map-makers and Tan to the folk in and round the Vale. Of course
I made the mistake of believing that the two names were really
one—that, in local speech, St Ann's had been simplified into Tan.
The date of the fair, 6th August, is St Anne's Day in the calendar
of saints, and so all seemed plain. This, I discovered, had at one
time been accepted as what might be called the orthodox explanation. I also discovered that there were some to whom the matter
had not seemed plain, though their explanation of why the hill had
two names seemed fantastic enough for a doubter to feel justified
in writing the sentence at the end of the passage I now quote from
the *Wiltshire Archæological Magazine*, Volume IX, 1869:

". . . the conspicuous eminence . . . commonly called St Anne's
Hill, is by a natural corruption, Tan Hill. Here an annual fair is
held, chiefly for the sale of sheep and horses on August 6th, the
festival of St Anne, mother to the Blessed Virgin. Many have
been the theories respecting the first origin of this fair, and the
real meaning of the name given to the hill. The late Mr Bowles
would fain tax our credulity by assuming that the original name
was Tan Hill, and St Anne's Hill a perversion of it, and that in
this fair we must recognise the ancient holiday of some Celtic
Jupiter whom he calls Tanaris, to whom he believes the hill was
once sacred. And the late Mr Duke would fain lead us on a
similar track. . . .

"It will not be deemed presumptuous, it is hoped, if we venture to pass over with a smile these lucubrations of very worthy
men."

This is from a "History of All Cannings" by Canon Jones.
The derided belief was that the origin of Tan Hill Fair lay far
back in pre-Christian times when Celtic pagans made the hilltop
a place for performing the rites of one of their fire festivals, probably a festival connected with ripening crops; that the gathering

together of people for the religious festival would, as a matter of course, lead to the addition of trading to the activities on the hilltop; and that the hill's oldest name had come down to us in folkmemory from these remote times in spite of the Church's attempt in the Middle Ages to christianise the fair by linking it to the name and day of a saint.

I quote again from the *Wiltshire Archæological Magazine*, this time passages from "Tan Hill Fair" by T. Story-Maskelyne:

> "*Tan* means *Fire*, and the date of the fair falls at the very time of the year where Fire worshippers are known to have celebrated their rites on hills. . . ."

> "Fairs are held in Brittany on the same day as the fair on Tan Hill, August 6th, at St Anne d'Auray; at St Anne de Palve early in August; and at Carnac on St John Baptist's eve."

> "*Tan Hoel* (Fire of Helios, or the Sun) became changed into *Tan St Jean* (St John Baptist), on the eve of which day fires are still lighted in Norway, Brittany and other places, and a tinge of Christianity given to the old customs by giving a saint's name to the day on which they were observed. In this way Tan Hill has been altered to St Anne's Hill; and it is greatly to be regretted that modern maps all perpetuate the error."

That was published in December 1906. In 1940 was published an edition of the Ordnance Survey One-Inch Map, and on it St Anne's Hill had at last become Tan Hill. The fair was held very early in the morning. The writer I have just quoted mentions being told that in former years shepherds were guided through the night to the hill by beacons lit for that purpose. But it is no use setting out to see the fair on any 6th August now: no sheep have been driven across the downs to be bid for at Tan Hill Fair since 1932. The fires and the fair have gone, leaving only the magical strangeness of a name.

Chapter VIII

THREE SMALL CHURCHES

I. MANNINGFORD BRUCE

THE Manningford villages—Abbots, Bruce, Bohun—are small places alongside the middle mile or so of the Avon between Pewsey and the gap in the Plain. The main road from Pewsey to Upavon passes by them in succession: to reach them we must leave this highway, for the people who live there do not, as Edward Thomas put it, "dwell in all men's dust". From north to south there are the river, the villages, the road and then the scarp slopes of the Plain, with the road running as a division between the riverside fields and the much larger fields that make a broad belt of cornland edged by the downs. On the road's downland side there is unshaded openness, on its inward side are the valley trees, at first standing up rather thinly above the hedges around the roadside fields, but becoming denser towards the river shut in by its fringes of willows, poplars, alders and hawthorns where it is not darkly overhung by the three stretches of woodland along its banks. The villages lie close together, and as well as being tree-sequestered they straggle in a way that, by contrast with the easily taken-in compactness of most villages in the Vale, makes them seem formless. I have been going through and about them for a year or two now, and still find the ramifications of their lanes and footpaths puzzling. The Manningford villages must have left a similar impression with Edward Thomas: in his poem "Lob" he remembers

> "Their churches, graveyards, farms, and byres,
> Lurking to one side up the paths and lanes,
> Seldom well seen except by aeroplanes."

It is chiefly of Manningford Bruce's Romanesque church of St Peter that I wish to write here. Until 1291 the parish itself was called Manningford St Peter, but became Manningford Bruce after the manor had been given to William de Brewose. I had read about the church and several times caught sight of its flint-grey shape among trees near the main road before I went to find out for myself what it was like. This was on a day in April, and I approached the Manningford villages from within the valley, reaching them in the afternoon by way of a footpath leading from Swanborough Tump and down the side of Frith Copse. After crossing the railway beyond the end of the copse the path goes along the edge of a small arable field which, when I passed it once before, had caused me to stand and examine its appearance with surprise, and to say to myself, "Surely, there can't be chalky soil in this part of the Vale?" A man was turning over the field with a single-horse plough, but instead of being the dark grey of green-sand the earth was almost as chalkily grey as that of many a downland field. I could not believe it—something was geologically wrong! So, waiting on the headland until the ploughman came to the next turn and gave his horse a breather, I told him what was puzzling me. A tall, spare, bony-featured man, middle-aged and deliberate in both movement and speech, he saw and appreciated my point; and with a fleeting twinkle of amusement in his eyes he explained that he had given the ground a thorough liming the previous year. Whilst remembering this I came to the first cottages of Manningford Abbots, the time of day being already afternoon. There had been so much of April in the paths and byways I had followed from Pewsey that my walk had become a loitering saunter at little more than a mile an hour. Later on I discovered that this was not to be my day for seeing the inside of the church: the stubbornness of the great key in its locked door left me no time for that.

Manningford Bruce has the middle place in this puzzle of villages and is the closest to the main road. Its church is only about a hundred and fifty yards from the road but screened from it by a line of roadside beeches as well as by the vicarage among more trees behind the beeches. The turning to it leads also to a tree-screened house in grounds just beyond the west end. It is least shut in on its north side, where the width of a meadow reaches from the churchyard wall to a press of trees in parkland ending in riverside trees backed by the denser timber of Lock Wood. Small

Alton Barnes Church

though the church is, the difficulty is to stand away from it in a place from which it can be well seen as a whole. Village churches are frequently sited on a swell of ground, sometimes the highest place in the village, that reveals them prominently, if not completely, as the steadying feature among the groupings of dwellings about them. I am remembering such places as Chirton, Marden and Milton Lilbourne, where the church has this interest as well as any it may have as architecture. At Manningford Bruce the attraction comes from the church alone.

So I came at last to this church, walked among its gravestones, and saw the downs in its walls. In plan and character it is Romanesque, thought to be either tenth-century Saxon or pre-Conquest Norman. The authorities are unable to agree about the date. Hutton, for example, in his *Highways and Byways in Wiltshire* cannot believe that the English before the time of Normanised Edward the Confessor were capable of building such a church, and is convinced "that we owe this to Norman art and craftsmanship". Between sixty or seventy feet long and about twenty-five feet wide, it consists of a nave with belfry and south porch, and a chancel with its east end rounded into a semicircular apse, the nave taking up something less than two-thirds of the length, the chancel roof being stepped down a little below the nave roof. Except for stone quoins, window openings and doorways, and the wooden belfry, it is built of courses of rough flints, though they are more neatly trimmed and more closely set in the upper part of the gable under the belfry. The rough-textured, grey mottling of flint rising to the smoother greyness of leaded roof-slopes makes the church seem to hold and reflect the daylight with a frosted kind of coldness. It is highwalled for its length and width, but this may not be so apparent now as it must have been before the original plainness of its unbuttressed walls was taken away by the Gothic tracery and coloured glass of the three windows we now see in the west and south walls of the nave and the south wall of the chancel. From the outside the original Romanesque windows are simple openings hardly more than narrow, round-headed cell lights close to the eaves. At first there were probably five, one to each wall, the apse being left blind, as it is today. Those remaining are the two in the chancel and the

6*   81

Chirton Church

one in the north side of the nave. The original doorways, one each side the nave, are tall, round-arched and narrow for their height, entirely without moulding and other ornament, and are flush with the wall-face. The north doorway is blocked with flint; the south doorway, with its massively oak-timbered, iron-clamped door, is reached through the pointed and simply moulded entrance arch of a sheltering porch. The only ornamentation on this church exterior is later embellishment. There is the tracery of the newer windows and the arch-moulding of the porch—all the rest is two or three carved finials on gable points and the Gothic curves and cusps that make the open sides of the wooden belfry an arcade under a pyramidal roof.

When I had seen and noted these things I did not go into the church at once, but stood for a while at a gate through which a footpath enters a meadow beyond the north wall of the church-yard. Intending to walk a little way across the field to get a more distant view of the church from that side, I was about to go into it when the behaviour of a mistle-thrush on the grass a few yards inside caused me to stay where I was and watch the bird. What made me look at it with particular interest was the beakful of dead grass it held sticking out on each side like a ragged moustache. It continued to pick up grass and make the moustache bushier and more ragged. But then, instead of flying off with the beakful to some nearby tree to weave the grass into the nest I assumed the bird was building, it seemed to lose interest in such work and let the whole bunch fall to the ground discarded. Immediately after-wards the bird began to pick up and drop a short succession of small tufts of grass-roots tangled in earth, lifting each one up, holding it a moment, and then letting it fall. This ended when, having dropped a tuft, the bird cocked its head to eye the ground in true thrush fashion, darted its beak to the turf, and drew out and swallowed a worm. It did this several times, with an air of ab-sorbed diligence, as if the gathering of material for building a nest were forgotten completely. Indeed, when this mistle-thrush flew away its bill was empty.

The bird had drawn my attention from the church, and there was not, I discovered then, too much time left for seeing the inside if I was to catch the most convenient bus for taking me home.

Still, I should see what I could in the time remaining and come again on another day. That was what I thought as I went to the church door and found that although it was locked its great key had been left in the lock. Yet any other key, or no key at all, would have been less troublesome. Try as I might I could not turn it in a way to make it throw the lock so that I could raise the latch and swing open the heavy door. "There must be some knack in doing it," I told myself, "some sort of persuasive touch that makes the old lock work easily when you have it." If so, I never caught the trick. I went from the porch to the churchyard and looked about to see if I could find someone used to the key, but the place seemed as deserted as if no human being ever came there. I returned to the porch and struggled with the key again, but with as little success. "There *must* be a way of moving the lock," I kept thinking. After this effort I took a rest and went to see if the mistlethrush had come back to the meadow, but the field was then as blank as the church door, the churchyard and its surroundings as deserted as ever, though there was noisy animation in a rookery towards the main road, and behind the cawing the voice of an April cuckoo sounding constantly. A last attempt to turn the key proved that this was not to be my day for seeing the inside of this church. I caught the bus—but only just.

It was summer and June before I came back to see what I had been prevented from seeing in April, and this time the door had been left unlocked. I went in hoping to find as much of the original unadorned simplicity within the church as without, or at least enough to offer the imagination a chance to visualise the interior as it was before the three Gothic windows were shaped in the walls. My hopes were not disappointed: if the added windows make the church lighter and less cell-like they do this without changing its character too much. The putting in of one of them, that in the south wall of the nave, meant the destruction of a Romanesque window, all of it but the small round arch still in place above the pointed window-head. It seems likely, too, that another was lost when the west end of the nave was brightened with a fourteenth-century three-light window. Entered from midsummer sunshine, the church must have seemed dim and close-walled when its only windows were the few openings outwardly narrowed by being splayed through the thickness of the walls, the crown of each round head almost at the top of its wall. Much of the simplicity remains. The grey walls of the nave are plain under the timbering of a roof in which the principal trusses have horizontal tie-beams, whilst the secondary trusses between them are tied to give an arched effect echoing and leading to the semicircle of the chancel arch, beyond which the arching is carried along by the more modern tunnel-roof of the chancel to a rounded close in the half-dome of the apse. The ceilings of chancel and apse are evenly surfaced with small rectangles of wood. To come nearest to the impression I wanted of the church, I put the west window out of sight by sitting under it and looking eastward. The other Gothic window in the nave was more than half concealed by foreshortening, the one in the chancel out of sight altogether. I saw the simple severity of the original door and window shapes set in the bare though short perspective of the nave, this framing the chancel arch, and the arch in turn framing the apse beyond. Apart from the one glimpse of window-tracery, the only ornamentation I could see was an unobtrusive line of wooden moulding along each wall-top of the nave, a plain moulding at the springing of the chancel arch, and an unusual patterning of joints in the face of this arch where, instead of single voussoirs, there is a double row of stones with their inward ends wedge-shaped and interlocking. This church has been so well cared for and repaired that its nine hundred years neither burden nor antiquate it.

Late in the afternoon my way home took me to the little bridge over the Avon at Manningford Bruce in a gusty west wind that sent a straggling drift of crisply-white clouds billowing across a very blue sky. The sun was still well above the west end of the Vale. With it behind them the clouds in that direction were outlined by the gleam of their bright edges, but when their drift took them away from the sun and against a deeper blue their dazzling lustre reminded me of sunshine on the softness of new snow. This sky-drift found a visual echo in the continual and quick alternation of sun-gleam with cloud-shadow in the Vale. At one moment the river towards the sun would be all shimmer, glint and sparkle, and the next moment be dulled to the grey of dimly reflected cloud-colour. For its very attractive setting the bridge is an unimaginatively ordinary structure set on brick piers at each side of the stream, and with white posts and rails instead of parapets, and similar posts and rails leading to the crossing. On the east side the river comes to it from a white-railed footbridge at a tall, red-bricked millhouse several hundred yards away. The river banks are the most open on that side, the view less quickly closed by trees than it is in all other directions. The road to and from the bridge is a twisty lane between banks and hedges. It is perhaps a little wider than the stream, but not much. Pines, beeches, alders, willows and slenderly towering poplars stand close to the bridge, and on the west are backed by the trees of mixed woodland in which a vista of unkempt marshy ground is like a corridor with the river flowing along the south side. The bridge spans the river in one of the swampy corners of the Vale that give no glimpses of the downs and seem farthest from them in spirit.

Sky, trees and stream were all movement, fluctuating light, and brightening and darkening colour. There was always the rushing, sibilant sound of the wind, and everywhere the swaying of high boughs. The wind gave a silvery greyness to the green of willows and poplars by turning over so many of their leaves and keeping the pale undersides showing. The wood along the side of the corridor of marshy ground away from the river is edged with conifers. As they were towards the afternoon sun their shadow sides faced the bridge and I saw them in very dark silhouette against sky-blue and the gleam of cloud. The sunlight which put the conifers into shadow slanted over their tops and brightened the two or three willows standing a little forward in the open, so that against the shadowed conifers the airy leafiness of each willow was shaped in a mist of silver-green radiance which was also a shimmer of sun-reflecting points when its leaves quivered in the wind. They were seldom still. Wherever I looked the green of mid-June was the dominant colour, not one green but many, from its darkest tones on the conifers to its palest and greyest on the willows. I could pick out little flower-colour in the green of the riverside and roadside herbage near the bridge: a few yellow irises between river bank and open water, a sprinkling of the white umbels of cow-parsnip, parsley and angelica raised on their tall stem-columns, and the sometimes cream, sometimes purple clusters of drooped comfrey-bells almost lost in a jungle of horse-tails at the south end of the bridge.

2. ALTON BARNES

Excepting war-ruined, abandoned Imber, isolated on Salisbury Plain, the Ridgeway passes through no village on its way over the downs north and south of the Vale of Pewsey; but its upland world above the spring-line is cut by the two valleys it must cross in keeping direction—the narrow valley of the upper reaches of the Kennet between Silbury Hill and Marlborough, and, lying two or three miles south of this, the wider Vale of Pewsey itself. It is in these valleys, with their streams, springs and not too deeply subterranean waters, that we find the Ridgeway passing through its few villages. Its Kennet village is East Kennett, to which it descends from Hackpen Hill and Avebury Down but quickly rises again to downs that bring it—though diminished from the marching width it has on Hackpen—first to a gap in Wansdyke and then to a *col* between the neolithic camp on top of Knap Hill and the long barrow on top of Walker's Hill at the lip of the Vale. Here it drops down the steep of the escarpment to cross the second valley, and at the foot of the slope comes to the Alton villages, Alton Priors and Alton Barnes, that are so close together as to seem one; after which it ceases to be a green road and perhaps any road that can be identified with certainty, until, behind Wilsford at the far side of the Vale, it breasts the rise of another chalk scarp and runs on downland again. Its course across the Vale must be more or less closely followed by the metalled road that converges from Lockeridge in the Kennet valley, and after cutting Wans-dyke about half a mile east of the Ridgeway's gap in the earth-work, joins the Ridgeway at the edge of the downs above the two villages. Alton Barnes, with its diminutive Saxon-walled church of St Mary, lies very comfortably between Alton Priors and this metalled cross-valley road.

The lower sweep of today's road down the scarp under Walker's Hill is a good place for a first view of the Altons. The hillside below it, still keeping its downland bareness, shallows into a gentle tilt of arable fields ending at a scarp-foot road that separates them from the nearest edge of the villages and makes a sharp division between the openness of the valley-side and the clustering of trees, many of them elms, among which these two little places are dispersed. Here, again, as at the Manningfords, though with no suggestion of their wooded riverside seclusion, are farmhouses and cottages whose scattered grouping seems formless except that each of the two parts has a church in its midst, though the Alton Priors church of All Saints is now in decay and disuse. The two places together do not make a large village, and certainly not one that overcrowds a site that must have been chosen by its first Saxon settlers as much for its accessible water as for the farmable land around it and the already ancient highway across the Vale. The root word of the name gives a clue, I think, to the explanation of why these twin places are shaped as we find them today. In the look and the sound of the word "Alton" it is easy to see and hear Saxon *æwielle-ton*, meaning "the farm by the springs"; which suggests that there is something in a name after all, and that if the original settlers had to build on the drier places among the damper ground about the springs and along the brooks running from them, later people would be obliged to do the same, and this would account for the loose and irregular dispersal of their farmsteads and cottages. The main brook flows south through the field separating the two churches and runs on across the Vale to join the Avon at North Newnton opposite the river-gap in the Plain. I recall and quote a passage from a letter written at Alton Barnes on 15th October, 1829. Augustus Hare had been appointed to the living, and during their first week at the rectory his wife wrote:

> "The day has been beautiful, and before we began our morning's work we took an exploring walk, and after wading through a bed of mortar we did get to a dry walk up the downs. Our great object is always where to find a place tolerably dry for our walks, and our first errand to Devizes has been to beg the shoemaker to come and measure us for waterproof shoes."

The Alton footpaths and roads are better surfaced and better drained today, but the waters still rise and separate and flow.

From the Walker's Hill road the Altons are places I like to see in the cold clarity of mid-winter sunshine. I am thinking of the kind of temperate day that has its hours of open, tranquil sky from which the sun brightens their side of the Vale and its downs with lucid radiance, whilst in the distances towards sun and Plain the brightness loses this clarity in a mistiness it makes in the air. By contrast with the colour-quenching fall of light among the trees and fields to the south, and upon the downs rising behind them, the winter colour in and about Alton villages is luminously revealed, and at close range the eye discovers a vivid crispness in the details of the shapes into which things have grown, or have weathered in decay, or have been fashioned to human needs. It is a revelation of colour, form and texture that is like being given new vision for seeing such familiar things as the downland mat of turf, the shaggy tangles of herbage on a roadside bank, the bark of a tree, the close parallels of stubble with, perhaps, an undergrowth of clover, the knots and crevices in a field gate-post, the surface of a ploughed field. The downs of the escarpment above the Altons never seem more bare, open and lonely than they do when the winter sun is proving their colour to be not so much the green of turf but the pallidly sere, almost blanched hues of sapless, brittle relics of blades and stems that sprang from and flowered above the turf in the previous summer. A distant shoulder of down can seem incandescent with sunlight then. Between these slopes and the village trees there is the open sweep of cornland in which some of the great fields will have been ploughed and be showing the chalky pallor of downland furrows, and some where the sun will reveal that not quite all the sheen and mellowness of harvest-time has faded from weather-tarnished stubble. There is, as well, a similar and immediate openness of cornland to west and east of the Altons, a more level westward expanse to the next scarp-foot village, Stanton St Bernard, and an eastward rise that steepens smoothly in becoming the base of Woodborough Hill, that bare but tree-tufted outlier from the downs. The Alton elms are almost an island in these cornfields. In the winter radiance, with the sun-misted, tree-darkened undulations of the Vale behind them, the most luminously clear colour glimpsed among their trunks will be the jewel-like green of the little fields round which they stand.

The church at Alton Barnes is out of sight of the cross-valley road, but a short byway leads to it, first going between some bright new council houses on the right and the old brick-and-tile rectory that is much larger than the church and fronts it across the open green of a small meadow on the left. A tree or two almost screen the south side of the church from the road, and then there is the garden between the churchyard and another house of warm-toned brick and tile close to the large group of farm buildings and yards where the road ends. Most of this mainly brick-and-thatch village lies in the quarter of a mile between this byway and the road along the foot of the downs. The church is even smaller and simpler than the one at Manningford Bruce, the Saxon-walled nave as old, if not older. It has a nave only twenty-five feet by fifteen feet inside, a smaller chancel without apse, and no porch, buttresses, tower or belfry, its two bells being hung side by side in openings in the west gable. One bell is inscribed "Anno Domini 1626", the other "Robert Wells Aldbourne Fecit 1788". At Manningford Bruce the clean-lined, unified simplicity is rather coldly severe, at Alton Barnes the unsophisticated, rough-hewn simplicity is that of rustic homeliness which makes it look the kind of village church that should be embowered in a Bewick vignette.

Under steeply pitched roof slopes covered with stone slates that have weathered to a creamy brown overlain with patches of grey and yellowish lichen, the nave walls are whitishly grey with a crumbling surface of coarse plaster and a few peeling vestiges of cream-coloured limewash. This conceals most of the stone surface except the long-and-short work of the quoins and the two pilaster strips spaced without projection along each side wall. Where the decaying plaster exposes other stonework the pieces are so very crudely shaped and set that it can hardly be called masonry, though where the east gable end—which is not plastered—projects above the chancel roof, it shows a mixture of roughly shaped flint and stone, roughly coursed. The little chancel, whatever its original fabric, was entirely rebuilt of brick in the eighteenth century, and although the brickwork is much overgrown with ivy, particularly the gable, enough is left bare for the discovery that the headers, ranging in colour from dark reddish-brown to vitrified blue-black, chequer the warmer shades of the other bricks. The east end and each side wall has a masonry window with mullion and head tracery. Not one of the church's earliest doorways and window openings has survived. The blocked-up north doorway is fourteenth-century, the south doorway seventeenth-century, the west window, originally fourteenth-century, was altered in the seventeenth century. There is a square wooden-framed window with plain leaded lights above the south door, and on the right of the door one that is a wooden imitation of Gothic in both senses of the adjective. The church has, in fact, the oddest hotch-potch of doors and windows, yet this does not weaken its rustic attractiveness.

There is no disharmony between the outward appearance and the inward: the spirit of gentle homeliness pervades the interior. Its narrow smallness gains a kind of upper airiness from the steep pitch of the roof and the three tall triangles of its collared and braced trusses with their slightly cambered tie-beams spanning a nave in which the lower part of the walls has panelled wainscot to about a foot above the tops of the pews, and all the upper part is smoothly cream-washed, though these surfaces have a surprising number of small marble memorial tablets, often to former rectors, relieving their blankness. Not much of the west window is to be seen, as its wall is behind an old-fashioned gallery across the end of the nave. The pointed chancel arch is wider and taller than it was at one time, but this only makes chancel and altar seem the closer. Here all is close and intimate, and if all the people in the village came to church it would look very full.

One of the memorials in the church bears the following inscription:

"Sacred to the memory of the Rev. Augustus W. Hare, M.A., sometime Fellow of New College, Oxford, and Rector for five years of this Parish, who, having gone to Italy for the restoration of his health, died at Rome, Feb. 18, 1834, aged 41.

"The parishioners of Alton-Barnes and Alton-Priors, sorrowing deeply for his loss, have placed this tablet in thankfulness to God who gave and spared him to them a little while, and in affectionate remembrance of the love wherewith he loved and tended the flock of Christ committed to his charge."

I quote it because it is not, I think, an empty, formal tribute, but one that truly reflected the feelings of his parishioners. In a period when there was great poverty among farm labourers and other rural workers in the south of England he did what he could to increase the temporal good and comfort of the Alton cottagers. He used to say, "We must get at the souls of the poor through their bodies." In acting up to this he portioned off as allotments part of his glebe and encouraged the men to cultivate them properly. He also opened a shop once a week in the rectory barn where, with his wife as shop-assistant, "he sold at two-thirds of the cost price all kinds of clothing and materials of clothing". These and other things are told in *Memorials of a Quiet Life*, a life of Mr and Mrs Hare written by Augustus J. C. Hare and published in 1872. The author, a nephew of the Alton Augustus, was adopted by Mrs Hare after her husband's death. She had no children of her own.

The Hares moved to Alton Barnes in October 1829. For a few days in November 1830, life was not quiet in and round the Alton villages. This was the time when the south-country farm labourers, struggling to exist in the poverty caused by skinflint wages, found their discontent boiling up from apathy into a passion of resentment that drove them to destructive rioting. The increasing use of threshing machines was a grievance, too, the men believing that these machines were, as Cobbett put it, "robbing them of wages that they should have received". So they went about the countryside in bands to seek out the machines and smash them. They also —to quote Cobbett again—"resorted to the use of fire, secretly put to the barns and stacks of those who had the machines, or whom they deemed the cause of their poverty and misery". Such a band came one November afternoon to the farm of Mr Pile close by the church and rectory at Alton Barnes. What happened then is told by the rector in the following letter I quote from *Memorials of a Quiet Life*:

"Nov. 24, 1830.—For fear you should be alarmed by cross-country accounts in the newspapers, I write a few lines to say we are all safe, after one of the most painful days I ever went through.

"About two o'clock we were summoned by two half-drunken men who professed to be *sent on*. They came to the door, and asked for money, 'any trifle', announcing that two hundred were coming at their heels. After failing of their errand, they went down to Pile's house, opposite us, whither I followed them. He was gone to Marlborough, and there were none but women in the house. As the only chance, I had the church bell rung, but none of the labourers came; perhaps they were too far off, and did not hear. About ten minutes after the troops arrived. The machine had been taken to pieces, but *that* did not satisfy them; they must break it. And breaking it they were, when Pile on horseback dashed in among them, and fired. They would have dispersed, perhaps, in a fight, but in a place where they could close with him, his gun went off a second time. They dragged him down, and have nearly killed him. They then burst into the house, and broke everything to pieces, and for some time I expected they would serve us in the same way; so irritated were they, and so mad with drink. Indeed, they talked of coming back tonight, and burning all his ricks and barns. But the news had reached Devizes even before I could send a messenger. The Yeomanry were here by six, and I have just heard that they have surprised several of the rioters in the public-house at Woodborough. On the Marlborough side ten men were taken today; and a regiment of Lancers were to be there by eight o'clock tonight. So we feel safe again."

As a tailpiece in a more peaceful mood I add a quotation from another letter, printed in the same book, the writer this time being the rector's wife. She says:

"I had such a delightful ramble over the Downs; the sun shone so bright, and the air was clear and reviving, and I pushed on till I turned a point of the hill, and there sprawling beneath me lay the great White Horse in all its chalky glory. I could not go back ignominiously when so far, so I went on, and soon planted my stick in the White Horse's tail! Far beneath in the hollow the sheep were collected together, and the shepherd boy was seated on his knoll of grass. What a time for meditation! No wonder the great poet of Israel was a shepherd, or rather, to give the cause before the effect, *vice versa*. I dare say, however, no very sublime thoughts are conceived on the Wiltshire Downs, and I should fear the mind was as inactive as the body in the boy I saw stationed on the hill with that wide view all below him."

Which reminds me that about a century earlier the poet Stephen Duck, who was born only a mile or two away on the other side of the Vale and began his working life as a thresher and ended it as a parson, must have had somewhat similar thoughts about downland shepherds when, after a journey across Salisbury Plain, he wrote:

> "Propt on his Staff, he indolently stands;
> His Hands support his Head, His Staff his Hands;
> Or, idly basking in the sunny Ray,
> Supinely lazy, loiters life away."

There are many more machines than shepherds in the Vale of Pewsey nowadays.

3. CHIRTON

From the Altons I go now to Chirton, a village between the west branch of the Pewsey Vale Avon and the Devizes–Andover road at the foot of the Plain in the Vale's southwest corner. Patney is just across the river to the north, Marden a little less than a mile to the east, and Wedhampton about the same to the west, the latter being, to me at any rate, the last village definitely within the Vale on this side. I can never make up my mind whether Urchfont, a mile and a quarter beyond Wedhampton, is just within or not. It always seems a place that is neither quite within nor quite without, a place on the corner, as it were; for behind it the scarp of the Plain, with Urchfont beech clump as a landmark, begins to swing away from the Vale and face the wider and lower valley of Wiltshire's other Avon. A byway loops Wedhampton to the inward side of the Devizes road, but the way to Chirton from this main road continues right across the Vale, bridging the Avon to enter Patney and the railway to leave it, then winding on across the former Cannings Marsh to skirt All Cannings and bridge the canal before reaching the northern scarp-foot road where it passes the out-thrust end of Clifford's Hill.

Chirton is a long, open village. Opposite to it, and about a mile away, the scarp-crest of the Plain gives a smoothly flowing sky-line to upper slopes in which the lateral sweep is through wide and shallow bays in the downs rather than the deep hollows of coombs, and the first fall from the crest quickly shelves into a very gentle tilt of cornland that is almost level when it comes to the main road, and then, in the threequarters of a mile between road and river, swells up again into a low fold parallel to them but with its ridge nearer the river. The road that is the village street crosses this fold and rises so gradually with the longer or downland side that it never steepens into a noticeable hill. It hardly seems to be a rise at all until the church on the crest of the fold is reached and the shorter, steeper dip from the churchyard to the river is revealed. Here are pastures with a few elms standing in their hedge-rows, the ground beyond the river rising again between Patney and Beechingstoke and gaining a wooded look from its greater concentration of trees. In front of the church the street goes sharply right for about a hundred yards and then as sharply left in beginning its winding descent to the river bridge at Patney. To turn from the main road under the plain into the straight length of the village street is to see its grass-bordered width as an approach to the church raised above its end, though the church's grey stone shape does not stand completely exposed because the brick-walled, slate-roofed vicarage screens its west end. All the same, it is clear that this is one of the villages where the church is set upon the highest place. The same fold of ground stretches along the river eastward towards Marden, the next village, and there, too, the village street on the downland side is an approach to a church overlooking the river from the crest.

No village in the Vale reveals its shape more clearly than Chirton, none is sunnier and more open. It is, as I have already suggested, a place that can be taken in by walking along its one street. Its greater part, the part south of the church, is on a sunward slope, hardly noticeable though the slope may be. There are few tall trees to give shade. The many elms in the parkland immediately west of the village are a background contrast that makes it seem all the more open to the sun whatever the season. Even winter sunshine, particularly the kind of day I spoke of in connection with the Altons, seems here to add a less reluctant warmth to its colour-revealing clarity. It can be felt as a most pleasant radiation from every sun-brightened wall along the street. I remember standing not far from the church one January afternoon and for a moment or two thinking myself surrounded by hive bees. Then I noticed that the roadside wall nearest me was of chalk-mud or cob, and that the insects were not hive bees but mason bees the sun was beguiling from the small cavities they shape in a crumbling cob wall. They appeared to be doing nothing but fly about rather aimlessly in front of the wall, as if they had been prematurely roused from winter inertia and felt no instinctive urge to do anything but exercise their wings in the brief January foretaste of April warmth and brightness.

Until the street turns aside in front of the church its width and not too rigid straightness, together with the uncongested way in which the village is lined along it, give the place openness without disunity. The roadway itself has ample width and grassy margins as well, and as often as not there are gardens behind these margins, so that the house-frontage to the street is neither regular nor continuous. Most of the larger houses are close to the church. The cottages stand singly, or in semi-detached pairs, or in short rows of three or four, and have enough difference in structural detail to keep one's interest in them lively. Brick without timber framing is the building material here, with thatch on one or two roofs only, and either tiles or slates on the others: indeed Chirton today has less thatch than is usual with villages in the Vale, and if any of its walls are timber-framed I have not yet caught sight of them. In general tone the brickwork is a pinkish red that brightens to a soft richness in the sun and is really a fusion of many shades, for it would not be easy to pick out two bricks exactly alike in their tinge of redness. There are some cottage walls in which the general red comes out through a not too insistent chequering formed by the use of bricks with darkly burnt ends as headers in the bonding. Their colour ranges from a brownish red to a purple almost black. They are used in another way on a pair of cottages that have their front doors side by side but each recessed within its own

95

porch entered under a semicircular arch shaped in brick of normal colour. A second arch of similar colour is set round this, and a third, formed of the dark bricks, encloses the second to complete an arch-within-an-arch effect reminiscent of Norman Roman-esque. The flatter segmental curves of ground-floor window-heads, one each side the twin porches, are also repeated in an upper arch of these dark bricks.

Towards the downland end of the village street a gateway is the entrance to a farmyard. A long, lofty barn with weather-boarded sides and tiled roof takes up the whole of the farther or west side, a square-built farmhouse of brick, quietly formal in style and with 1843 on a porch facing the yard, is set back a little in its grounds on the south side, and lesser buildings, mostly of brick and tile, line the other two sides. Under the long ridge and plain steeps of its roof the barn is made a double one by a central wagon-way, tall as the eaves, that leads right through it. To right and left of this each part has a gabled projection in which double doors give access from the yard. For the first three or four feet above ground-level the barn is brick-walled, but from the red of brick to the paler red of roof tiles the colour is the black of its boarded sides. When I walk into Chirton from this end of the street, and go on towards the church after stopping to look at the barn, the single cottages I pass seem very small.

The church here is less simple in design than the other two, but although the nave is aisled and has a battlemented tower at the west end, this only makes it large by comparison with their small-ness. In character I find it neither as intimately homely as the one at Alton Barnes, which, for a church, is all too human, nor as austere as that at Manningford Bruce, which still shows how it once shut out the world. To me its outstanding quality is charm, and I do not see why a church should be any the less a church in possessing it. There are parish churches as well as cathedrals that give wings to the spirit by their soaring grace—as at Bishop's Cannings in this Vale, for example; but there is also a place, I think, for those that hold the spirit to earth by the no less real though perhaps more elusive quality we call charm. Whether in a person, a flower, a place or a building, it is something that seems to fade under analysis, yet lives again the moment we cease trying

96

Marden Manor House

to account for its presence. With this church at Chirton I feel that
it is partly the result of balance of proportions in the unity of the
whole and on just the right scale—on a larger scale it might be
dulled by heaviness; and partly the result, whether accidental or
not, of restoration in which the rebuilders did nothing to upset
this unity and balance—they have preserved not only the masonry
of the Transitional Norman nave but its original roof-trusses as
well; and as an exterior, partly the result of seeing the pale, soft
grey of its stone in contrast with the warm brick-tones of the
village below it.

As well as being on higher ground the church is not so shut in
among trees as the other two. The south half of the churchyard,
its old gravestones sunk in the grasses of its turf, makes an open
approach across which the church-walk continues the line of the
village street, and within a pace or two sets the south porch perfectly in the eye at a distance not too close for seeing it as a whole,
yet close enough for the texture of its stone to be seen. From the
verticals of the fifteenth-century tower rising at the west end in
three stages to a crowning fret of battlements, to the ball-finial on
the chancel gable at the east end, with the porch gable's acute apex
and terminal cross cutting the horizontals of aisle and nave though
not the line of the roof-ridge, no part overmasters another. In the
balance of their contrasting lines and shapes they rest in the happy
composure that must be a source of the building's charm. Another
source must be such a feature as the tower buttress diminishing in
two bevelled steps against the outer corner of the lowest stage,
thus basing the tower firmly but not ponderously on earth before
it rises to the simplicity of plain quoins; and another must be the
felicitous placing of a two-light mullioned window, closed with
perforated stone slabs below a tracery-head, in each face of the
battlemented stage. Then there is the creamy grey of the stone
itself and its light-holding texture, and the darker grey of the
stone-slatted nave and chancel roofs, the roof of the nave
steepening from the narrower leaded roof of the aisle that is like
a footslope to it. And in the end there are those completing
touches—the thin encrustment of greenish-grey lichen hardly to
be distinguished from the stone surface it covers, and the small
round patches of dark brown moss dotted and clustered about the

7

Beechingstoke Clump

stone roof-slopes—that nature gives like a benison to the work of craftsmen whose material is the limestone quarried from hills within sight of the chalk downs enclosing this part of the Vale.

Alton Barnes has its Saxon-walled nave, Manningford Bruce its pre-Conquest Anglo-Norman walls, windows and doorways, Chirton its Norman nave, south door and font. The porch at Chirton was a fifteenth-century addition to the south door and was partially rebuilt later; but the doorway it shelters takes all the attention as soon as it is seen within. Like the nave, it is of the Norman Transitional stage in which, in the middle of the twelfth century, the mason-architects were feeling their way forward from the limitations of the semicircular arch to the pointed arch and a change of style. The height of a semicircular arch is fixed by the width of its span—for a given width the builder cannot make it higher or lower; and the wider the span the greater the weakness of the crown, the part where the joints are nearest the vertical and therefore the part in which the wedge-shaped stones are the most likely to push the abutments askew and sink under the pull of gravity, as appears, for example, to have happened in some Norman chancel arches. The pointed arch can be blunt or acute according to the builder's requirements and is stronger at the crown as well. The change was, of course, the transition from Romanesque to Gothic.

In the arch-within-arch effect of the Chirton doorway the opening itself is shaped by a pointed arch inserted in the fourteenth century, but though the members enclosing this are pointed their crowns would not need very much flattening to become the rounds of semicircles. The tunnel-like severity of the purely Norman doorway has been lost and some lightness of form gained, whilst the plainness of the quarter-round moulding of the innermost arch sets off the ornamental enrichment of the older part. There are two bands of continuous zig-zag and their echo in the beads or pellets in a hollow behind them, and outside this a roll moulding, along the arch of which are little, closely spaced reliefs of human heads, two human hands, animal heads, a bird's head and the upper half of a mannikin under another moulding with very worn and now indefinite ornament. There are, as well, the usual Norman beak-heads on the doorway, those grotesque, formalised shapes which, it has been suggested, may have originated in the idea of adding eyes and ears to the zig-zag triangles. The other figures are neither formalised nor fantastic, but were, I should say, straightforward attempts at realism. Within the church something of the same feeling for the natural, though here turned descriptively to a formal subject, is found in the carved decoration of the font, probably the one made for the original church. It is a cylindrical limestone block, nineteen inches high, and shows the Twelve Apostles each in his own bay of an arcade in which round arches span columns with capitals representing clusters of pine cones. Ten of the robed and rather stiffly standing figures hold books, the eleventh holds what looks like a roll, and the twelfth a key. There are bands of interlacing plant stems and leaf ornament above the arches. The repetitions and rhythms of the patterning are perfectly adapted to the continuity of the cylindrical surface, but the carving lives by its naive realism.

The nave is not only Transitional Norman in its arcading but is also believed to be this in its timber roof as well, so that when we stand in it the original twelfth-century roof is overhead. Such a survival of roof-timbering is very uncommon. The steeply pitched rafters are close together, each pair strengthened with the kind of intermediate crosspiece known as a collar and by a pair of curved braces between wall-top and collar, their curves meeting to form an arch under rafters and crosspiece. Four of the frames—one at each end of the roof and two in between—are made into triangular principals by means of tie-beams, though these beams hardly obscure the barrel-vaulted effect the curved braces give to the nave. The roof principals and the arcade pillars divide the nave into three bays. Except for their base-moulding and capitals the pillars are plain under plain arches, each capital having different ornamentation that varies from the formality of simple scallops to the freer curves of foliage. These church masons were never the slaves to unessential repetition, and their work gains charm because of it, especially in such capitals as these. Nor is there anything of Norman dourness in the build and bearing of the nave to weaken the unaffected charm of the whole church, as can be seen by standing under the tower arch and looking east. The tall west window brightens the shape and sculptured detail of the font in the foreground and the nave arcades and the creamy smoothness of the side walls rising from the arches to the greyish-brown roof timbers spanning them. The pale masonry shaping the almost semicircular chancel arch is like a frame that reveals the farther end of the chancel's boarded, semi-hexagonal ceiling as another kind of arch, and close under this the pointed arch that contains within its deep splay the triple lights of the east window below tracery in which a cusped circular light is centred between two narrow trefoils.

CHAPTER IX

MARDEN

MOST of the parishes in Pewsey Vale are long and narrow, with one end low in the valley and the other well beyond the crest of the downs, each with its village lying towards the end farthest from the escarpment. This was the usual pattern of Saxon settlement and land-sharing in the kind of countryside where, from a wide valley bottom, the land rose gently at first and then more steeply to the edge of open uplands. So it was in the Vale of Pewsey. Water, the most fertile soil and the sheltering position of lower ground among trees determined the site of the village. Round its cluster of homesteads were ploughland and meadow reaching back to the uncleared inner parts of the valley where there were woods for swine and glade pastures for cattle, and forward in the opposite direction to the footslopes, with the earth becoming too thin or too steep to plough, and up to the breezy sheep-pastures of the high downs. It can be half a day's walk from the church in the village to the downland end of the parish and back. The outlines of the pattern remain, though the valley woodland has been reduced to small copses and hedgerow trees, and today's ploughland follows the easier gradients of the scarp, often beyond the crest of the downs; which, after all, is only a return of the plough to hillsides where corn was grown in times long before the Saxons settled here.

The evidences of prehistoric cultivation can be seen on the hillsides flanking the Vale either as the tiers of long narrow terraces with their country name of Shepherds' Steeps and their archæological name of strip lynchets, which form gigantic steps curving to the contours of the steeper slopes, or as the rectangles the Ordnance Survey Maps name Celtic Fields, which are outlined by dim balks or banks on the turf of shallower slopes and are to be seen the most clearly when the sun is low enough to cast revealing shadows along the divisions. Shepherds and sheep are not today

the familiar sight they used to be only a few years ago on the
downs above the Vale : changed farming is fencing the open sheep-
walks to form cattle pastures. But change or not, few must find it
possible to live in these villages under the escarpment of Pewsey
Vale and not look up to and be drawn by the downs, feeling as
well as knowing that though the parish acres begin close by in the
valley on one kind of soil, they lift to the turf and thorns and
beech clumps of the chalk hills and end at a known mark—a barrow
or an ancient embankment, perhaps—out of sight in the downland
world beyond the crest of the scarp. The downs are there: they
lie back, but not remotely. Something of their spirit pervades
these villages and the whole Vale. It is a fact, too, that most of the
villages close to the downs lie on cross-valley byways leading to
the hills, and not on roads that pass along the Vale. This is very
noticeable with those under the edge of Salisbury Plain. A highway follows the foot of the Plain, and from Easton to Chirton
every village except Rushall lies a little back from it, on one side
or the other, along byways that change into tracks up the side of
the downs.

Marden is one of these villages between the west branch of the
Avon and the Plain, with Wilsford nearly a mile to the east, Chirton not quite as far to the west, and the highway from Upavon
to Devizes running between them and the downs.

There are few better places for discovering how much of the
downland spirit is in Pewsey Vale than the footpath from Marden
to Chirton. Both villages are set among trees, but the path quickly
runs clear of them into an opening out of cornfields on each side
under a wide sky above the width of the Vale. Here, between
stream and downs, this part of the valley floor is curved across in
the low swell of a broad, rounded fold, so that leaving the trees of
either village is like a sudden stepping forward into almost the full
spaciousness of the downs. From the path a very gentle upward
reach of tillage to the top of the fold hides the valley north of it,
making a near crest beyond which the upper slopes of the northward downs from Tan Hill to Knap Hill rise to a skyline about
four miles away. The Alton Barnes white horse is plain upon the
slope there, and the great mound of Adam's Grave gives a peak to
Walker's Hill in a way that shows why, in the Vale, it is always

Adam's Peak. The Plain is closer, only about a mile and a half to the south, with all the escarpment visible in its flow from Wilsford Hill to Urchfont Clump and in its rise from the footslopes towards which this side of the fold in the valley bottom falls. The Plain here is not entered by deep coombs. The scarp-slopes lie back in a lateral sequence of long and shallow bays with gradients that have permitted them to become a mixture of ploughland and pasture saved from bareness by a few lines and clumps of beeches. Occasionally the trees break the skyline, but not often. The tracks I have already mentioned, some of them scored deeply into the chalk, lead up from the valley.

The openness into which this footpath between the two villages seems uplifted belongs to the Vale as a whole: although the slopes from the downs are often steep, the change from downs to valley is neither abrupt nor final. It is always a descent, whether come at from north or south, but only to a lesser spaciousness within the greater. It is simply that the one is part of the other but at a lower level, keeping the flow of continuity across the Vale from the higher world of downland beyond the scarps.

Several things drew me to Marden one morning in the middle of May. I had been close to it once or twice but never in it, and so had still to discover what the village was like and how it held its ground in the Vale between the western branch of the Avon headwater and, farther away than the river, the main road along the footslopes of the Plain. Then there were the remains of the embankment and ditch of an earthwork which had enclosed an area of about fifty acres, and there were records of a vanished tumulus that stood within the earthwork, "the largest circular tumulus in England if we except Silbury". I had read, also, about a strange relic of folk-memory lingering in the village until recent years, a tradition of battle and the interment of slain fighters that might have reached us from prehistoric times. The name "Marden" takes us back no farther than Saxon times. According to experts in the interpretation of place-names, one of the earliest forms of it, *Marc dene*, signifies "boundary valley", whilst another, *Merh dene*, may mean "fertile valley". The things I have mentioned—earthwork remains, records of a destroyed tumulus, lingering battle-traditions—are definite indications that when the Saxons took the place it was already a very ancient settlement. On the downs above Pewsey Vale and on the slopes that descend to it there are numerous relics of prehistoric occupation from the Neolithic Period to the Early Iron Age, yet Marden today is the only one among the villages in the Vale standing side by side with prehistoric remains that suggest the full length of time through which people have made it a dwelling place.

The stream meanders into a loop past Marden mill in the little open hollow between what is now the least diminished part of the earthwork's bank and the north end of the village, the road from Woodborough bisecting the ground originally enclosed by the bank before dipping into the hollow, crossing two small bridges and rising gently up the other side to become the village street. This damp hollow is a gap between the amplitude of two low swells in the valley bottom, with the earthwork at the edge of one which, still rising, opens out into a broad, airy spread of arable and pasture towards Woodborough, and Marden beginning at the edge of the other and following its almost imperceptible fall towards the road under the Plain. The highest part of the village is above the gap. There, among trees and behind the unselfconscious mellow and homely attractiveness of a cluster of brick and thatch cottages set a little above the roadside, the church stands on the highest ground of all, though the cottages and trees surround it so intimately that hardly more than its tower is to be seen when the trees have broken into leaf.

The village street goes on past several larger houses and two or three more cottages, all uniform in material but pleasingly varied in shape and in their garden settings along the wayside. About halfway down the village a plain and substantial brick farmhouse, shaped into two wings like the letter L, is roofed with a spread of thatch as great as any I have seen on a house in the Vale or beyond its borders. There are long and deep slopes of thatch on many of the old timber-sided barns in Wiltshire, two such barns in Marden itself. One of these, lately rethatched and still with hardly a weather-stain on its pale, golden newness of straw, stands near the roadside opposite the farmhouse in the middle of the village, the other, its old thatch dark and sunken, in a roadside farmyard at the end away from the church. Very few houses have anything like such wide spans of thatch as the barns or such sweeping tilts of it from ridge to eaves. In regions like Pewsey Vale, where thatched roofs are traditional and thatching continues to be a living craft, many an old house that is nearer to a barn than a cottage in size will have had its early thatch replaced with tiles or slates. Fear of fire and sometimes fire itself were probably the chief reasons for the change, though today the cost of rethatching is another, for tiled or slated roofs resist wind and rain longer than thatch before falling into leaky or unsightly decay. So it comes about that a fire-damaged roof is not usually thatched again; which is why the large house next to the thatched farmhouse has a tiled roof now. But to return to the farmhouse—neither dormers nor gabled projections break the sweep of its thatch to eaves lifted well above ground-level by brick walls that carry their span and weight of roof very comfortably without seeming overburdened or pressed down by it. A small thatched cottage with dormers and low eaves often appears to be all roof, its windows peering like eyes from under the rim of a hood.

The lower half of Marden is not as it used to be. T. S. Cunningham, in a contribution to *Wiltshire Notes and Queries* for March 1913, stated that within the previous fifty years "No less than fifteen ancient thatched cottages have been utterly destroyed and their places taken (in part only) by red brick erections." The last three words quoted show, I think, what the writer felt about the change. There may have been good reasons for the demolition and replacement, but he gives none. It is obvious that he did not like the loss of mellowness and unity of appearance which the raw brick and slate caused in a village he must have loved. In whatever ways the new dwellings have been more convenient and comfortable to live in than the old, time has not yet mellowed the contrast between their rigid, angular rawness and the smoothly varied contours and shy tones of the cottages nearer the church. All the same, they are part of the village as I have come to know it; yet their lack of ease and homely graciousness has been lately re-emphasised by three pairs of council houses that have been built as a northward extension of the village just beyond the river near the mill. There is no doubt about it, a lightness of spirit, a gaiety, almost, is appearing in much of the council-house building that is going on in the village today. These new houses at Marden, with their cream window-frames and duck-egg blue doors set in the warm yet not strident red of brick walls and pantiled roofs, are the best criticism of those at the other end of the village. At last, it seems, we are learning to design and build village houses that do not clash too intrusively with ancient comeliness. We have yet to see how time will mellow and settle them among the quiet harmony of the countryside.

With the contrast between the brick and slate cottages I have just been looking at and the grouping of thatched cottages below the church still fresh in mind, I came to the end of the village towards the Plain. I was hoping for, but not expecting, another contrast that would, as it were, put the village into balance again, not only in the way it holds its ground, but in spirit as well. Marden had begun to seem as if, in this direction, it might dwindle weakly to a vague ending among the fields. I was half expecting it to peter out like that when, after turning into the lane to Chirton, I found myself looking over a hedge and across a short vista of parkland at the grey stone front of a manor house about a furlong away. In the scale and proportion of its simple rectangular shape, and in the proportions and spacing of its door and windows, it was just right for the area of tree-dotted green that lay between it and the road. The parallel ridges of its low-pitched, slated roof with a chimney stack on each side of a small white dome came against the sky without emphasis behind the level upper edge of the grey front. Centrally placed, a portico with two pairs of columns shaded a white door under a semicircular fanlight. The only ground-floor windows were two, each balancing the other to right and left of the portico and showing their white-bordered panes between white-louvred shutters opened wide to the wall. White railings enclosed the roof of the portico, making it a balcony in front of a tall, white-framed french-window. This, like the porticoed door, was centred between two white-framed sashed windows, and set vertically above those lighting the ground-floor. These upper windows were arched, in contrast with the straight lintels of the lower, and were within a very shallowly inset panel which echoed the whole window-shape, giving it a broad but unobtrusive border of grey wall. They also had two splayed sills, one at the base of the window, the other forming the base of the recess, the oblong surface between them saved from blankness by a simple, framelike pattern in low relief. This downward extension kept the break between the upper and lower windows from being too wide and abrupt. It was one of the touches that set me thinking how sensitively the symmetrical balance of the front had been conceived and how well and surely achieved without losing simplicity among an overload of ornament.

Perhaps this detailed description will suggest something of the tranquil but not coldly austere dignity of the house as I first saw its grey and white brighten and darken in the varying sunshine filtering through the high, smooth cloud of a May sky clearing after rain. Spread before it were green levels of spring grass under the open spacing of mature trees—oaks still in the amber-green stage of leaf, elms thinly covered with clearer green, horse-chestnuts more densely covered, and one or two beeches that looked bare then, but which a week or two later were rounded shapes of dark, coppery brown among the other trees in June's fullness of green. The hedges along the lane in which I stood—along all the lanes then—were in the tender coolness of green that follows the first spangling of buds on the hawthorns. In front of them the waysides were lined with narrow jungles of tall chervil stems and their feathery leaves, a green that would soon be lost for a time under the white laciness of umbels of flowers just beginning to expand. A blackcap's notes sounded gaily buoyant in trees on the other side of the hedge, whilst blackbirds were lingering over their phrases as if the spring were going to last for ever. The house has no long history, having been built in the early nineteenth century on the site of some old cottages. It certainly proves that its architect was one who did not believe "the severe directness of well-related wall and window to be too nakedly unashamed". It is also truly a part of Marden, and there is no disdain in the way it turns its back on the village to face the south and the sun.

Back round the bend where the village street changes into the lane which leads past the manor house there is an old cob or mud wall along the side of a farmyard. To puddle chalky mud and mix chopped straw with it, and then to build it up layer by layer as each becomes dry and hard enough, finishing it off with a thatched "roof" and perhaps a limewashed face, must be a very ancient way of making a wall. In his book *The Development of English Building Construction*, Mr C. F. Innocent suggests that this form of walling developed from "double wattlework, filled in between with mud" after the solidity of the filling had shown, "probably by the natural decay of the wattlework exterior, that the latter was not a necessity". A few farmyards and gardens up and down the Vale still have these thatched cob walls along one side or more, although some of them are now in decay, their surfaces flaking and crumbling, their thatch ragged and sunken under the projecting bends of the withy "spikes" that once held a full thickness of straw. Those in good condition stand with a look of solid permanence and ancient rightness at all seasons and in all weathers. I have often thought that farmyards and gardens never give the impression of being as warmly enclosed by brick or stone as by this chalk mud that is called cob. The capping of thatch must help to deepen the impression, though this is an accidental effect: its purpose is to be a roof to protect the top of the wall from rain, snow and frost. To protect cob from the weather is also the chief reason for giving a wall-face thick coats of limewash, even when the wash is tinted.

The wayside wall at the south end of Marden was in decay. Its first few yards were of brick, not cob, though capped with a ridge of thatch like the remainder, but with a difference. Dilapidation revealed that the thatch on the brick part had a wooden support under it resembling, on a small scale, of course, the triangular trusses and ridge-piece in the framework of a very simple roof. The cob-thatch did not have this—one proof, I think, that the cob length of the wall was very much the older; and as an illustration of what could happen to a mud wall going into decay I found it much more interesting.

The blunted ridge was becoming green with herbage sprung thrivingly from wind-blown and bird-carried seeds that had lodged in the crumbling straw. It was turning into a wayside roof garden of wild plants. Dandelion, sowthistle, chickweed, shepherd's purse and one poppy were already there, with little tufts of

grass—rye, slender foxtail, sweet vernal—among them. The green
of leaf and blade hid as much of the greyish-brown weather-
stained remnants of thatch as it left showing under the plant stems
caught against the sky. Below this the wall's five feet or so of
height was based on a steep-sided bank that raised the top another
two or three feet above the edge of the road, the lower two-thirds
of the wall being faced with brick set on edge, the upper third
showing the grey of cob that had once been smoothed off flush
with the brick. Where the cob still remained flush there were
flaking traces of thick coats of limewash on it as well as on the
brick face below it. The rest, the greater part, was gradually being
cut and tunnelled back by a large colony of mason bees, a gathering of individuals brought together by the attraction of a suitable
breeding place, not a community in the hive sense. They were not
unlike hive bees in shape and colour, though perhaps a little
smaller, and on the sunny spring and summer days when I watched
them they were very busy at the cavities or cells, in each of which
an egg is deposited together with pollen for the grub to eat when
it emerges from the egg. There were hundreds of the cells, side by
side, pitting the face of the cob, some with the entrance open,
others with it closed by a stopping that looked like rough, dark
grey mortar. Each that I could look into was shaped as a finely
curved cylinder with a bluntly rounded inner end, the whole being lined with a wafer-thin covering of mud-cement smoothed
off to the texture of a dull glaze. The cells were about an inch long
and a quarter of an inch in diameter. What I took to be disused
cells had little more than their inward halves remaining hollowed
in the wall-face. But there were also as many cells in use. A bee
would alight, run about for a moment or two until it found the
entrance it seemed to be looking for, and then disappear through
it. I was watching one kind of slow, persistent attrition that something other than the weather can carry on year after year against
a cob wall.

The church, now, beguiles me away from the manor house and
the old wall back to the other end of Marden. It is one I always
like to revisit, even when the return is only a brief passing-by and
all that I see on my way through the village is the top of its battlemented tower above the thatched roofs and the trees standing so

intimately close. The grouping is not a congested huddle but a companionable cluster that conforms with easy naturalness to the low swell of ground on which the church quietly, almost retiringly, holds the crowning place. The tower is Perpendicular and, literally, has had its ups and downs. It was lowered in the eighteenth century because the foundations were thought to be insecure. This did not make it safe, so in 1885 it was taken down and raised again, the original stones being carefully numbered and replaced. There has been other rebuilding and restoration, but after it all this little church of tower, nave and chancel, whether seen from inside or outside the walls, has been left with a well-proportioned, simple unity in which the Norman doorway and the oddly flattened chancel arch—neither of them decoratively overburdened by their several stepped bands of characteristic ornament—fall into place as symbols of age and continuity without the crumbling hoariness of decay.

I have known one or two village churches that chill the heart—damp, melancholy places from which I have been glad to hasten back to the sweet airs of the countryside. Marden church is not one of them. The mouldering earthiness of the tomb obtrudes no farther than the churchyard, where green turf conceals it though gravestones do not let us forget it. Here, with the starker symbolism of earlier times, a carver of sepulchral ornament continues to remind us that this is indeed its place. Stand near the porch in afternoon sunshine and look at the graves in front of the thatched roofs that almost reach down to the eastern edge of this little churchyard. Among the headstones is a cluster of four box-like vaults of stone, each with an end that will be full in the slant of sunlight across tree-tops opposite the south corner of the tower. Because of shadowed places behind them and the lichen encrusting them, the sun will make these four squares of grey stone stand out with a kind of cold incandescence; and whilst three are blank, the fourth is a panel on which, in spite of weathering, a crudely simple carving of cross-bones with a skull above and an hourglass below will be thrown up into strong relief by its own shadows. After seeing that, it would perhaps be best to walk round the church tower to the north side of the churchyard and discover how the Vale beyond it opens out and reveals the northern downs, so that the eyes may be lifted up to these hills and find unexplainable comfort in the harmony of their smooth slopes and flowing skylines.

The immediate fall of ground north of the churchyard is one side of a little shallow gap that takes the river past Marden mill at the end of the village. Along the edge of the opposite side of the gap the only easily recognisable remains of Marden Earthwork are now a hen-run among the trunks of tall trees covering them. The river is looped into two meandering channels in the flood-plain separating mill and earthwork, the outer channel being part of the boundary between the parishes of Marden and Beechingstoke, so although the earthwork takes its name from Marden it is within the other parish. This earthwork, or what is left of it, is one of the least common kind which have the ditch on the inner side of the bank, as it is found, for example, in the Avebury enclosure. Until 1818 Marden Earthwork contained a mound called Hatfield Barrow, "the largest circular tumulus in England if we except Silbury", to repeat the words of its excavator, William Cunnington of Heytesbury, as quoted by Mr O. Meyrick in a recent number of the *Wiltshire Archæological Magazine*. William Cunnington was the first of the well-known Wiltshire archæologists in this family and helped Sir Richard Colt Hoare to obtain the material for his famous volumes on ancient and Roman Wiltshire published early in the nineteenth century. Commenting on Colt Hoare's dismay at finding this great mound completely levelled by 1818, Mr Meyrick ironically points out that "It is highly probable that he and Cunnington were indirectly responsible for this through their excavations a few years before. They sank a shaft from the summit through the unstable greensand and had cleared a space of about 24 feet square, when suddenly the whole of the centre caved in, leaving a much lowered and unshapely remnant ready to be spread out to fill in the deep and wide surrounding ditch." It is a pity we can only find out what we want to know about these ancient landmarks by methods which mutilate and even destroy them.

Neither urns nor bones of prehistoric burials were uncovered there, only British pottery near the earthwork; yet this and the dwindled embankment and the completely vanished mound make it reasonable to think that the village was there centuries before it had church or parish bounds or a Saxon name. In the background there is also the dim folk-memory of battle I have mentioned. It takes us away from stream and valley up to the downland heights of the parish. The contributor to *Wiltshire Notes and Queries* who tells about the pulling down of the old cottages at Marden tells also how he heard in the village "that a great battle had been fought ages ago on Marden Down between men with red heads and men with black heads, and that the red-headed men won. . . . The dead are buried in a large cave on the down and nobody had ever dared to enter it." On the downs such a cave could hardly have been anything but a long barrow. If so, where was it? And what of the black-headed men and the red? The whole thing is full of questions. Can it be that in this legend we are hearing faintly, across a span of more than three thousand years, of dark-haired neolithic people who lived on the downs above Marden and of their losing fight against Bronze Age invaders? Through how many generations of Marden ears may this memory have passed in coming within earshot of our own times?

CHAPTER X

AROUND BEECHINGSTOKE CLUMP

WHEN, on a spring day, I came along the footpath that leads from Chirton to Marden, I began to pick out and name the hilltops of the northern escarpment of the Vale westward from Knap Hill above Alton Priors to Easton Hill near Bishop's Cannings. There was nothing to hide them—no farm buildings and hardly a tree—along the opposite side of the cornfield reaching away from the footpath in a gentle rise towards this edge of the downs. All the hills were in view, though set back by the two or three miles of valley lying out of sight beyond the lift of the field, which was then becoming tinged with the green of springing oats. I should have denied it if anyone had suggested that, from this viewpoint, I did not know the shapes and order of these hills well enough to name them without hesitation, and yet that is what I soon had to tell myself. The flat cap of Knap Hill, the peak with which Adam's Grave appears to tip Walker's Hill, and the broad shoulder of Milk Hill with its straggle of bushes were easy, but the contours of Tan Hill, and of Clifford's Hill projecting in front of it, had grown strange. Rybury Camp, showing very indefinitely on Clifford's Hill, was concealing the tuft of conifers near the crest of the slope at Tan Hill's western end. Caught from where I stood, there seemed to be nothing convincingly familiar in the shapes of these two hills.

A man at work spreading chemical fertiliser among the oats came to the path to replenish the hoppers of his tractor-drawn machine. I went up to him and said: "I'm trying to pick out Tan Hill." Then, pointing along the line to it: "That should be it—what do you think?"

I assumed that anyone working day after day in the fields in this part of the Vale would know the shape and skyline of this hill almost as well as he knew the build of his best friend, but he seemed no more certain of it than I was. He scanned the range of

Kennet and Avon Canal above All Cannings

downs and replied, pointing to Walker's Hill: "That's Adam's Peak—but what's the next hill to it on the right?"

"Knap Hill," I said.

"Then the one on the left, past the White Horse, must be Milk Hill."

"Yes," I agreed. "And the next one to the left of that is Tan Hill, with Clifford's Hill sticking out in front of it and getting in the way."

At this point his interest suddenly changed to impatience. He turned towards me and said, as if puzzled exasperation had forced the question from his lips: "If you want to find out which is which, why don't you go up there and have a look at them?"

As he did not turn away to go on with his work but appeared to expect an answer, I explained that I had done so, frequently, and that I liked seeing the hills from a distance and recognising them in spite of the way a different viewpoint changed their shapes. My impression was that he thought this reasonable if odd. We talked a little longer, chiefly about the hills. I mentioned that prehistoric farmers had grown corn on the downs and that the shapes of their fields could still be seen on the turf there.

He had often wondered what they were, these groups of green rectangles outlined by low banks which seem to fade into the slope as you approach them. His comment was: "I wonder how they managed to grow corn up there without artificials?"

He was young, little more than a youth, in fact. An older farm-worker, born and bred within sight of Tan Hill, would not, I feel, have seen the hill as a place remote from his valley-world, and I also feel that he would have smiled sceptically at the young man's notion that the land's best source of fertility is in a manufacturer's brown-paper bag.

As I pointed out in the chapter about Marden, this footpath leads across one of the parts of the Vale that are gently upfolded in broad swells of cornfield and pasture on which, in contrast with the tree-shaded villages and lower ground along the streams, one has the feeling that the openness and skyey space of the downs are here in the valley as well. These upfolds do not steepen into definite hill-shapes like the three—Etchilhampton Hill, Wood-borough Hill and Picked Hill—so often sighted from different parts of the Vale and its escarpments. From the valley they reveal themselves more by the widening of the view round them than by standing out as landmarks; from the downs they are the open places among the dark press of elms. This one lies within a triangle of three villages: Marden, Beechingstoke, Woodborough. In crossing it the road from Marden to Woodborough passes a small group of pines in the angle of a fork to Beechingstoke—but I am going on too fast, as I have still to mention something that for me, at any rate, makes the footpath a vividly remembered part of the Vale. The cornfield margins along it are the one place where I see the corn marigold or yellow ox-eye growing. Though often abundant where it appears, it is a local flower and not common. I had looked for it hopefully in many places for many years before I caught sight of it here springing up among the corn.

I suppose the farmer, when he sees its yellow beginning to open among the green corn, looks upon it as merely one weed among the others that will share the field with his crop, do what he may against them. Of weeds and not-weeds, Anthony Collett wrote: "The same soil nurses both alike; and when man chooses to intro-duce his distinctions, he has to work to make his wish good. . . . Weeds are simply plants growing where we do not want them." I hope that no farmer will ever succeed in making his wish good, especially with the corn marigold. The only kind of countryside without weeds would be an absolute desert, I imagine; for where they cannot grow, neither can any other kind of plant. After all, we do not want everything springing from the fertility of the land to be a crop. So let us rejoice when, as well as poppy and pansy, Venus' looking-glass and Venus' comb, mayweed, pimpernel and all the others, we are fortunate enough to discover a field in which the corn marigold is growing.

For me this was a discovery made whilst going along the path in mid-June. The oats on one side and the wheat on the other were less than half-grown then, so that it was easy to see the weeds among the close ranks of blades. The marigolds were here and there, some of them already in bud—top-flattened shapes too tightly enfolded yet to be disclosing the first tinge of yellow, but perfect for revealing the bluish glaucous bloom on their pattern of light-green scales, a bloom that would shortly be matched on the necks of the green-eared wheat stalks around them. This year, then, the summer promised to be, and was, my first corn-marigold summer. A fortnight later they were coming into full flower either along the path or else in another place not far away. I learnt this as I passed through Marden village one afternoon and saw a child carrying a bunch she had gathered on her way home from school. She was shyly proud of her handsome yellow flowers when asked where she had got them. Another three weeks took me well into July before I came to the footpath again and caught their yellow among the corn.

The chosen day could not have been better for revealing the beauty of those flowers and their setting. I came up to them about noon in gentle westerly airs with a cool touch under a sun whose dazzling burnish, high above the edge of the Plain, was more like silver than gold in the scintillating resplendence of his light. His glow filled the Vale, the sky's only trace of cloud being the sunny vapouriness of a semi-transparent drift that hardly dimmed the lustre of pale blue along the Tan Hill skyline. Marden elms and Chirton elms and those near the road at the foot of the Plain had now darkened to their deepest tones of summer green, with the side away from the sun almost black, so dense were the shadows among their boughs. The scarp of the Plain lies only a mile or so from the footpath. On the part that I could see rising behind the trees at its foot some of the cornfields were already becoming tinged with the first pale brown of oncoming ripeness. They stood out more brightly in the sun-glow than the olive-green turf-slopes and the fields in which the corn was still green or roots were growing. The scarp of the northward downs is at least three miles away. Most of its upper slopes are too steep for ploughing, so there, instead of cornfields reaching to the skyline, I saw downland turf covering the bluffs and hollows of hillsides on which, at that distance, the sunlit yellow of large patches of ragwort was like a smoulder of dull gold in the green.

Such were the margins of the summer world in which this footpath along an old wire fence rising from a fringe of tall, seeding grasses divided the two cornfields. Here, at this moment of high noon, there was no more shade than a beetle could find in a tussock of grass, only such a radiance and sheen of sunlight as makes colour—and flower colour above all, especially the reds and yellows—seem to glow with inner as well as surface brightness. The day's sounds were like an undertone to its radiance—the continual insect hum, as if the sun's light and warmth were vibrant, the intermittent cooing of ring-doves in trees towards Marden, and always a faint rustling from the wheat, but no sound from the oats except when the gentle airs strengthened enough to stir the loosely hung awns into slow, swishing sibilance. The oatfield stretched away from the sun and was shadowless. Early ripening had changed its colour from silvery green to pale fawn, its crowded multitudes of panicles holding the sunlight as if misted by a blond glow. The wheatfield was almost under the sun. In looking across it I faced the sunlight slanting down steeply into a close array of vertical ears. Their shadow sides being towards me, the fall of light turned them into a level forest of lance-heads glisteningly tipped and edged with silver, and with a cold bloom still making them blue-necked.

A sprinkling of poppies had raised their lax, scarlet petals clear of the oats, but the yellow ox-eye or corn marigold, the handsomest of all the daisy flowers, had made these cornfield margins and the day its own very much more by the beauty of its sun-echoing shape and colour than by outnumbering the poppies. At first I did not realise how many of these yellow flowers had opened there, as they were among, not above the corn, and, unlike the poppies, were on both sides of the footpath, in the wheat as well as in the oats. Pale green stems, the upper parts often branching into as many as eight flower stems, leaned and straggled a little in contrast to the upright cornstalks, so keeping the flowers within the height of the corn. The widest open were about two inches across, yellow discs encircled by yellow rays set close together and with a slight backward curve. Their clear, rich colour came out more brightly from the green wheat than from the fawn-tinged oats. Below them in the oats were many mayweed flowers, another daisy-like shape, but with white rays and a dull, rather dingy yellow centre. Corn-marigold yellow looks as if the very spirit of sun-colour and sunshine were glowing in it. Its centre is a shade deeper in tone than the rays encircling it, yet takes nothing from the clarity of colour in the whole flower. The colour is warm and clear, rich and bright at the same time—neither cold like lemon, which is too close to green, nor flushed like orange. It has the light-holding and light-reflecting softness of texture that gives its purity a powdered quality like that of the clear colour on a cock yellow-hammer's head. Under this sun-disc—for that is what the corn marigold is—the pale green calyx has a complementary beauty of tone in the bluish-grey, glaucous bloom that is like a patina upon the bract-scales and extends to the neck of the flower stem as well.

When I broke off to look at the corn marigolds I was saying that the footpath from Chirton to Marden crosses one of the open un-dulations in the floor of the Vale which deepen the impression that there is no real division in spirit between Vale and downs. Less than half a mile into the valley this one is cut by the river flowing east from Patney to the mill at Marden. Then comes an-other and wider swell of land in the triangle of the three villages I mentioned earlier—Marden, Beechingstoke and Woodborough —with the road from Marden to Woodborough leading over it and passing a group of Scots pines isolated in the angle of a road-fork to Beechingstoke. This is Beechingstoke Clump, a cluster of red-tinged trunks rising bare to a high branching of boughs curved in gale-flattened toughness under horizontal crowns of dark green foliage. It is also known hereabouts as the Seventeen Sisters, which was the original number of pines in the group. Today fourteen are left, though if any magic is to be evoked by counting up to seventeen there, it may still be done by including two hawthorns and a gorse-bush. The clump stands at the edge of the plateau, on the side towards Marden, and must be at or near the highest part of its broad and very slightly rounded top. Except for another half-dozen or so hawthorns dotted along the field margins these pines are the only trees on it. They stand out in a way that seems to make an already spacious sky wider and loftier and this gently uplifted part of the Vale more airily open. Even on a calm day their shape as a group always appears to have the wind in it.

I have been walking about the Vale of Pewsey for months now, gathering material for this book, seeking new impressions and re-viving old ones, talking to all kinds of people and sometimes ask-ing what must have been thought curious and even tiresome questions. It has proved to me that the people of the Vale are too good-mannered and tolerant, even when mystified, to ask out-right what I am up to when loitering about this place or that. It is perhaps not strange that the only direct question of this kind I remember came from a policeman with whom I spent a pleasant few minutes on the canal bridge at Wilcot.

"I suppose you are on holiday?" he enquired.

"No," I had to reply; "I may look as if I am, but . . ." And I told him what I was doing. So, he getting on with his work and I with mine, we parted.

When a corner in the countryside interests and excites me— such as, for example, the footpath from Marden to Chirton, or Beechingstoke Clump—I like to return to it now and again in different seasons and weathers, perhaps to renew the pleasure of seeing a particular flower, bird or building, or perhaps simply because I enjoy being there at any time. This may keep me at the place for an hour, often a whole morning or afternoon. The night hours, too, have their attraction. I have often noticed that passers-by and any workers in the fields near me, especially the latter, are more than a little curious about the one sitting there, or perhaps strolling about the spot, and occasionally writing in a notebook; though if it should be necessary to raise binoculars to look at a bird, I imagine this makes them feel able to identify my pursuit, even as I the bird—for nowadays everyone knows that to carry binoculars in the country means birdwatching.

I was conscious of this interest taken in a loiterer when I spent a warm, sun-hazy September afternoon under the pines of Beech-ingstoke Clump. Harvesting was going on in adjoining fields, with the nearest corners reaching almost to the grassy bank under the trees. In one field two men were cutting oats with a reaper-thresher, in the other field about half a dozen were carrying stooked oats with a cart and a wagon, both horse-drawn; and every time the progress of the work brought them to this corner of their field I saw them glance now and again in my direction as though thinking after each interval, "Still there! A good way to make an easy afternoon of it, that is!" Perhaps there *was* quiet but salty comment in warm-toned Wiltshire speech. All the same, I think my interest in them was greater than theirs in me; for as I watched them at work I saw them in the foreground of an ages-long vista of harvest-times that faded away, not here in the valley, but on the slopes of the downs flanking it. I saw shadowy harvesters, with flint sickles in their hands, bending over ripe corn on their little hillside plots, and remembered that we are told they performed rites to propitiate the corn-god who was perishing under the sickles of the reapers. I remembered, too, being asked earlier in the year, "I wonder how they managed to grow corn up there without artificials?" And here, in the immediate forefront of time, I watched the newest mechanical method of taking the corn harvest ousting an older by doing the work more quickly, less tiringly and with fewer hands, but amidst how much persistent and ear-dulling noise!

In one field two men and a reaper-thresher, a scarlet juggernaut of a machine, were steadily transforming acres of standing oats into a straw-littered expanse of stubble. To me the continual droning drive of this machine, hour by hour until the transformation was complete, suggested a kind of sacrilegious ruthlessness, as if the ancient corn-king had at last been dethroned and banished from the land for ever. The tractor driver intent upon his course, the man on the platform making sure there was always a sack in place to catch the flow of grain, both also, it seemed, watching the machine and listening for signs of erratic running, had no time for talk even if they could have heard each other without shouting. In the adjoining field the oats were being harvested in the older and more leisurely way. The reaper-binder had strewn the stubble with sheaves, not with mangled straw. The sheaves had been stooked, and now they were being piled high upon horse-drawn cart and wagon and taken off to be built into ricks at the side of the farm. Threshing would come later. The loading and carrying went on quietly as the long lines of stooks dwindled away with deceptive gradualness, leaving the stubble bare. All the sound that came to me from this field was an occasional creak when the cart or the wagon moved on, sometimes a call to a horse, and sometimes the men's voices in conversation. It came very close to silence, and closer still when the men on the reaper-thresher finished their piece and rode the machine out of sight beyond the far edge of the field and stopped its insistent noise.

The other harvesters kept on and were moving away from me. There was now the glow of cloud-diffused sunshine everywhere on this open plateau of cornland round Beechingstoke Clump, giving sheen and lustre to the stubble and the discarded straw, and a definite shadow side to the remaining stooks. This brighter sun-glow became duller and hazier beyond its rim, above which only the upper parts of the elms crowding the lower ground showed their sombrely green and densely shadowed foliage. Margined by such heavily dark tones these cornfields round the pines seemed the one place in the Vale full in the sun. Two miles to the north-east the twin points of Woodborough Hill and Picked Hill lifted their tree-tufts clear of the surrounding elms, Woodborough Hill with a base of pale stubble under a dull green summit, Picked Hill all dark turf. Eastward beyond them, in the direction of Pewsey, I could see nothing but the press of trees fading into the haze. Turning westward I looked across more elms, with Beeching-stoke church and roofs among the nearest, and a little to the south of them, far away at the Devizes end of the Vale, the very dim shape of Etchilhampton Hill. The Vale's downland margins were a little less dim. Being under the sun the rise to the Plain loomed behind a brighter yet more obscuring haze of light than that through which the opposite scarp could be seen. I could pick out no field-shape or crop-colour along the side of the Plain, but along the Vale's northern side, where the broad sweeps of cornland be-tween the canal and the downs ended below turf slopes too steep for the plough, the change from light to dark would have been revealed more radiantly but not much more plainly by clearer sunlight.

CHAPTER XI

WILSFORD

WHEN the west branch of the Avon in the Vale of Pewsey has left the gap between Marden and the remains of the earthwork north of the village, it winds through level bankside pastures to Wilsford, about a mile away, and on past the villages of Charlton and Rushall in coming to its confluence with the east branch of the river at Scales Bridge on the road from Pewsey to Upavon. Could there be a more pleasant meanderer than the Avon in these reaches, especially in summer? The river does not flow through Wilsford or through any of the villages from Patney to Rushall —they are close beside rather than on it. At Wilsford its banks are about a furlong from the east end where, at the church, a lane leads to a wooden footbridge flanked by an old ford. The west end of the village is about twice as far from the stream and another bridge. This was the bridge I was making for when I came to Wilsford along field-paths from Marden one July afternoon.

Just within the village a short lane quickly reaches a gate at the edge of the riverside pastures, across which it continues as an open field-way to the bridge and other pastures beyond. From the gate it first traverses a small field that is like a hedged approach to an elm-shaded, gateless gap in the corner nearest the openness along the stream; and this feeling of being brought gradually to the full opening out of the flood-plain levels of grassland and their sky is deepened by two slightly divergent lines of close-growing elms beginning one each side the gap and leading away to ends about a hundred yards on, yet well short of the river bank. Willows just behind the first elms give more shade to the entrance gap. All the elms are full-grown trees at the towering height they reach in the Vale, their boles and lower limbs darkened with many a year's growth of ivy. The eastward line has one or two ashes in it, their spreading grace reaching as high as the elm-tops, and they too are ivied.

Before walking clear of the elms into the shadeless, sun-drenched pastures between them and the river I stopped to look back. The sun was high above the south, a burnished, glowing scintillation around which the cloudless sky was too bright with the sun's radiance to be blue. The trees at the field-gap and beyond it, particularly the elms, were shaped as much by the shadows among their boughs as by the summer-deepened green of leaves crowded into foliage contours. The gap was a darkness of shade under its elms, and this and the narrow band of shade under those lined convergingly towards it made the breadth of grass they margined seem at that moment the brightest place in the sun. I could see nothing of Wilsford and no part of the rise of downs to the edge of Salisbury Plain a mile behind the village. There were too many close trees that way.

The way to wider views was out from between the lines of elms and towards the river. The course of the stream could be traced through its west-to-east meanderings by the rushes, sedges and reeds standing higher than its banks, or else by the tall and bushy growth and deep green of the other waterside plants in contrast with the grazed turf of the pastures. The nearest trees beyond the river were ranged like a wood along the first gentle rise of ground to the broad fold of cornland between Puck Shipton and Woodborough. Their tops came against the sky, but gaps among them gave glimpses of the downs along the Vale's northern escarpment from Walker's Hill to Tan Hill. The Alton white horse, a distant, sunlit chalk-shape on the side of an olive-green down, was framed by an opening in the dark green foliage near the brick chimney of a thatched cottage among the trees. There was no shade in this little valley that is so shallow in its half-mile of width from the elms behind me to those against the sky beyond the river as to seem no valley at all. The sky over it, at the zenith and northward, was too far from the scintillating dazzle of the sun's blaze for its blue to be lost in the intensity of sunlight. As I walked towards the river the greatest glow and brightness seemed to be on the fields round me, not in the sky. Above me, the sun-glow giving it lustre, I found the pure blue of sky-space flecked and filmed with the whiteness of airy vapour almost too tenuous and wispy to be called cloud.

The bridge, an old one of brick, is very slightly hump-backed in spanning a stream about eight yards wide. It has two semi-circular arches and parapets which are barely higher than the crown of the rise and have little more than room for a wagon on the roadway of chalky earth between them. A sandstone block, shaped like a truncated wedge, is set on its base at the ends of each parapet to protect the brickwork against the impact of wheels turning into the bridge too much aslant. Grey lichen and some patches that are rusty brown make a scumbled overlay on the dark red of the brick. They give it the weathered, rain-cleaned texture that seems to hold the sunlight in its fabric and there transmute it into an infinite variety of colour tones within and between the red, brown and grey which set the key. This old bridge looked as naturally in place as the rushes in the water on each side of it.

Together with reeds and sedges the rushes were crowded into a broad band, five or six feet tall, along the middle of the stream, leaving only a narrow strip of open water on each side, and this overhung by plants growing on the banks. I must confess that, with me, this forest of stems and blades rising from the water, magnificent in luxuriance though it was, is chiefly remembered as a somewhat colourless but natural background to river banks made so very attractive by the profusion and variety of the plants flowering on them. All the same, I do not forget that when the long green rush-blades were seen against the fall of sunshine they appeared to fill with light and brighten to a golden green in contrast with the dark green of those not lit up; and that there were also many dragon-flies, large and small, planing and darting about between the rushes and the banks, among them the small, slender one, the demoiselle, which seemed to become a streak of iridescent kingfisher-blue as it darted. But, as I said, the streamside flowers are what I remember the most vividly. None was uncommon, and only one surprised me a little by appearing in that kind of place.

The creamy-white foam of meadowsweet was there, and droops of cream, green-tinged comfrey bells hanging above spreading clusters of large leaves, and upright arrays of the water-side willow-herb called codlins-and-cream, the sun giving its roseate purple flowers a lustred richness that made them look like jewels set in clear green. There were the yellow sun-discs of marsh ragwort, a more delicate and spreading plant than the common ragwort, anything but tough-looking or rank, and the richly yellow five-rayed stars of St John's wort, and the deep, dusky red of figwort flower-spikes tapering like spires, and the small white flowers of gypsy-wort forming ruffs about square stems at each pair of pointed and pointedly cut mint-like leaves, the whole plant otherwise a yellowish green. Teazels stood at full height, their spiny flower-heads still in the pale green stage before they break into purple, their thin, needle-pointed bracts completing the decorative effect of the flower-head by an alternation of those which curved outward and upward to overtop the head with those which were shorter and more horizontal in their outward curve. Thick spikes of purple loosestrife stood tall above forget-me-nots with the quality of pure enamel in their blue, and above fleabane with its dark yellow discs in paler fringes of thin rays.

These were not all, though I was never more than a hundred yards from the bridge. The open margins of the stream had yellow water-lily cups on the surface. In one place where the bank, rising behind a young alder, was lost under meadowsweet, codlins-and-cream and purple loosestrife, the fieldward side of its top was bordered by a patch of meadow-cranesbill. It was the only one I saw, and its shallow cups of purple-tinged blue were the flowers I did not expect to find in company with the others. Water bedstraw straggled its stems and their leaf-whorls and inconspicuous white flowers along the water's edge. At the bridge a clump of valerian had opened its pink corymbs almost touching the lichen-encrusted brickwork. And in the stream, after missing it for a succession of years, I found water-plantain in flower again. It shapes erect central stems and straight side-shoots into airy pyramids of small, three-petalled flowers of palest lilac. I have always felt that if any flowering plant rising above the surface of pond or stream appears most in love with the sun, this is it—though some may feel the same about water-crowfoot, arrow-head or the flowering rush. The river and its flowers kept me there most of that July afternoon, and often I could hear the thin plaints, and now and again see the staccato wing-beats, of peewits restless over other fields along the river towards Marden.

As a contrast I should like to picture a glimpse of Wilsford village—not the river this time—at another season, and pass from the turn of high summer to late autumn, from July to November. In the middle of an early November afternoon I approached the east end of the village by the road which enters it almost opposite the church. What wind there was came across the Plain from the south, never strong, but varying with a sky sometimes darkened by ragged clouds with a shower pelting from them, but as frequently opening into expanses of thinly vapoured blue among cumulus banks gleaming with the whiteness of distant snow as the sunlight flooded them from behind other clouds passing before the sun not far above the Plain. These clouds were shadowy, hazy shapes in the sunlight streaming past their edges, its downward break a radiating slant of beams behind which the rise of the Plain appeared as a grey silhouette in a luminous light-mist. Wilsford is only about half a mile from the scarp-foot of the Plain. In the misted sun-glow on the scarp the lynchets stepped up the lower slopes of Cleeve Hill were silver-green strips of turf separated by shadowed rises, and a little to the west of them the valley-facing embankment of Broadbury Banks was shadowed along the skyline.

I followed a fenced road that leads away from the Plain across a broad ribbon of level, treeless pastures between the scarp and the village. Near the village a left-hand turn swings it abruptly aside, but another to the right soon swings it back again and sends it along, now lined with elms, curving past a farm to the first cottages and the church. The elms stand close together and soar up to make an archway shading the road and ending in front like a frame to a cluster of thatched roofs with the church tower rising close behind them, and behind roofs and tower a glimpse of sky fretted by the elm boughs. If I looked back the first elms along the bend of the road screened the Plain, to the right I could see only farm-buildings just behind the elms, and to the left the narrow corner of a field between the elms and the patchily caught side of a white house.

On this early November afternoon there was yet no winter in the Vale. If the sun was a waning fire, the air was mild. The deep-toned coppery brown of the beeches had become a dwindling smoulder in the smudgy darkness the groves and clumps made on the open valley-sides; but the elms were still leafy, and whilst the sun shone it was their colour, not the sun's, which made the inner valley golden. It was as if the sun, growing weak, gave the light and the elms the colour, changing the cold pallor of silver into the warmth of gold. The impression was of gold, but brightened and richened with the glow of clear, ambered yellow. To stand under elms like those at Wilsford was to be in amber-golden light even when there was no direct sunshine. The hedgerow hawthorns brought paler tones and the maples deeper tones of the colour closer to the ground, and it covered the ground under them all; for the leaves already fallen were lying there unsullied, whilst others floated down continually, one here, two or three there, still leaving many to follow in this gentle way.

It happened that before I reached the elms at Wilsford the afternoon's last and longest shower had ended and left behind it calm air and a more evenly and thinly clouded sky. The sun, above Urchfont Clump, seemed in and not behind the smooth films of cloud, glowing in them with a silvery radiance that filled the Vale with the lucent clarity of light in which no colour, even the most sombre, is dead. Under the elms the middle part of the road, where wheels had crushed the wet leaves into mud, was like a ribbon of black between wider, amber-golden borders where the leaves remained as clear and warm in tone as when they came down. Along the outer edges of these borders the dark elm-trunks towered into golden clouds of foliage full of sunlight which also gave an upward glow of reflection to the colour of the road-margins. In the arch against the sky at the end of the elms the greyish-brown thatch of cottages, darkened by much rain, subdued the sunlight to its darkness, but there were variations in tone as well as shape in the different slopes from the main ridges and the curves on hipped gables and hooded dormers. The deep red of brick in the chimneys made the thatch look more brown than grey and helped to reveal that it was old enough for tinges of moss-green to be caught on the most weather-stained slopes. Near the middle of the group the slant of two gable-ends met and formed a deep notch in front of the church tower, so that, instead of being cut off horizontally by a roof-ridge, almost the full length of the south side was exposed. For a few minutes the cold clarity of sunlight on the pale grey stonework with its detail of buttress, battlement and corner turret, and the simple tracery of its two-light window, seemed incandescent in contrast with the darkness of brown roofs and the golden-amber glow in the elms. When an uprising of denser cloud weakened the sun, I saw how bright this November afternoon's last flood of sunshine had been.

Wilsford village is an uncrowded spacing of cottages along a quarter of a mile or so of street from the church and a farm at the east end to another farm at the west end. There are one or two more cottages a few yards down a side-turning towards the river at each end. Except for the two farmhouses and a white-walled house standing a little apart from the church end of the street, and the cream-washed Old Malthouse with its timber-framed back to the street at the other end, the village is all cottages. Most of them are along the south side of the street, with half a mile of large, almost level fields, chiefly cattle pastures, between them and the main road under the edge of the Plain. These fields are more frequently fenced than hedged and have few trees to weaken the feeling of openness which links them to the downs. The village, too, does not give the impression of being a tree-shaded place. The extreme ends have their clusters of elms, but apart from these there are only one or two along the outskirts. In this bit of the Vale the trees begin farther inward, north of the village and the river.

In many villages the cottages are interspersed among larger and more elaborate houses, almost, I sometimes feel, as if they had sidled into humble contiguity and kept their places by permission of condescending patronage. I have never had this impression at Wilsford: the cottages make the village. Most of them are ranged along the south side of the street and not set back from it, some singly and close together, some with a length of garden between them, and some joined in twos under a common spread of roof, though not in the symmetrical balance suggested by the word "pair". The longest gap is a break which gives those at the west end the look of a separate group with the farm-cluster of elms rising behind them. The village makes a simple whole which finds unity in brick that is often cream-washed, in timber-framing

Kennet and Avon Canal near Bristow Bridge

that is usually painted black to make panels of the cream, and in straw thatch. They wall and roof cottage shapes which avoid monotony by being so naturally and unselfconsciously varied. The differences are in character with the materials and cottage style, as though they grew from the sites, the builders accepting them and working under their control, here completing a right-angle by adding a short wing at full height, there attaching a ground-floor outhouse, and sometimes stepping down from one to the other. No two plans are quite the same, yet every cottage is a piece of the true vernacular of local building, with never a hint that any freakishness or oddity has been dared in avoiding sameness. These country builders were simply using traditional knowledge and craft in making the best of each site. Of course, some of the wings and out-parts may have been later additions to the original cottages, but it would be difficult to say which.

Such variety of shape must be very clearly reflected in the roofs, and when—as it is here—the roofing material is thatch, the problems set for the thatcher, if they are solved properly, will not only give us the pleasure of admiring good craftsmanship successfully applied, but will make thatch seem the most natural as well as the cosiest roofing material in the world, even as it is the oldest. Put aside the notion that it is picturesque, and forget its Christmas-card associations. Think first of what a roof must do. Sound thatch will keep you dry in any rain or snow, warm at the right season, cool at the right season, a little too cool, sometimes—for I live under thatch and have known summer hours when I have gone out into the sun to enjoy more of his warmth than came into a cottage with doors and windows wide open. Then think of the look of a thatched roof, of the way it completes a house and with the chimneys gives it a skyline. The cottages that are Wilsford show as well as any how satisfyingly thatch can do this—through all the variations, from those which have straight up-and-down slopes and a simple gabled ridge, to those with inswept valleys under right-angled ridges, perhaps with a more or less central ridge higher than the others, with slopes curving round hipped and half-hipped gables, hooding dormers, and sometimes continuing the sweep from a hip-end to the low eaves of washhouse or woodshed. However simple the roof-shape, however complicated, a thatcher who

9   129

Kennet and Avon Canal near Brimslade Farm

knows his job will mould his overlapping layers of straw to the whole roof, rounding them at inward corner and outward angle, making the thatch appear to flow with the shape as well as cover it.

Wilsford is also one of the villages in the Vale where garden and farmyard walls of thatched cob are still to be found. Most of them are in good condition, the walling itself as well as the thatch capping. The path across the fields from Marden enters the village between cob walls, and the one along a garden on the right is very well preserved and its thatch wire-netted. Along its other side the way has first a small barn, thatched and weather-boarded, then the back of a thatched, cob-walled cartlodge, and then a length of cob wall going on for about twenty yards to a free-standing end. A weed-overgrown, forsaken-looking farmyard lies behind them. The cartlodge, as a cob-walled building, helps to make this the more interesting side. The first time I looked at it there was too tangled a growth of wayside herbage for me to discover the kind of foundation the cob had under it, so I went into the farmyard to see what the interior of the building would reveal. It has, of course, three walls and an open front. It is four cart-bays long, divided by single posts each set on a stone base and supporting the end of a roof-truss under the thatch. The earthen floor did not cover the foundations and I was able to see that about half the length of the mud-walling stood upon courses of brick and the remainder upon irregular blocks of chalk, some of them very roughly squared. It looks as if the builders ran short of bricks. The walls are low, not more than seven feet, but there is plenty of height between the roof-trusses.

The thatch-capped boundary wall begins flush with the corner of the cartlodge, and what should have been a corner of the building's hip-slope of thatch is diminishingly shaped and continued without break into the ridge of thatch along the wall-top. Cob is tough: here the chalk mud has small fragments of broken flints mixed with it. Properly based, such a wall will stand as long as the thatch sheds the rain and melting snow—on this one, though the thatch is not new, the overhang is not less than a foot. Any cob wall now standing must have had its thatch renewed at intervals of a few years, and some today, like one or two at Wilsford, can be seen with old coats of limewash or an old skimming of plaster flaking off patchily under new thatch. The face of the wall adjoining the cartlodge may be crumbly with weathered age and the burrowing of mason bees, but its thatched mud will be a substantial wall for a long time yet. I have come across no new cob. Brick is the material used today when the surviving walls are repaired. The decayed end of this wall was rebuilt with brick very recently, and a garden wall at the opposite end of the village has been given the support of several brick buttresses. When cob walls were being built in the Vale there must have been much carting of chalk from the downs. The distance from Wilsford to the nearest chalk of the Plain is about a mile.

Cob walls, like other walls, have gateways. Because it was the first of its kind I ever saw, I have never forgotten the one in this farmyard wall at the west end of Wilsford. Perhaps I should call it a doorway, for it is just about wide enough for a wheelbarrow, and its opening is framed with rough-hewn timber jambs bearing a lintel which takes the wall-thatch across the span like a roof above the primitive wooden door of boards and battens and a wooden latch. The fissured, hard-seasoned wood has never been painted, and has the silvery-grey patina given by age and exposure to all weathers. The wall looks ancient, and the doorway as ancient as the wall.

From summer flowers, autumn elms, cottages and cob walls I came back to the east end of the village, to the church with its satisfyingly proportioned and featured tower, its high-roofed, narrow and rather severe nave, and its lower chancel. Its masonry has the light-holding texture of pale grey stone encrusted with grey lichen. The shape of the whole church, but especially of its tower, is always in contrast with the sombre green of its churchyard yews and the brown tones of the thatched roofs near it however dull the day. The tower rises to its battlements from buttressed angles, one of which, that next the church door, is shaped into a stair-turret. It begins square, but at a little more than the height of the normal buttresses is chamfered and diminished into a semi-octagon carried up to a battlemented top higher than the tower's main battlements. Its interior is circular and holds the stone spiral of a newel stairway.

The turreted angle, in the rightness of its change from the

weightier square to the lighter octagon, is one of the tower's graces. So are two bands of carved ornament, one forming a frieze of stemmed trefoils just below the battlements of its west and south walls, the other, near the ground, divided into squares, each filled with a kind of quatrefoil of circles in an enclosing circle, though much of this band is lost under ivy. Other graces, one in each face of the tower, are the two-light window shapes of broad trefoiled tracery and mullion where the upper walls would look very blank without them. These window openings are closed with stone slabs perforated with even rows of small round holes or else with one or two oblong slots. In *The Development of English Building Construction* Mr C. F. Innocent says: "The pierced slabs of English window openings, whether of wood or stone, had their origin in the pierced marble slabs with which window openings were filled in the Mediterranean lands."

The lofty nave has no aisles. Though it has large windows the impression it leaves is one of grey-walled height to where the principals of its dark-timbered roof are corbelled on stone heads of prelates and kings. Its chancel arch and tower arch, by their tall simplicity and narrower span, make the impression stronger. And so do the long, single chains suspending homely brass oil-lamps and pre-paraffin iron candle-holders from the roof. For this church is still lit by oil and candle: when the days grow shorter a wooden candlestick appears on pulpit and lectern. The lamps hang in the chancel and the part of the nave towards the pulpit, the candle-holders in the part towards the tower, three of them, a little rusty now, but as serviceable as when they were made. They are simply hoops of iron, two and a half inches deep, with four-inch cylindrical candle-sticks attached by riveted loops of metal, one to each, at equal intervals round their outsides. The candle-stick tops are cup-shaped to catch the runnels of waste. Three short chains of equal length, linked to the upper edge of the hoop, rise and converge above the centre and are there hooked to the rim of a small bell-like shape with a loop at its top by which the ring of candles is suspended on the single chain from the roof. Two are about twenty-eight inches across and hold twelve candles, the third, about sixteen inches in diameter, holds six. They are obviously blacksmith's work, and I have never seen their like anywhere else.

CHAPTER XII

THE CANAL

THE west end of the Vale of Pewsey is not the outlet for its many streams. With a more or less southward trend and a rootlike convergence they all flow inward towards the opening of the narrow cleft that cuts the chalk from Upavon to Salisbury and beyond, most of them coming from the foot of the Vale's northern margin of downs. The lowest part of the Vale is opposite this cleft, and there, after taking in the last of their tributary brooks, the east and west branches of the Avon unite at Scales Bridge in the mouth of the cleft and flow through the Plain to Hampshire and the English Channel. There is, though, a waterway, the Kennet and Avon Canal, which traverses the whole length of the Vale from Burbage Wharf below the tip of Savernake Forest at the east end to Horton Bridge near Bishop's Cannings at the west end and follows the northern margin of the valley bottom where the footslopes of the downs die away. As the canal's name implies, it links the Kennet (at Newbury) to the Bristol Avon (at Bath), the part in Pewsey Vale being the fourteen or fifteen miles of its middle reaches. It is now the only canal in Wiltshire that holds water, though as I see it in the Vale there can hardly be the depth above its muddy bed for the passage of laden boats. That kind of slow-moving traffic no longer sends the ripples of its wake into reedy margins. Several of the long, narrow canal-boats are still to be seen in the Vale, but only as foundered wrecks such as the one by Horton with its wooden ribs sticking up from the green water-weed and with the lance-leaves and flower spikes of dock springing from fissures in the rotting timbers. As a waterway the canal is now a haunt shared by angler, heron, swan, mallard, coot, moorhen and dragonfly, and has settled into the Vale and become a part of it, almost as if natural.

The Act authorising the construction of the Kennet and Avon Canal was passed in 1794. This canal was the work of John

Rennie, one of the period's famous canal engineers. Its barges carried Somerset coal, Bath building stone, grain and timber, until railroad competition, aimed at putting the canal companies out of business, began to make it—and many another canal as well—unprofitable to maintain. When, in retaliation, the Kennet and Avon Canal Company threatened to build a railway along its course, the old Great Western Railway Company settled the matter in 1851 by buying out the Canal Company and then laying the railroad which runs through the Vale of Pewsey and is now the main line from Paddington to the West Country, whilst the canal has declined to the condition of disuse in which we find it today. Sir G. M. Trevelyan, in his *English Social History*, sums up the effect of this conflict between the canals and the railways in these words: "The canals, after half a century of prosperity and public service, were most of them ruined, and were many of them bought up by local railway companies that had in fact been started with the object of cutting them out."

The canal helps us to realise that the Vale of Pewsey is a downland valley raised above that of the Bristol Avon which is bottomed by the low-lying clays immediately to the west. Just outside the end of the Vale the market town of Devizes over-looks this other Avon valley from the edge of the outer scarp of the great chalk plateau that covers more than half Wiltshire. The scarp is the division between the county's upland and lowland regions, between the "chalk" and the "cheese", as they used to be called, though along the four miles or so opposite the Vale it is not as high and bold as it is elsewhere. In coming from the west to Devizes and then to the Vale the canal had therefore to be made so that its traffic could be lifted from the lower valley to the higher. The lift required about thirty locks, the middle fifteen, each a boat's length apart, forming a straight flight of steps where the slope is steepest. East of Devizes there are no more locks until the one or two that are spaced between Wootton Rivers and Burbage Wharf along the canal's last two miles in the Vale. They step it up to its five-hundred-yard summit tunnel at Savernake.

My first memories of the canal in the Vale are now nearly twenty-five years old. In those days the parts I knew best were the reaches from Horton Bridge to All Cannings and Stanton St

Bernard. I did not return during the war years and then came back wondering what changes I should see. I need not have wondered. The discovery I made was that the years between had brought far greater changes to myself than to the canal along which I had first loitered during that bygone summer. It was the same peaceful, reed-fringed and weedy waterway under the downs in the quietude of the Vale. It had, perhaps, grown to look even less like a work of human engineering, much less like, I thought, than the many centuries older Wansdyke high on the downs above it. Their makers took them both onward with such conformity to the flow of the land as must have put their lines in harmony with the natural scene from the beginning; yet after a millennium and a half the great embankment is still obviously man-made, whilst after only a century and a half the canal in disuse could not look more like the flexible windings of a very lethargic stream.

For on its course through the Vale the canal seldom stiffens into rigid straightness, and where it comes nearest to doing this—in the reach at Wilcot, and in a second from Brimslade Farm, east of Wootton Rivers, to Burbage Wharf at the Vale's end—the change from a succession of closed views between bend and bend to the perspective of a long vista makes a pleasing contrast by which the canal sets one aspect of its charm against another. It was sited for levelness along the winding contour of the lower edge of the footslopes under the Vale's northern scarp; hence the flexible curving of its course. It is a division between the chalk slopes and the greensand valley bottom. There is usually a perceptible fall to its downland bank, and where the field on that side is a pasture the bank is cut away for a yard or two to form an incline down which the cattle come to drink at the water's edge, each place showing the white of hoof-trampled chalk. Except along the Wilcot reaches from Lady Bridge to Bristow Bridge the opposite side has the towpath raised above the waterway and outwardly margined with a bank, often hedge-topped, that is low on the towpath side but much deeper in a rather steep fall to the valley fields. The canal is thus shelved on the very edge of the chalk. Northward from the canalside pastures there is the gently rising tilt of the almost treeless, unevenly undulating band of great cornfields to the turf steeps of the scarp where the field margins curve with the base-contours of the slopes, the farthest acres sometimes deeply embayed within the smoothly inswept sides of coombs hollowed between shoulders of down. Little can be seen of the similar openness of cornfields and downs along the south side of the Vale. Beyond the first field below the canal the elms and other trees look so deceptively crowded together that the Vale seems full of woodland, though it is really a valley of milk and corn. Its northern flank of downs is seldom more than a mile from the towpath, but its southern flank, the scarp of Salisbury Plain, as well as being lower and less boldly built, is at least two miles away across the Vale at the east end and at least four towards the west end, and for much of its length is screened by the intervening trees.

Today the canal is not an obtrusive feature of the Vale whatever it may have been like in the years before it was doomed to disuse. If boats were still on the move along it the activity at Burbage, Pewsey and Honey Street wharves would be noticeable enough from the bridges at these places, but I doubt if more than occasional glimpses would be caught of the boats between wharf and wharf except where the canal could be overlooked from a bridge. At first I used to be surprised at not being more aware of its presence; for it is, as I have pointed out, shelved along the very edge of the chalk at its side of the Vale and has the inward valley fields a few feet below the level of the towpath, which would seem a position that should display rather than obscure its course. Yet I have grown to think of the canal almost as a secret way through the Vale, its course never very clear from a distance and most likely to be discovered if one of its grey-lichened brick bridges happens to be in sight. I have seen more of its continuity from the top of Martinsell than from anywhere else, tracing it by a bridge or two and the silver-grey streaks of sky-reflecting water in parts where, narrowed by its margins of reeds and flags, the canal surface was not covered with weed and the floating leaves of lily and persicaria and not hidden by canalside trees.

The canal banks are neither monotonously uniform in height nor bare. Along some reaches they heighten with the swell of ground on one side or the other, and at irregular intervals sink waterway and towpath between the slopes of a cutting that deepens until it is arched by a bridge and then gradually shallows again. To walk along the towpath is to experience a continual narrowing and widening of view and sky. Here a bank shuts out the downland view, there the width of the Vale is shut out and the downs revealed, and at the approach to a bridge there may be no downs, no Vale at all, only the bank-narrowed sky overhead. The grasses of shaggy, tussocky turf and the luxuriant growth of waterside and fieldside plants cover the banks whether high or low, the higher banks sometimes overgrown with tangles of thorn, bramble and briar. The towpath has its thorn-hedge, and this in many places is overhung or backed by lines and groves of elm, ash and willow intermingled; whilst the opposite bank, though much more open to the rise of fields within the valley, has here and there a springing of willow-wands behind the jungle of flags and reeds at its foot as well as parts with lines of full-grown trees—again elms, ashes and willows—along its top. It is no wonder, then, that the canal, left to nature, has become such an unobtrusive feature in a valley of many trees.

Yet the canal has one short reach that always gives the impression of belonging to the downs rather than the valley. It lies immediately to the east of All Cannings Bridge, where, in conforming to the outward-curving edge of the cornland under Clifford's Hill, the canal swings through the shallowest of bends towards Stanton St Bernard, and for about a quarter of a mile has no trees and very few bushes to shut in its banks. This is a reach where both bank-tops are mounded above the canalside fields, the towpath being a broad green way, almost four paces wide, with the outer slope of its bank falling to a hedged turf-track beyond which the mid-valley fields begin. After a short line of thorns near the bridge the towpath hedge dwindles to an isolated bush or two and some patches of bramble on the slope to the track. When I walk from under the bridge the spaciousness that opens out between the Vale's downland margins—for here they are both in sight—makes the path seem more elevated than it is anywhere else: it curves onward as if the embankment under it were not that along a canal in a valley but one shaping an Early Iron Age camp on the downs. I experience the same kind of stimulation, though to a lesser degree of intensity, as when, coming to a camp or a barrow on a high downland place, I climb the bank or the mound and feel that the full spaciousness of the world it crowns is open around me.

Two villages lie behind the bridge—Allington several hundred yards north of the canal, All Cannings a little farther away from it to the south—but the most that can be seen of them is a roof or two among the trees darkening the Vale inward from Allington. Forward beyond the bend another village, Stanton St Bernard, is as close to the north bank but completely lost among the trees at which the open reach of the canal ends. In this direction, seen from a point near the bridge, the massing of trees seems the denser because the bare upper slopes and tree-tufted summits of the two small outliers from the scarp, Woodborough Hill and Picked Hill, jut up in the distance as if islanded among woods. The opening out southward and northward puts the towpath under a span of sky arching the Vale from one downland flank to the other. The scarp-crest of Salisbury Plain, revealed from Urchfont beech clump to the Avon gap, is four or five miles away, that of the downs between the beech clump on Roundway Hill and Adam's Grave on Walker's Hill is only a mile or so. But what can such a statement of measured distance convey except that the Ridgeway on Chirton Down and Wansdyke on Tan Hill are these few miles apart? It is only convincing when straddled on a map. Here, on the towpath between All Cannings Bridge and Stanton, the convincing thing is the corridor of spaciousness connecting them across the Vale. To know how far this or that point lies from the canal leaves the imagination unstirred, the spirit cold. It is better to see how the cornfields reach away from the track under the towpath and gradually swell up to shape the low hillock-dome of the Ball as they recede into the Vale, with the hillock rounded against and overtopped by the distant rise of the Plain and concealing all but the crowns of the many elms between it and the Plain, and in the opposite direction to follow the lateral sweep and outward rise of greater cornfields to the foot of the nearer scarp where they steepen abruptly into downland turf ending in the continuity of a bare skyline which links hilltop to hilltop with a subtlety of flow that eludes description.

As a contrast I think of a reach at the east end of the Vale where Brimslade Farm stands almost midway between Wootton Rivers and Burbage Wharf. I have said that to me the canal is like a secret way through the Vale, and now add that it is never more so than where it curves closer to the downs in approaching Brimslade Farm and then, the farm passed, goes dead straight in the three-quarters of a mile to the wharf. Here the canal and railway run side by side along a smaller valley within the larger, its north side coming down to the canal as a gently shelving dip from the ground along the foot of the greatly diminished chalk-scarp below Savernake Forest, its opposite side rising as gently beyond the railway. This shallow little valley contains them both until, west of Wootton Rivers and almost in front of Martinsell, the southern width of the Vale begins to open out and the railway diverges to Pewsey and the middle of the Vale. Its skylines, often tree-crested, are seldom more than the width of two fields from the canal. Like the main valley it has many trees. They stand along the field-hedges, thicken here and there into copses and spinneys, and often line the canal banks variedly. One sequence along the towpath begins with a great horse-chestnut dome followed by six towering elms, and ends with the grace of two well-grown ashes. The elm-tops look as high as, if not higher than, the valley-sides. Despite the secluding effect of its trees the valley gives the impression of being a raised hollow at the Vale's upland head. That it is also a rising hollow is made evident by the four locks which, after the canal's level winding from Devizes, are spaced between Wootton Rivers and Burbage Wharf and step the canal towards its summit-reach beyond the Vale.

This small valley is the setting in which Brimslade Farm stands on both sides of the canal where the straight from Burbage Wharf flexes into the shallow bend to Wootton Rivers, the farmhouse close to the towpath, the barns and other buildings on the oppo-site bank and connected by a cartway across the parapeted arch of one of the canal's characteristic brick bridges immediately below a lock. There is a similar bridge at a lock two or three hundred yards nearer the wharf. I like to come to the farm from the direc-tion of the wharf, so that as a prelude and contrast to the farm group I enjoy first the grouping of a lichened-greyed brick bridge and lock, the massive timber levers of the lock-gates, and a lock-keeper's red-tiled cottage of one storey with white walls, green door and green window-frames seen at the end of a short perspective of bankside poplars and willows, with the highest steeps of Martinsell brokenly revealed through gaps in the tree-tops behind the bridge. After that the towpath, still straight and now screened from the railway by ash trees and willows, leads to the next bridge and the farm.

The farmhouse could hardly be more different from the small, low box of a cottage. It is Elizabethan. Among the surrounding trees the clear, warm-toned red of its tiles and brickwork takes form as a many-gabled homestead centred about a great rectangular chimney-stack bearing a line of six square chimneys, set corner to corner, which were saved from a too vertical and severe plainness when each was finished off with the simplest of caps by corbelling several courses of its brick under the same number of courses stepped back again to the chimney-top. It is the kind of chimney-stack that seems to rise from the heart of a house, to firm the house by its broad-based solidity. This one, from the way the roof-slopes and gables surround it, seems to be gathering every part of the house closer to itself and the sheltered warmth it symbolises. As well as being tile-roofed the farmhouse is tile-hung almost to the ground, a protective covering which takes away plainness from the walls and becomes a decoration on the double-gabled west side, for there the tiles are not straight-edged but rounded, giving scallop curves along each course and a fish-scale pattern to the whole. The red of these wall-tiles is the clearest between the patches of grey lichen thinly encrusting them. On the opposite side of the canal the brick walls and tiled roofs of barns and other farm buildings are toned with a similar warm clarity of red. It makes the brickwork of the connecting bridge and the lock look greyishly dull.

The cutting of a canal means the severing of roads, the sundering of farm lands, and therefore the building of bridges. Along the Vale the Kennet and Avon Canal is spanned by about twenty-five, nearly half of them crossed by smoothly metalled roads, the remainder by rougher farmways linking canalside fields. I cannot think of the canal and not remember its bridges, especially the smaller kind that carry the field tracks and byways. These are similar in shape and fabric—strong, plain structures with the look of having been designed not merely to bridge a canal, but to be a harmonious feature of the waterway as well. They are brick bridges, the only masonry being a rounded capping of limestone along the lead-in splays and the parapets. As seen from the tow-path there are the curving splays of the lead-in rising to the spring-ings of the arch, and behind them the main brickwork from bank to bank with the ends vertically buttressed and in the middle the arched waterway narrowed to little more than a boat's width. A course or two above the crown of the arch the parapet base is marked by an outset course of brick casting a thin shadow-line that follows the lift of the road across the bridge and is echoed by the parapet top. These bridges satisfy by their simplicity and the way their lines and surfaces grow into the whole span from the stability of the canal-banks, the verticals giving them the look of strength and sufficient height, the horizontals bent into the shal-lowest of curves across the central support of an arch in which, and very fittingly, the fullness of a semicircle is slightly flattened to an ellipse. Their colour is grey-toned rather than red. The bricks were originally burnt to surface-tones of dark red and pur-plish-black, and these have become so weather-stained as to seem further darkened, whilst the brickwork as a whole is greyed with a patchy scumbling of lichen.

There is one bridge, though, that differs from the others in be-ing an ornate span of stone. Called Lady Bridge, it is crossed by a farmway at Cocklebury where the canal lies between Picked Hill and Swanborough Tump. It has stone parapets balustraded at each end, arch-stones with reticulated surfaces, similar reticula-tions on the buttresses at each end of the bridge, and an orna-mented oval panel on each side of the arch and one above the crown. If a contrast were needed to help us to appreciate how naturally the plainness of the others grew into shape from the necessity of bridging the canal, this ornate bridge provides it. To me it looks out of place, yet I remember that the first time I came to it—which was from the direction of Honey Street—it certainly prepared me for the discovery that the canal between it and the next bridge towards Wilcot is different also. This reach widens into what is more like a sweep of ornamental water than part of a disused canal, the towpath a green walk between the waterside and a low hedge beyond which there is the gentle rise of two or three fields to the foot of Picked Hill, and in the opposite direction the open water ending at a broad fringe of reeds in front of beeches edging the wooded park of Wilcot Manor.

Not knowing why this bridge at Cocklebury was built fancy when the others were plain, or why it is called "Lady Bridge", I asked about it one day at Wilcot. The explanation was, I learned, that in planning the course of the canal its engineer wished to make the cut across the grounds of Wilcot Manor, but at first the lady of the manor would not agree to this, as the canal would then be within sight of the manor house. In the end she granted way-leave if, along the edge of her park, the canal were made wide, like an ornamental water, and if the bridge required at Cocklebury were made ornamental. This was done, and the reach of the canal along the edge of the park came to be known as the "widewater" or "broadwater", and her bridge as "Lady Bridge", meaning the Lady of Wilcot Manor's bridge.

We realise the most vividly that this is an abandoned waterway when we come to the canal wharves. They leave the impression that their once quietly busy activities, the leisurely comings and goings of the narrow horse-drawn boats, the loading and un-loading, the accompanying talk, banter and argument, have stagnated into the shadowy kind of stillness that is halfway to oblivion. At Burbage Wharf in the little valley within the Vale, where the edge of Savernake Forest crests the slope to the north and the village of Steep Green, leading on to Burbage, crests the southern slope, the brick buildings that were once storehouse, office and wharf-keeper's dwelling have not yet been left vacant, and the yard between them and the Marlborough road is kept open; but the part of the yard on the other side of the storehouse is a dump littered with derelict carts, wagons and other debris among tangles of waste-ground herbage. On the waterfront is a crane, built of massive timber baulks, which time has made the very symbol of disuse. Green with moss, it slants away from the canal as though long since immovably fixed in the final turning of its back to the empty wharfside. The canal passes about half a mile to the north of Pewsey, and where it is bridged for the Salisbury road Pewsey Wharf, opposite the curiously named public-house the French

Horn, has a deserted grass-grown blankness. The third of the canal's wharves is at Honey Street about the same distance west again and beside the road from Woodborough to Alton Barnes. According to *The Place-Names of Wiltshire* the name Honey Street was given to the Ridgeway where it crossed the Vale, probably because it was a muddy road. Honey Street is now the name of the small group of houses about the canal bridge, the disused wharf, and a timber-yard. Stone cottages with slated roofs, brick quoins, doorways and window-openings line both banks of the canal more or less continuously for a quarter of a mile westward from the wharf on the north bank and the timber-yard on the south bank to the Barge Inn alongside the towpath. It is obvious that the cottages were originally built to house people whose livelihood lay at and around the wharf. They are not typical of the Vale, their stone, slate and brick a canal-borne importation. One row is dated 1874. Today the timber-yard on the south bank, with its saw-mill and carpentry, keeps the place alive.

The wharf-yard has warehouse buildings of brick, a timber-shed and, in piquant contrast with its surroundings, a low wooden clock-tower. It is square and has weather-boarded sides and a slated pyramidal roof truncated to bear a second, lantern-like stage with clock-face and slate-hung sides under a completing roof-pyramid with a weathercock turning above its apex. There is also a wooden crane like the one at Burbage Wharf but constructed of less massive timbers. It looks a later as well as a lighter version that may still be workable. Two foundered canal boats rot at the wharfside.

The canal's open water is narrowed by the varied jungle of reeds, reed-grasses, rushes and sedges that grow along the foot of each bank, and between them much of the water-surface is dappled or patched or filigreed with the greens and brownish-greens of duck-weed, pond-weed and the leaves of arrowhead, persicaria and yellow water-lily. Often the whole ribbon ceases to mirror the sky or reflect the daylight: in October I have seen it a golden-brown mosaic of fallen leaves where, for two or three hundred yards on the Wilcot side of Bristow Bridge, the canal banks are overhung by woodland trees. One of the water-covering plants, *Azolla filiculoides*, spread to the Wiltshire reaches of the canal only a few years ago. My friend J. D. Grose, the Wiltshire botanist, whose Flora of the county will soon be published, tells me that *Azolla* was first noticed at Limpley Stoke near Bath early in 1939, and by the autumn had almost completely covered the canal there. Describing it then, one of his correspondents wrote: "It looked from a distance like a red asphalt road and I heard evacuated Londoners solemnly telling newcomers that the weed was a subtle device of the Government to prevent the enemy seeing the water from the air." It travelled eastward along the canal, taking three years to reach Devizes. In 1945 it was noticed at Pewsey Wharf and in 1949 at Wootton Rivers. The greatest quantity has always been found in the van of its movement. To quote J. D. Grose: "By the time it had reached Pewsey it had become relatively scarce at Devizes where, three years previously, it was so abundant that swans had an obvious difficulty in swimming through it; when Wootton Rivers was reached it had become much less common at Pewsey." I saw a stretch of it at Honey Street in the summer of 1952. The narrow footbridge that sags to water-level opposite the Barge Inn was like a path across the red-tinged green of the weed. In that summer many of the locks in the stairway below Devizes were coloured unbrokenly by it.

Every year there is a little cutting of the varied border of reed, rush, flag and sedge along the towpath, chiefly, it seems, for the benefit of anglers. The border along the other bank is not touched and so has the tallest growth on it. In places on that side of the canal the reeds are eight or nine feet high when their greyish, glaucous green leaves, band-like and sharp-pointed, arch from a close array of upright stems at the tops of which the silky, wine-red panicles of flowers have broken out and are like flexible plumes. That is the side of the canal on which the dabchicks, moorhens and coots platform their nests and at all seasons find the cover in which they pretend to hide as we approach and pass them, particularly when their lively broods have appeared on the canal. Yet the weed-cutting, as the anglers call it, does little more than make a quickly passing, shorn-looking untidiness, and it certainly gives a more open view across and along the water visible from the path; all the same, it spoils the characteristic flowering of the plants that grow with reed-grass, bur-reed, bulrush, club-rush, flag and

144

greater pond-sedge, and are cut down with them. I think of their attractive variety—codlins-and-cream, figwort, water-plantain, angelica, hemp-agrimony, meadowsweet, flowering rush, St John's wort, skullcap, water-bedstraw, forget-me-not. But they recover and persist, even that upstanding pink-flushed beauty the flowering rush.

There used to be a heronry in tree-tops a field away from the canal between Horton and All Cannings. It is not there now, but herons—rather fewer of them today, I think—still haunt and fish the waterway, mostly as solitary birds, though I have sometimes put up two together and very occasionally three. I am always on the lookout for them, yet they usually see me first, if we do not glimpse each other at the same moment, as on the September afternoon when, by way of the canal between Bristow Bridge and Pewsey Wharf, I was going to Pewsey to watch the illuminated procession that winds up Pewsey Feast. Soon after leaving the bridge I sighted a heron standing in open water. Almost at once the slow beats of its blue-grey wings, broad across and arching to their rounded tips, were carrying it just above the canal to the edge of a very green pasture on the farther side. It stood there watching me as I advanced slowly to see how close a view I could get of it without the help of the binoculars I usually have with me but on that afternoon had left at home. Too uneasy to remain in full view on the grass, the heron flapped away and disappeared round the bend concealing the canal's next reach. I went on to stalk the bird and rediscovered it standing in the flags that came into view along the path as I began to round the bend. Had it seen me? I stood and watched it step slowly into open water, but it was still too uneasy to stay there. Its next move took it from sight round another bend where, after following very cautiously, I spotted it again about a hundred yards from the road-bridge at Pewsey Wharf. For a few moments we both stood looking at each other until the bird lifted itself clear of the canalside tree-tops and swung into a leisurely course that took it farther to the other side of the bridge than I had time to go. Another heron, watched in another September, was picked out full in the harvest sunshine of early afternoon and at a distance at which binoculars brought it close enough for al-most intimate observation whilst—judging by its behaviour—

10*   145

Statue of King Alfred in Pewsey

leaving it in unapprehensive tranquillity. This heron stood where a wide sweep of stubble ended in a shallow dip to the foot of the bank on the downland side of the canal at All Cannings Bridge. I was coming along the road from the downs to the bridge. There were willows on the low rise of the bank behind the bird, peewits in a large flock were dotted about the middle of the field, starlings were running about among the peewits, and rooks were walking about near the heron, who stood as if contemplating and pondering the busy, rather rook-noisy foraging of the other birds. He may, of course, have been comfortably digesting his latest meal. Sometimes he kept his head sunk upon his shoulders, sometimes elevated it a little to peer about him, and once he raised a long leg and scratched his ear with a claw. There I left him, still undisturbed, the sun revealing him to the unaided vision as a white and blue-grey shape hunched against the silvery green of the canalside willows.

CHAPTER XIII

CHARLTON AND STEPHEN DUCK

CHARLTON is about half a mile from Rushall and the Avon gap, the west end of its one street almost touching a bend of the river that has curved towards and then away from the scarp, which is there pushed forward in the broad shoulder of down called Cleeve Hill, the base of the hill having been cut back to keep the main road shelved on firm ground. After swinging through this deeply curved bend and under a bridge at the end of the village, the stream winds in shallower curves a furlong or so behind the village and roughly parallel to it. There is about the same distance between the village and the main road, though its inn stands apart on the open side of the road opposite Cleeve Hill. On each side of the inn, but a little away from it, a byway leads down to the village street, one of them the roughest of narrow lanes with unkempt hedges that make it just the sort of way for stealing unobserved to and from the riverside end, the other a direct and broadside approach with the village always in view.

The inn is called "The Charlton Cat", an odd name, even for a pub. The animal pictured on its signboard today is a white cat: the probability is that it should be a heraldic leopard. For the inn was formerly called "The Poore's Arms" and then had this name and a leopard rampant on its board, the device being the arms of the Poore family, once lords of the manor of Rushall, the next village to the east. It has been suggested that the signboard was so crudely painted or repainted by a local artist that the creature soon became known derisively as "The Charlton Cat", and that this name for the inn took the place of the earlier one.

The place for a first view of Charlton is the highway on the Rushall side of the inn before the scarp of the Plain steepens above it into the shoulder of Cleeve Hill and is a more gently swelling rise of sheep-pastures to a farther-off skyline along Rushall Hill. Here the road could not be more obviously terraced at the foot of the downs: on the side towards Charlton it is banked up like one of the ancient cultivation terraces called strip-lynchets, and is also like most of them in fronting a wide outlook. From it there is a very gradual slope of fields to this small village that lies parallel to the road, with its church tower showing in the middle place and too few trees either in front of the village or inside it to obscure the clustering of its thatched roofs and brick walls. It is not one of the Vale's elm-shaded places. Most of its elms are in the grassland between it and the river, and these, with the tall willows and poplars on the river banks, make a background fringe beyond which is the open breadth of a low swell of cornland reaching away to North Newnton and a group of hamlets south of Woodborough. This leads to distances where villages, though not the neat, tree-tufted shapes of Woodborough Hill and Picked Hill, are lost among a multitude of trees, chiefly elms, behind which the Vale's northern flank of downs rises to close the view. The road reveals Charlton as if in a double setting, a lesser and a greater. The lesser surrounds the village with its own fields, the greater displays the village and its fields as the foreground of the full width of the Vale from Cleeve Hill to Adam's Grave peaking the top of Walker's Hill. Only glimpses of the wider setting are caught from within the village, and these chiefly from its east or more open end where its one street changes to a footpath leading between cornfields to Rushall. At the west end, less than a quarter of a mile away, the street passes into riverside shade and dampness, there narrowing to the lane already mentioned as leading up to the main road, and there as well sending off a turning that leads to the river bridge and then becomes a green drove across the swell of cornland beyond the river.

From end to end of its straight and comfortably wide street Charlton is a small, mellow-toned place of brick, timber and thatch. Neither congested nor scattered, but with a sufficient spacing of garden room, its cottages and farmhouses conform to an even site in their irregular placing and varied grouping along the street, some edging it, some set back, their timber-framed brick walls and thatched roofs sometimes in contrast with weatherboarded and thatched barns and cartsheds round an intervening yard. The church stands on the corner where the byway from the main road enters the street. Its stone-grey is a different and cold colour-note in the general mellowness. At Charlton the typical cottages are not plainly rectangular but have full-gabled or else half-hipped wings that make each roof a ridge-and-valley cluster which may also have a dormered eaves-line and, where there is an outshut or lean-to at the back, one slope that sweeps from the main ridge almost to the ground. For such village roofs there is no more satisfactory covering than well-laid thatch—it defeats the weather, it pleases the eye, and its putting on has proved a craftsman's skill. Thatch at its best is only equalled by Cotswold stone slates, but these should, of course, have stone walls under them, not the Vale's brick and timber, nor its cob, nor the interesting combinations of local materials occasionally discovered in its villages.

There is one of these combinations at Charlton. Facing a side-alley in the part of the street west of the church, the end of a cottage has a bedroom window hooded under the thatch of a half-hip. The wall round it is of brick. Below this window, at a level slightly lower than the eaves of the cottage front, the wall is thickened outwardly by three or four inches under the slant of a splay that is covered with several overlapping boards to cast off the rain. I have never seen weather-boarding used in such a position anywhere else. The brickwork is continued down each wall-angle to the ground and across the base of the wall, thus framing a surface which, in surrounding a lower window, shows an alternation of very rough courses of squared flint, courses of much bigger lumps of chalk rock, and courses of thin brick. Whether the builder thought he might find himself short of bricks, or whether he simply had a mind to try how the mixture would work out, such a bit of wall is one of the things which do not let us forget that the Vale of Pewsey is a downland valley. The church, too, by its flint-walled nave reminds us that we are close to the downs. Here again there is a mixture of materials—stone quoins terminating courses of small irregular flints banded at intervals with a course of stone or brick. The church has a west tower, nave with oak-screened chapel, and oak-screened chancel, mainly fifteenth-century work with a nineteenth-century rebuilding of nave and chancel; but it is the solidly square, keep-like tower with its battlemented parapet and corner pinnacles that holds the eye.

Charlton is a village where, in 1705, Stephen Duck was born to be first a thresher, mower and reaper, and then a poet who proved, as Edward Thomas put it, "that an agricultural labourer could write as well as ninety-nine out of a hundred clergymen, gentlemen, and noblemen, and extremely like them", and in doing so found himself transplanted from the very rural seclusion of Pewsey Vale to the court of Queen Caroline and the London of Pope and Swift. Under the Queen's patronage he was given various offices which left him all the leisure he needed for writing, whilst the clergymen and gentlemen who, discovering his talent, had encouraged him to exercise it, continued their encouragement. The result was sufficient to fill the three-hundred and twelve pages of his *Poems on Several Occasions* with the beat of the heroic couplets fashionable in his day. The copy I have before me is the second of the book's numerous editions and is dated 1737. The poems are offered to Queen Caroline in a flowery dedication that begins:

"The great Honour Your Majesty has done me, in giving me leave to prefix Your Royal Name to the following Poems, does not encourage me to presume they are worthy to be laid at Your Feet on any other account, but only as they are a humble Tribute of Duty, offer'd from a thankful Heart to a gracious Benefactress. Your Majesty has indeed the same Right to them, as You have to the Fruits of a Tree, which you have transplanted out of a barren Soil into a fertile and beautiful garden. It was Your Generosity which brought me out of Obscurity, and still condescends to protect me."

In a preface following the dedication Duck proposes

"only to bespeak the Reader's Good-nature, and to say something which may incline him to pardon what he cannot commend. I have indeed but a poor Defence to make for the Things I have wrote: I don't think them good, and better Judges will doubtless think worse of them than I do. . . . I have not myself been so fond of writing, as might be imagined from seeing so many Things of mine as are got together in this Book. Several of them are on Subjects that were given me by Persons, to whom I have such great Obligations that I have always thought their Desires Commands."

Following the preface there is "An Account of the Author" written as a letter to a friend, "By J. Spence, Professor of Poetry in the University of Oxon", in which is given "all the circumstances I could learn from a Week's Conversation with him in all his Simplicity". The letter was written in 1730, the year in which some of Stephen Duck's verses were brought to Queen Caroline's notice and read aloud in the drawing-room at Windsor Castle, the poet being described as "lately a poor thresher in a Barn in the County of Wilts at the wages of four shillings and sixpence per week".

From this account we discover that after a schooling which grounded him in the three R's Duck went to farm work at about the age of fourteen, had wife and child before he was twenty, and at some time in between, "when he reflected within himself on his want of Education, he began to be particularly uneasy that he should have forgot something of what he had learnt, even at the little School he had been at". He therefore resolved to recover what he was losing, also to try to increase his learning. With the very little extra money he could get by working overtime he managed to buy a book or two. He had a village friend as well, one who had been in service in London for two or three years and, having "an inclination to Books", had bought a few which he kept when he returned to the country. Between them the two men had perhaps twenty or thirty books of various kinds, including an English dictionary, an English grammar, *Paradise Lost*, a volume of Shakespeare containing seven of the plays, and some issues of the *Spectator*. Duck frequently took the *Spectator* with him to work, and "when he did so, his Method was to labour harder than anybody else, that he might get half an hour to read a Spectator, without injuring his Master. By this means he used to sit down all over Sweat and Heat, without regarding his own Health, and often to the Prejudice of it." *Paradise Lost* was difficult going at first, but with the help of a dictionary he read and reread it until "the new Beauties in that Poem, that were continually opening upon his Mind, made all Labour easy to him".

It was, the letter tells us, the verses in the *Spectator* that moved Duck to try his hand at composition. The professor explains it thus:

> "The copies of Verses scattered in those Pieces, help'd on his natural Bent that way; and made him willing to try, whether he could not do something like 'em. He sometimes turn'd his own Thoughts into Verse, while he was at Work; and at last began to venture those Thoughts a little on Paper. What he did of this kind, was very inconsiderable; only scattered Thoughts, and generally not above four or five Lines on the same Subject; which, as there was nobody thereabouts that car'd for Verses, nor anybody that could tell him whether they were good or bad, he generally flung into the Fire, as soon as he had pleas'd himself enough in reading them.
>
> "Whatever care he took to burn these little Pieces, he found it not sufficient to conceal them. The Thing took Air; and Stephen, who had before the Name of a Scholar among the Country People, was said now to be able to write Verses too."

This is where the clergymen and gentlemen come into the picture. A "young gentleman of Oxford", hearing about the farm labourer who writes verses, sends for Duck, talks with him and asks Duck to write him a letter in verse. He does so and opens with the lines:

> "Sir,
> I have, before the Time prescrib'd by you,
> Expos'd my weak Production to your View;
> Which may, I hope, have Pardon at your Hand,
> Because produc'd to Light by your Command.
> Perhaps you may expect some finish'd Ode,
> Or sacred song, to sound the Praise of God;
> A glorious Thought, and laudable! But then
> Think what illit'rate Poet guides the Pen:
> Ill suit such Tasks with one who holds the Plough,
> Such lofty Subjects with a Fate so low."

The complete effort was "the first whole Copy of Verses that he ever wrote". It later fell into the hands of some local clergymen, who were so well pleased with it that they gave presents to the poet and strongly encouraged him to go on writing. His next piece was a slightly longer one entitled *On Poverty*. Then came *The Thresher's Labour*, a still longer poem on a subject suggested by one of the local clergymen already mentioned. It is Duck's best work. This is as far as the professor's account takes us.

Stephen Duck's compositions were soon being talked about in London. Queen Caroline listened to them in her drawing-room at Windsor, gave him an annuity, made him a Yeoman of the Guard, keeper of Duck Island in St James's Park, and finally had him educated for the Church, and in 1752 gave him the rectory of Byfleet in Surrey. On 21st March, 1756, he drowned himself in the Kennet at Reading. His end leaves us wondering whether the patronage given to him, however well meant, had been the right way of providing him with the opportunity to develop his far from great talent. It might have been the better for the man and his poetry if the "clergymen, gentlemen, and noblemen", whilst giving him ease had given him less encouragement to be like themselves and more to be naturally himself. We are left wondering what kind of distress drove this sensitive, modest and sturdy spirit to the extremity of suicide.

Most of his verses make dull reading now, not from lack of skill in the handling of their metrical form, but because he too readily accepted the conventional second-hand literary verbiage of his day, with its clutter of classical imagery and allusion, as the only language for his poetry. If, as Edward Thomas suggested, he could somehow "have thrown Cuddy and Chloe on to the mixen and kept to the slighted homely style", and if, as well, he had been left to discover his themes in and around Pewsey Vale, he might have given the life to his verse that would have made the thresher a poet, if a lesser one, whose work would have been readable today. Stephen Duck, the countryman, was too deeply submerged beneath the artificiality of the birthday odes and other adulatory efforts, the satires, the pastorals and the rest, too much "dissolved in his floods of Alexanderpopery", for his voice to carry pleasingly into our century. His book contains too much verse like the following passage from *On Richmond Park, and Royal Gardens*:

"Of blissful Groves I sing, and flowry Plains:
Ye Sylvan Nymphs, assist my rural Strains.
Shall WINDSOR Forest gain a deathless Fame,
And grow immortal as the Poet's Name;
While not a Bard, of all the tuneful Throng,
With these delightful Fields adorns his Song?
Thy Gardens, RICHMOND, boast an equal Theme,
And only ask an equal Muse's Flame.
What tho' no Virgin Nymphs, of Cynthia's Train,
With Belt and Quiver grace the verdant Plain?
What tho' no fabled consecrated Floods
Flow o'er thy Fields, or murmur thro' thy Woods?
My Song thy real Beauties shall pursue,
And paint the lovely Scenes, and paint 'em true;
A pleasing Task! Nor slight shall be the Praise,
If Royal Caroline accept the Lays."

and far too little verse like the passages I now quote from his best poem, *The Thresher's Labour*:

"Divested of our Cloaths, with Flail in Hand,
At proper Distance, Front to Front, we stand:
And first the Threshal's gently swung, to prove
Whether with just Exactness it will move:
That once secure, we swiftly whirl them round;
From the strong Planks our crab-tree Staves rebound
And echoing Barns return the rattling Sound.
Now in the Air our knotty Weapons fly,
And now with equal Force descend from high;
Down one, one up, so well they keep the Time,
The Cyclops' Hammers could not truer chime. . . .

"In briny Streams our Sweat descends apace,
Drops from our Locks or trickles down our Face.
No Intermission in our Work we know;
The noisy Threshal must forever go.
Their Master absent, others safely play;
The sleeping Threshal does itself betray. . . .

"When sooty Pease we thresh, you scarce can know
Our native Colour, as from Work we go:
The Sweat, the Dust, and suffocating Smoak,
Make us so much like Ethiopians look,
We fear our Wives, when Ev'ning brings us home;
And frighted Infants think the Bugbear come.
Week after Week, we this dull task pursue,
Unless when winn'wing Days produce a new:
A new, indeed, but frequently a worse!
The Threshal yields but to the Master's Curse.
He counts the Bushels, counts how much a Day;
Then swears we've idled half our Time away:
'Why, look ye, Rogues, d'ye think that this will do?
Your neighbours thresh as much again as you.'
Now in our Hands we wish our noisy Tools,
To drown the hated Names of Rogues and Fools.
But wanting these, we just like School-boys look,
When angry Masters view the blotted Book:
They cry, 'their Ink was faulty, and their Pen';
We, 'the Corn threshes bad, 'twas cut too green.'"

and later, when he modulates from threshing to hay-making:

"Soon as the rising sun has drank the Dew,
Another scene is open to our View:
Or Master comes, and at his Heels a Throng
Of prattling Females, arm'd with Rake and Prong;
Prepar'd, whilst he is here, to make his Hay;
Or, if he turns his Back, prepar'd to play:
But here, or gone, sure of this Comfort still;
Here's Company, so they may chat their Fill.
Ah! were their Hands so active as their Tongues,
How nimble then would move the Rakes and Prongs!

"The grass again is spread upon the Ground,
Till not a vacant Place is to be found;
And while the parching Sun-beams on it shine,
The Hay-makers have Time allow'd to dine.
That soon dispatched, they still sit on the Ground;
And the brisk Chat, renew'd, afresh goes round.

All talk at once; but seeming all to fear,
That what they speak, the rest will hardly hear;
Till by degrees so high their Notes they strain,
A Stander-by can nought distinguish plain.
So loud's their Speech, and so confused their Noise,
Scarce puzzled Echo can return the Voice.
Yet, spite of this, they bravely all go on;
Each scorns to be, or seem to be, outdone.
Meanwhile the changing Sky begins to lour,
And hollow winds proclaim a sudden Show'r:
The tattling Crowd can scarce their Garments gain,
Before descends the thick impetuous Rain;
Their noisy Prattle all at once is done,
And to the Hedge they soon for Shelter run.

"Thus have I seen, on a bright Summer's Day,
On some green Brake, a Flock of Sparrows play;
From Twig to Twig, from Bush to Bush they fly;
And with continu'd Chirping fill the Sky:
But, on a sudden, if a Storm appears,
Their chirping Noise no longer dins your Ears;
They fly for Shelter to the thickest Bush;
There silent sit, and All at once is hush."

The Thresher's Labour is, as I have said, an early piece. The theme
was suggested to Duck by the Rev. Mr Stanley, Rector of
Pewsey, who, in proposing the subject and particularly when
reading the poem, must have realised that this was a promising
track for the poet to follow. It seems a pity that Mr Stanley did
not persuade him to keep more closely to it.

Charlton people, though they may never read Stephen Duck's
poems, do not forget the man. They still celebrate his memory
in the Duck Feast held every year at the Charlton Cat on the first
of June. The feast dates back to his lifetime, to the year 1734, when
Lord Palmerston gave a small field—afterwards called Duck's
Acre—on the borders of Charlton and Rushall so that the rent
from it could be used for giving a supper to the Charlton threshers
in honour of the poet. Twelve men sit down to the meal, one of
them, the Chief Duck, wearing a ceremonial hat that is a sort

of pointed skull-cap made of coloured segments. It has a crest of coloured feathers from side to side, and on its front a square of parchment with a margin of painted ornament framing a painting of a thresher wielding a flail. At the end of the supper the toast "In remembrance of Lord Palmerston and the Rev. Stephen Duck" is drunk from a goblet passed round the table. Each man must empty the goblet in one swig or pay a fine; but it holds a swig that is appreciably less than a pint, so very few fail. In the supper-room, too, is a handsome leather-bound edition of the poems, which, I fear, usually remains in its glass-topped case unopened. Yes, Stephen Duck is still remembered at Charlton exactly as he himself prophesied when, after revisiting the village, he rounded off an account of the feast with these lines:

"Oft as this DAY returns, shall Threshers claim
Some hours of Rest sacred to Temple's Name;
Oft as this DAY returns, shall Temple chear
The THRESHER'S Hearts with Mutton, Beef, and Beer:
Hence, when their Children's Children shall admire
This Holiday, and, whence deriv'd, inquire;
Some grateful Father, partial to my Fame,
Shall thus describe from whence, and how it came.
   'Here, Child, a THRESHER liv'd in antient Days;
Quaint Songs he sung, and pleasing Roundelays;
A gracious Queen his sonnets did commend;
And some GREAT LORD, one TEMPLE, was his friend:
That LORD was pleas'd this Holiday to make,
And feast the THRESHERS, for THAT Thresher's sake.'
   Thus shall Tradition keep my Fame alive;
The BARD may die, the THRESHER still survive."

CHAPTER XIV

SHARCOTT

SHARCOTT is a hamlet on the Avon about a mile west of Pewsey. For several months it was to me only a name at the turning that leads to it from the Woodborough road, though I began to feel that instead of always walking past I ought to turn aside there and let the name be transformed from a word into a place. A name on a guide-post arm pointing along a quiet byroad to a hidden village will, sooner or later, beguile you into going the way it points. Less than a quarter of a mile from the Woodborough road I could see a row of thatched cottages, and beyond that nothing but the side of a high railway embankment across the gently shelving hollow in which Sharcott and its brook lie. From this direction, then, the only way of seeing Sharcott is to go there. In the end it seemed as if the instinct, or whatever it was, which kept making me think, as I came to the turning, "No, not yet—not Sharcott today", had been a subconscious prompting to wait for the right day. After a long, very wet, stormy and sunless winter had brought the year to mid-April, a quick change, almost, it seemed, between sunset and sunrise, cleared the sky and flooded a backward spring with the kind of life-giving sunshine that makes the end of every winter a joyous festival. I had already seen swallows and martins, and heard chiff-chaff, willow-warbler, blackcap and cuckoo, but with little sun to brighten their return.

Then the sudden change to this mid-April daylong sunniness liberated a spring in which hardly a bud of blackthorn blossom had broken into white and the hawthorn leaf-buds had only begun to break into the green points that are like a spangling on bushes close at hand but make a green mistiness among the twigs of those in the distance. This was the season and weather in which I loitered along the Woodborough road from Pewsey knowing that the day for Sharcott had come.

It was good to be in the sun's increasing warmth again and feel

158

once more the elation and the sense of well-being that is the stimulating response to the springtime magic of life resurgent. The only traces of cloud on the pale, sun-lustred blue were no more than tenuous films of vapour seen as a faint milkiness high overhead where the blue seemed at its remotest above the brightness of the morning; and though the air was clear where one happened to be, it held the sunlight as a tangible glow in the distances across the valley fields, but as a definite sun-haze on the downs along each side of the Vale. The infrequent breezes died away almost as soon as they were felt. So, in the kind of warm and shining calm that only settles upon the countryside when the ground is being warmed from its winter chill, I walked to Sharcott between roadside banks on which the new growth of herbage had risen above almost every sere remnant of the old. It was covering them chiefly with the different greens and leaf-shapes of chervil, Jack-by-the-hedge and cuckoo-pint, all too young, yet, to be flowering; but in the grass along the foot of the sun-facing bank were newly opened dandelions, a long drift of them, their richly yellow rounds dotted closely on the grass-green. They were true sun-disks and a radiant margin to their side of the road. For birdsong, I do not think there was one moment when every blackbird was silent, yet even they were too spring-excited for settling down to the leisurely conversations which, later on, will carry so mellowly across the fields of a greener world. Skylarks, also, were too excitedly restless and too often in chase of each other near the ground to be filling the air with the shimmering, silvery web of song that would be heard under May skies. A cuckoo sounded a far-away vagrant. To me the willow-warbler was this day's singer as it flitted and darted among green-budded twigs, dropping the cool, gentle sweetness of its notes into clear shadows but no shade.

I saw my first young bird of the season under the hedge on the roadside bank opposite the dandelions. The thick rubber soles I wore brought me along quietly enough to surprise a song-thrush feeding a fledged young one there. The parent bird gave a quick, warning cluck as it flurried to an ash overhanging the road and left me and the apparently unconcerned youngster looking at each other, its eyes surveying me with the calm, bland interest a very young bird shows when it is not afraid. The parent was still cluck-ing an occasional warning as I backed slowly across the road and then leaned against the other bank to watch. In a minute or two both birds were together again, the young one, its beak wide open, being fed. It was noticeably lighter in colour than its parent, and by contrast looked very callow and new, its browns paler, its greys warmer, with a thin sprinkle of downy hairs among the feathering of its head. I could discover no other young thrushes there, so concluded that it was the only one of the brood still alive. The odds seemed against the survival of this one; for when I passed that way the next morning a very agitated thrush was flying at and round a carrion crow flapping about that very part of the hedge. The crow left the hedge, of course, when I appeared, but flew no farther than a tree-top near the road, and probably watched me as I looked into the hedge and discovered the young thrush perching in the upper tangle of its twiggery. Wondering what the crow would do next, I went on for twenty or thirty yards to where I could keep an eye on him from behind one hedge and have the thrush's part of the hedge in view at the same time. His peering, uneasy poise showed that he doubted if I had gone. He endured this uncertainty for perhaps five minutes before drift-ing across the fields, and this young thrush in the hedge lived to grow a little older.

On the first of these two mornings I followed the Sharcott turn towards the row of cottages I have mentioned and the railway embankment beyond. The closer I came to the cottages the more I found myself admiring them; and then, as I passed the middle of the row, I saw their name—Sharcott Barracks, 1845. Nothing in their shape and appearance had led me to expect a name such as that. Barracks! Why that name for a row of five cottages which could not have been less barrack-like? A few minutes later I put the question to a countryman I met coming along the road. He lived in one of the cottages, and though on his way home to dinner he very courteously stopped to listen to and answer my enquiry. He told me that an old soldier had built the cottages, giving them the name that is still on them in the original lettering. That this old soldier remained a tough, crusty warrior in his retirement was plain from what I heard next. The cottages were built on hospital

land (Pewsey Hospital, I inferred) and for this reason the hospital claimed them. Then another man built three more cottages nearer the Woodborough road and derisively named them Sharcott Free Barracks. (Here I began to sense the humours and bitterness of a feud.) But the old soldier, his anger, no doubt, constantly asmoulder just below flame-point, watched for a chance to hit back. It came when the three cottages were to be sold. He bought them, demolished them, and so—to use a phrase that takes us back to Alfred's Wessex—held the field.

Such was the interesting answer to my question, but it would have been equally interesting to learn who designed Sharcott Barracks, and whether the designer, when he saw the finished work, realised what a comely piece of building in brick and thatch he had brought into existence. One can see that it was never meant to look like anything but what it is—a row of cottage dwellings. It is not feebly picturesque either in conception or because of its century of weathering. In its proportions as a whole, and in the balance and arrangement of its parts, it looks modestly yet surely right. Length and width, height to eaves and to gable points, the area of brick wall in relation to the area of thatched roof, the rather steep angle of the roof-slope, the overhang of thatch at the eaves all combine in quiet harmony. The walls carry the roof easily under eaves that would perhaps seem a little too low if the thatch sloped from its ridge to a continuous edge; but the bedroom windows are higher than this line, and the eaves rise and fall to hood each in turn under dormered thatch. The recesses thus formed by the deep overhang of the thatch are narrow triangles, the middle one showing a brick surface, the others boarded. There are five of these windows, small square sashes, the central one under a taller and more prominent hood. Behind it, rising from the main roof-ridge, is a grouped stack of three brick chimneys, square but set in line and corner to corner in the Elizabethan manner, plain but for two courses oversailing below the top course. These two features—the bedroom window under the taller hood, and the group of chimneys—are the central shapes about which the whole is symmetrical. Single chimneys, like the others and set at the same angle, rise from the apex of each gable-end. On each side of the middle upper window are two others,

Thatch at Easton Royal

balancingly spaced, whilst below them the ground-floor windows
and the doors are also spaced to keep the balance. All the doors
and windows are flush with the wall. The old thatch is deeply
weather-stained, and weathering has dulled the dark brickwork
to a subdued red that seems the darker because the headers, or
brick-ends, showing in the courses are all of the kind to which
over-burning gave a tone that is nearly black. Afterwards I looked
at other cottages in the village with no less pleasure in their appearance and no smaller appreciation of their builder's traditional
craftsmanship, yet without the kind of admiration I felt for the
one who, designing a complete row of cottages, achieved the
symmetrical unity and rightness of Sharcott Barracks. Did he, I
wonder, consciously plan the effect he obtained by translating
brick and thatch from the rustic vernacular of earlier times into
the more sophisticated formalism of his own day?

The Sharcott hollow is, as I have said, crossed by a railway embankment a little beyond the cottages just described. A brook,
rising about a mile away at Wilcot, flows south along it, skirting
the west side of Sharcott to enter the Avon purling along past the
lower end of the village on its way from Pewsey to the three Manningfords. The road that brought me to Sharcott Barracks tunnelled
the embankment and soon became the village's one street. Within
half a mile it had bridged the Avon and left the village behind in
leading to the highway which keeps to a fringe of the Vale under
Salisbury Plain. Between railway and village, on a marshy wayside field threaded by the brook, I saw a contrast that was a vivid
revelation of the difference between dead winter and the quickening spring. More than half this waterlogged field was raggedly
covered with drifts of broken and leaning reed-stems intermingled
with flattened tufts of flag-blades—the previous summer's green,
upstanding hosts after autumn's chill and "the furious winter's
rages" had done with them. They were pallidly sapless in their
disarray, battered and bleached into a grey death. Yet among the
sere wrack, in the more open places there, life and colour were
springing and unfolding: this marshy field was a king-cup or
marsh-marigold swamp as well. The plants were crowded together, often in shallow water, spreading the clear, glossy green
of rounded leaves under the glowing yellow of flowers in all

stages of opening except the falling looseness of the full-blown. There were buds like golden balls, half-open petals curving into golden bowls, and petals lying back in the widest golden cups they could shape. This was the contrast—the colour and texture of brittle, spent tissue withering away, and those of pliant, living forms unfolding to the sun.

Sharcott lies comfortably spaced along each side of the road's quarter-mile from the king-cup swamp to the Avon. It is a well-kept homely little place consisting of one or two farms, two large brick and slate houses, both looking solidly four-square and manorial, one of them impressively so, and a few cottages, most of them timber-framed, with brick infilling and thatched roofs. In their timbering no strength is wasted in the over-massiveness which, in older examples of this construction, sometimes makes the wall-panels enclosed by the posts and beams appear too obviously what they are—merely filled-in gaps. At Sharcott, and usually in Pewsey Vale, the framing is not ponderously strong, yet is sufficient, and so does not emphasise too much the fact that the stability of the whole fabric is in the frame. This comes to light when, as in one of the cottages here, a brick panel has to be repaired. Something had loosened the bricks in one of these wood-framed rectangles and most of them had been taken out to be properly reset. This exposed the construction. The recess was backed by the close, stout lathing behind the internal plaster, and only one width of brick—a fraction more than four inches—was required to bring the face of the panel flush with the outside of the woodwork. Ordinary care and the mellowing of time have given those thatched and timber-framed homesteads at Sharcott an air of permanence which seems to have settled them in the country-side for ever. We know, all the same, that neglect will destroy this illusion long before it destroys the cottages.

A broad swell of pasture dotted with elms rises along the side of the village towards Pewsey, whilst beyond the side towards Man-ningford Abbotts is a lower parkland fringe where the brook flows in coming to the Avon a little west of Sharcott's Avon bridge. More than anything else this bridge and its surroundings made me glad I had not followed the byway through Sharcott to the river on a different kind of day. I knew at once that this would be a very attractive spot in any season, but felt that it should be first seen as I was seeing it then in the bright clarity of the sun's mid-April's radiance among the openness of budding trees, of which only the riverside withies and sallows had broken into their earliest green. The openness belonged to the springtime rather than to the lie of the land in this corner of the Vale. From the bridge I could look backward into the village but no farther, and forward a shorter distance to where, between lines of oaks, the road veered from sight. On each side I could see only short reaches of the river before its windings were hidden by trees. Either the massing of distant tree-tops or else rising fields shut off the farther parts of the Vale, so that the bridge, the piece of road leading to and from it, and the river approaching and flowing away from its arches were not only secluded from the rest of the Vale in this way, but were centred in a closer, more intimate seclusion of trees standing round them. This would deepen with the unfolding of summer leafage. Today, as I have said, only the riverside withies and sallows were showing green, the withies misted with pale points breaking from bud-scales, the sallows yellow-green with catkins. By contrast the oaks and ashes near the river and the alders along it were bare. Here again, on wet ground among the alders, I glimpsed the golden yellow of king-cup clusters. One of the grassy road-margins from the bridge to the first of the oaks was spangled with the paler yellow of wide-open celandines. When it was time to go on I left Sharcott bridge reluctantly. Its dark red, lichened brick arches and low brick para-pets span a current that is here little more than twenty feet wide— just the kind of bridge and water to beguile us into staying when we ought to be on our way. A continual cawing at the rookery in the ashes seemed threaded with a blackbird's leisurely sequences, whilst all the tones and semitones of April colour there, and the transparencies of running water, took the sunlight like an en-riching and clarifying bloom with an effect of gaiety heightened by the chuckling of the river. I shall not forget the moments when the cool, smooth notes of a willow-warbler flitting about the alders were intermingling with the cold, splashy water-sounds.

CHAPTER XV

PEWSEY AND THE SOUTHEAST CORNER

PEWSEY, on the east branch of the Avon, is the largest and busiest place in the Vale. With a population of about 2,000 it is the kind of large village that has the air of being a little town, whilst it certainly performs the function of a town for the villages round about. Six roads come to it, the railway passes its north end, and the canal passes it at Pewsey Wharf half a mile north of the railway. It is not quite at the middle of the Vale, there being eight miles between it and Etchilhampton Hill at the west end, but only four between it and Burbage at the east end, whilst it is nearer to the White Horse on the side of Pewsey Hill at the edge of the Plain than to the Giant's Grave on Martinsell at the edge of the northward downs. At Wootton Rivers, two miles and a half to the northeast, canal and railway are still so close together in coming west along the Vale that there is only enough room between them for the brook which grows into the Pewsey Avon. Half a mile nearer Pewsey the canal and the railway begin the divergence in which the canal keeps to the winding edge of the chalk footslopes whilst the railway swings inward to the middle of the Vale, thus giving the brook a gradually widening hollow in which to grow. Almost above Pewsey the hollow turns southward and is crossed by the high embankment carrying the railway to Pewsey station, the stream passing beneath the embankment to flow for half a mile to the south end of the village, where a westward curve takes it under the Salisbury and Devizes road at Swan Bridge and on to Sharcott, the three Manningfords, North Newnton and then to its junction with the other branch of the Avon at Scales Bridge.

That Pewsey is a village mainly disposed along a hollow is revealed less clearly from within than from without, the most clearly, perhaps, from a footpath across the meadows skirting its east side. One way to this path is a narrow lane that branches from North Street just below the railway station and leads to the north side of the railway embankment, there giving a view of the upper part of the hollow reaching back to the banked-up canal before it bends away towards New Mill and Wootton Rivers. To right and left there is the gradual lift from its shallow openness to fields among a scattering of elms, and behind it all is the long front of Martinsell making a downland skyline. In the bottom are marshy fields with their sedges and flags, meadowsweet and ragged robin, through which the course of the stream can be traced by the occasional willows along its windings to where, near the foot of the embankment, it broadens in passing what was once a small brick-built mill with louver-boarded windows. The wall rising from the water has no mill-wheel now, but the round of its shape is clearly marked by a chalky encrustment deposited on the brick-work as the wet wheel revolved. On the wall above it are also the markings which suggest that the wheel was housed under a ridged roof. Domesday Book records that there were seven mills at Pewsey, and according to *The Place-Names of Wiltshire* the forms of its name in Saxon and Norman times—Pefesigge, Pevesige, Pevesie—indicate that Pewsey was probably "Pefe's well-watered land", though nothing is known about Pefe, its Saxon owner.

At the mill the lane bridges the stream and changes to a path across the remainder of the hollow, reaching its edge at the beginning of the railway embankment and opposite the stiles of a level-crossing from which the footpath continues along the meadows I have mentioned. On this side of the railway the valley of the little river is not only deeper but is so crowded with trees that except for a roof here and there the village is lost among them. From the meadow-path it is not so much Pewsey as its containing hollow that we see. Some of the visible roofs are on the crest of the farther or west side, the raw newness of their tile and slate, and of the white walls under them, showing that the Pewsey of today is becoming too big for its earlier riverside confinement; but most that are visible—and there is thatch here—lie along and beyond the street to which the path leads, with a farther clustering of elms behind them towards the hamlet of Southcott, and away behind these elm-tops the downs of the Plain where a long barrow, another Giant's Grave, is caught on the Milton Hill skyline.

The more westerly of the two roads from Marlborough to

Salisbury crosses Pewsey Vale and passes through Pewsey in doing so, there coming to the Avon and following it down to Salisbury. At the canal bridge above Pewsey, with the grass-grown, abandoned wharf on the left and the curiously named public-house, the French Horn, on the right, it begins its dip towards the village, gently and between hedges at first, then more steeply between banks deepening under elms and other tall trees to where the slope eases again and the road crosses a brook which comes to it along a small hollow on the right and goes on into the larger hollow to join the Avon near the mill I have described. Where it approaches the road the brook is overhung by alders, aspens, hazels and ash trees and is fringed with much comfrey, whilst the marshy bottom of its hollow is overgrown with horsetail, meadowsweet and codlins-and-cream, with an intermingling of flags, figwort, marsh cress, hemp agrimony, water avens, red campion and herb-Robert, according to the saturation of the ground. White posts and rails enclose it from the road without diminishing the attractiveness of the spot. A relic at the bottom of the hill reminds us that the end of the horse age on our roads is still within living memory. Almost under the rails is a water-trough that today is as little used as the canal wharf at the top of the hill, though in its time it must have refreshed many a thirsty horse. Beside the trough a white-painted board speaks for some anonymous Christian in the clarity of the well-formed cursive script that is written there in black. With quiet firmness it told a generation who did not know that human beings were created bipeds because they needed one foot for the accelerator and one for the clutch that

> "A man of kindness to his steed is kind,
> A brutal action shows a brutal mind.
> Remember He who made thee, made the brute,
> He can't complain, but God's all-seeing Eye
> Beholds thy cruelty and hears his cry.
> He was designed thy servant, not thy drudge,
> Remember his Creator is thy Judge."

Two quieter roads converge on Pewsey along the Vale from the west, one from Wilcot and the Alton villages, the other from

Woodborough and the villages along the Avon's west branch. They meet in front of the Mental Institution, formerly the Workhouse, at the west end, continue as one across the railway that is there in a deep cutting, and descend the side of the river valley to enter North Street, which is what the Marlborough road becomes when it has tunnelled through the railway embankment. Lined with houses, shops and inns, with the river out of sight at the back of those on the left, and the side of the hollow lifting behind those on the right, North Street leads to the centre of the village where, as High Street, the road from Burbage bridges the Avon to make the junction in which a statue of Alfred the Great is islanded. This is Pewsey's most open part and unmistakably its centre; yet although called Market Place the area around the statue seems—today, at any rate—more of a road junction than a market place, gaining its openness chiefly because when the High Street has bridged the river it is the one part within the village where, for forty or fifty yards, the river banks are seen from the street, the one part, in fact, where it is clear that Pewsey is a place astride a stream. Instead of solid parapets the bridge has white-painted posts and rails, and these are continued along the roadside where the stream, shallow and several yards wide, flows between them and a pair of timber-framed cottages joined under a thatched roof and standing close behind the grassy slope of the farther bank. Next to these cottages, but almost opposite the bridge, there is the modernistic rectangularity of a cinema's red-brick façade. This is the only cinema in the Vale. Its presence in the village is as definite a sign as the shops, banks, inns, garages, bus office and fire station that Pewsey is the Vale's capital.

It has not taken Pewsey's statue of King Alfred many years to get its hoary, antique look. Inscriptions on the base tell us that it was "erected June 25, 1913", and that "This statue of his most illustrious ancestor is erected to commemorate the coronation of His Majesty King Geroge V, June 22nd, 1911." They also remind us that some of King Alfred's estates lay round about Pewsey. Armed with spear, sword and shield Alfred surveys the traffic—bus, coach, car, lorry—that passes his pedestal, and to much of which Pewsey must be chiefly a narrow village street that slows it down on its way across the Vale. Seen from the bridge, he has behind him the cream-washed brickwork of a tall row of shops rising to a thatched roof in which the eaves and ridge of the central part are stepped a little higher than those of the side parts. High on the wall a tablet names and dates these shops "Phoenix Row, 1825". From the statue North Street continues south as River Street for the hundred yards that bring it to a blind, right-angled turn to the west which, as Church Street, takes it between the church raised above it on the left and the newest part of Pewsey on the high ground to the right before it swings south again, leaves the village behind, and becomes a highway heading for Swan Bridge and the openness between the river and the downs of the Plain. Just beyond the bridge it offers a choice of ways— the main road under the downs to Devizes and Salisbury, or the road up to and over Pewsey Down to Everleigh and Andover, or the byway that soon changes to the deeply rutted green drove which leads straight to the Pewsey White Horse cut in the turf steeps of Pewsey Hill.

For a week in September the people of Pewsey and the neighbouring villages enjoy themselves at Pewsey Feast and Carnival— indeed, on the night of the procession at least, not only the people who live in the Vale but many from places well outside it. Originating long ago as the Church Feast and the pastimes and jollifications for which it became the occasion, the carnival idea of a fancy-dress procession along the streets appears to have been introduced towards the end of the 'nineties, to be followed later on with the idea of giving the procession a setting of galaxies of little lights of different colours hung about the streets and byways, the Market Place and its part of the river. Nowadays the festivities open on a Saturday evening with the crowning of the Carnival Queen, followed on the Sunday by Feast Services in the church, and throughout the week there are fairgrounds, sports and races, dancing and the culminating spectacle of the procession to be enjoyed. It all ends on the second Sunday evening with a Thanksgiving Service in the Market Place, and when the coloured lights have been taken down and stored away for the next celebration Pewsey is its everyday self again.

An hour before sundown on a recent September Saturday I walked to Pewsey along the canal towpath from the direction of

Wilcot to watch the procession. I knew that at this moment all roads in the Vale led to Pewsey, that the streets were beginning to fill with people, and that many more were on their way by bus, coach, car, motor-cycle, bicycle and afoot. Until I left the tow-path and became one of the people going down the hill to the village all this was beyond the tranquillity I shared with a heron along the canal between Bristow Bridge and the bridge at Pewsey Wharf. Before going into the streets I stood for a time to watch the coaches and cars follow each other into the parking-field by the station and the people streaming away from them. Pewsey was already crowded, and if many spectators had begun to line the pavements, many more were walking about and many still coming in. The great majority were country folk, all gay and happy, the number of family parties very noticeable. Some of these parties had a range of age from grandparents down to the youngest grandchildren. Youths and their girls were in high spirits but not rowdy. The sellers of toy balloons and oddly shaped, brightly coloured paper hats could hardly have been busier, nor could the pubs. When the sun had almost set among fine-weather clouds, and the first dimness of twilight was per-ceptible in the streets, men began to light the candles in the small, jar-like containers shaped in coloured glass that were hung every-where—on house fronts, in gardens and strung across the river at street level. By this time all wheeled traffic was being stopped at the outskirts of the village and the streets left to the multitude filling them and making walking about almost impossible. The only thing to do then was to stand and wait for the procession to appear. It chiefly consisted of electrically lit tableaux staged on vehicles, some of them drawn by farm-tractors. Several bands were spaced along it. There was no lack of humour, especially in the agricultural pieces.

After the procession I walked the streets again to see the lights in the dark of night. The candles made a soft brightness of their coloured containers. At the centre of the village the hundreds that glowed three or four feet above the river were very attractively reflected in its rippling darkness, whilst behind them the black-and-white riverside cottages were floodlit. At the other end of the bridge a "ducking stool" was in operation. A youth dressed as a girl sat within a framework so balanced that a wooden ball thrown hard enough and hitting the "bull" of a target by its side would loose a catch and drop him into a tank of water underneath. Many tried to do it, but the throwing—at about ten yards range—was so erratic that I saw only one ducking in a quarter of an hour.

There were two fairgrounds, both very crowded and very noisy with the machinery of the different kinds of roundabouts and the accompaniment of jazzed and crooned and much amplified music that was very different from the gasping, brassy sort of organ stuff I used to hear at fairs in my youth. At one ground I watched a "Hoop-La" stall where the attendants could hardly hand out the wooden rings quickly enough. A prize was won when a ring was pitched to fall so that it lay flat round the base on which, tantalisingly close, the object stood, the base's diagonal being very little shorter than the ring's diameter. A rosily market-merry countryman pitched a ring which lodged very lightly on one corner of a base, and seeing that no attendant was looking, quickly leaned across the barrier and flicked the ring flat. He said nothing, grinned mischievously, and waited. It seemed the understood custom for everyone watching to shout when a ring fell truly, the effect being somewhat like that of a unanimous appeal at cricket. This time it was a mixture of shout and very hilarious laughter. An attendant came round and handed over the prize without realising, or appearing to realise, what the laughter was about. The man went on playing—and, of course, paying—but I noticed that one or another of the attendants watched every ring he pitched afterwards. On my way to the other fairground I saw a youth drop a gaudily coloured plaster-of-paris statuette he was carrying. He picked up the largest fragment, looked at it as if he could not believe his eyes, and then flung it to the ground in exasperation. I could not catch what he said as he flung it down. The other fairground was more like those of an earlier day. It had a boxing-booth as well as several side-shows advertising the usual kinds of marvels. There was, too, a stall from which a rosy-cheeked, merry-eyed woman sold the toffee-apples she was making by first skewering the apples—all very red ones—and then dipping them into a hot, brownish, syrupy liquid. By eleven o'clock the folk from the outside places were going home. The streets, though still crowded by normal Pewsey standards, were again becoming walkable without pushing and jostling, the coloured lights were still glowing. The fried-fish shop had a long queue leading to its door.

The road east along the four miles of the Vale from Pewsey to Burbage passes the inward ends of a hamlet and two villages. The hamlet is Fyfield, the villages Milton Lilbourne and Easton, and in that order each is lined along its byway leading from the road to the rise of the Plain at the edge of this southeast corner of the Vale. The road follows the crown of a low fold in the valley bottom separating two small streams which are very erratic in flow and often dry, the stream to the north of it, Deane Water, rising towards Burbage and joining the Avon at New Mill about three-quarters of a mile within the valley from Fyfield, the one to the south rising at a pool at the downland end of Easton and passing the end of Milton and well below Fyfield in coming to the Avon at the southern outskirts of Pewsey. The second stream is the division between the elmy inner part of the Vale and the gentle upward tilt of the much more spaciously open cornfields, pastures and meadowland to the foot of the downs. Except in winter little of the two villages and hardly more than the skyline of the downs behind them can be seen from the road—its hedge leafage and the foliage of the elms along the field-hedges make too dense a screen, especially in the luxuriance of high summer. Fyfield, consisting of two large houses and several cottages, is not to be seen from the road at any season.

Its byway leaves the road about a mile from the centre of Pewsey and dips between very much ivied banks and thorn hedges under an arching spread of elm, beech, ash and sycamore, with a small mixed wood of old trees filling the angle it makes with the road on the Pewsey side, so that it has the look of a sunken lane disappearing into woodland. After about a furlong of this shade it widens a little and passes the side of the Elizabethan manor house, first the high-walled yard behind the house, then the side of the house itself, and then the wall enclosing the garden at its front. Next, and on the same side, come three thatched cottages banked above the lane, two with timber-framing and two with flint courses among their brickwork. Opposite the third cottage a drive leads to another large house almost hidden among the trees of its grounds. Here the lane changes to a rough-surfaced way leading between tall, untrimmed hedges to a pair of thatched cottages and eventually, after crossing the Easton brook, becomes a track to the downs where the slopes are stepped with strip-lynchets and the mound of the Giant's Grave is shaped on the bare skyline to the right of Milton Hill Clump. Another wood begins immediately at the side of the manor gardens towards Milton. Fyfield is indeed a small place secluded among trees.

With one side and its yard and garden walls flanking the lane the manor house faces south and is mellow with the warm tones of old brick and tile, except on the roof of the main part, where slates have taken the place of the tiles that must once have covered it. The kind of brick can best be discovered in the boundary walls. It has the thinness of former days, being two inches where later bricks are a little short of three, and there is much variation in shade from brick to brick, some having the bluish tinge given by over-burning. All are thinly and irregularly encrusted with grey lichen that softens the general warmth of tone. The house-front has five ridge-high gables each a little different in width, and behind this main part are three wings reaching back at right angles to it. There are nine chimney-stacks of brick spaced about this cluster of roof-slopes, seven of them double, all square and plain but for caps formed by stepping out the courses at the top. The double stacks are set corner to corner. At the back of the house a detached building has what looks like its original tiled roof, the ridge sagging through a shallow curve. The front windows have sashed frames and thin glazing bars, whilst some of the smaller windows alongside the lane have been shaped as if their wood were mullioned stonework. Stonework there is, though, in the walls of a dovecote that still stands in a corner of the gardens and reminds us of the time when fresh beef and mutton were not to be had in winter, the time when, because of the difficulty of keeping the summer flocks and herds alive through the winter months, all except the breeding stock were slaughtered and salted in the autumn. Pigeons were then a tasty part of winter diet, yet were not for everyone, as the privilege of building a cote and keeping it full of birds was reserved chiefly for landowners. This one is twenty-five feet square, with stone walls finished off with brick quoins under a pyramidal and tiled roof that is topped at the apex by an open-sided lantern by which the birds entered. It contains three-hundred and sixty-five nest-holes, but many were larger, having places for a thousand and more nests. Each host of pigeons fed on the surrounding countryside, and the birds were not to be touched for doing so: in the words of G. M. Trevelyan, their "function in life was to grow plump on the peasants' corn till they were fit for the lord's table". We can judge how the lord of the manor's pigeons were viewed by the farmers when we think of the damage done to crops by wood-pigeons today.

The small wood on the Pewsey side of the turning to Fyfield is a mixture of beech, ash, oak, sycamore and elm standing above the undergrowth of hazel, bramble and bracken on its rather hummocky floor. In the very corner of the angle between the two ways there is a mysterious oval mound, not unlike a long barrow, with its higher end towards the Pewsey road. The strange thing about it is that its flattish top is clear of undergrowth and is enclosed within a horseshoe colonnade of fifteen towering lime trees spaced at about two-yard intervals, with the bend of the curve above the main road and the gap between the open ends, about four yards wide, facing the eighth tree, in front of which the mound-top is heightened into a lesser mound. In spite of being raised among the other trees at the corner of the wood the mound is not easily seen from either road, and when I stand within its curving colonnade of limes, their trunks towering up and tapering to a height that causes me to lean back when looking at their tops, I have the feeling that it must be a secret meeting-place, the lesser mound in the deep of the curve suggesting a place of authority and perhaps honour. So far I have not been able to discover anything definite about the age and purpose of this lime-ringed mound. A woman who lives near said that it is thought to have been a burial-place of monks, a man said that an underground passage leading to a vanished priory began there. I shall not be surprised if it turns out to be the burial-place of somebody's favourite horse.

Milton Lilbourne, the next place east of Fyfield, is the village to which, on an August morning in 1826, William Cobbett descended from the crest of Milton Hill after his first view of "this valley of Avon, which was my land of promise". He was on his way to Fyfield and had, he tells us, passed Milton Hill Farm in riding across the downs from Everleigh, and so came to where his road—smoothly metalled today—changed from a green track to a deeply sunken, rain-scoured groove of chalk curving down the steep of the valley-side, the kind of chalk road that still leads down from Easton Hill to Easton, the next village. It had such a rough and crumbly steepness that he did not attempt to ride down but asked a boy to lead his horse. In another chapter I have quoted Cobbett's description of the valley that had opened out below him, and truly no place comes nearer to revealing the Vale of Pewsey as a whole than the bank above this road where it is curving round the head of the great west-facing coomb that, with the sweep of a green amphitheatre, is hollowed below Milton Hill and is all turf except for a small hanger of beeches on the downland side of its open end. The crest of the coomb-head just above the road reveals the flow of downs along the farther or north side of the Vale from almost the edge of Savernake Forest to Roundway Hill above Devizes, and on this side the other end of Milton Hill making a shoulder of down beyond the mouth of the coomb, and projecting behind it the lower shoulder of Denny Sutton Hipend, and behind that the continuous and even flow of the Plain's edge from Wilsford Hill to Urchfont Hill, with Etchilhampton Hill isolated among the elms in the Vale's western extremity between Urchfont Hill and Roundway Hill, whilst Picked and Wood-borough Hills, the only others isolated within the Vale, are close together among the press of elms in the middle distance before Walker's Hill. From this lookout the only completely unsighted part of the Vale is where, hidden by the crest of the coomb-head, the side of Easton Hill falls from its beech clump to Easton village.

The easing fall of the coomb's outer rim brings this downland road to the valley bottom. At once it turns from the downs to straighten into the lane which, almost half a mile on and with a border of elms on one side and beeches on the other for part of the way, becomes the village street where the yards of a large farm lie on each side of it. For a further half-mile, rising gradually and never rigidly straight, it is loosely and varyingly lined with the brick-and-thatch cottages, the larger houses and the two or three farm-houses that are banked up a little above its margins in making Milton Lilbourne another of the Vale's long villages of one street. At the Pewsey road it passes from the village and goes on as a narrow cross-valley lane that leaves the Vale by climbing the northern scarp at the east end of Martinsell.

Milton's small and solidly built church stands above the west side of the street towards the south end. It has a battlemented tower with crocketed pinnacles, a south porch, nave, north aisle and chancel, showing work of various periods from the thirteenth-century chancel arch spanning twelfth-century jambs to the fifteenth-century tower, as well as nineteenth-century rebuilding of the south wall of the nave, the porch and chancel. Except for the tower, and the buttresses, quoins and windows of the other parts, it is a flint-walled church with a curious patching of stone similar to that at Wootton Rivers on the other side of the Vale. Time and the elements have softened the differences in colour and texture between flint and stone in the north wall. The flints there are rough, uneven in size and very irregularly coursed, but in the south wall, rebuilt in 1875, they are much more squarely shaped to a uniform size and regularly coursed. There, too, the stone blocks set among the flint are more regularly squared, though of different sizes, some being two, some three and even four courses of flint deep. They patch the wall at fairly even intervals, their light grey smoothness giving the effect of small, flush panels dotted about the dark grey of the flint. I cannot leave the churchyard without mentioning the graceful beauty of the lettering inscribed on the tombstone of a musician. Dying in 1774, his epitaph reads:

"On Earth his tunes to Time confined was,
  Now to eternity thatt never ceafe;
  No more the Difcords of the World he hears,
  But the more Perfect Mufic of the Spheres;
  His Harmony whilft in this Life was fuch
  That it prepared his Soul at Death's approach
  To join the Sacred Choir where Angels fing
  Eternal praife to the Almighty King."

176

The Alton Barnes White Horse

Neither can I leave Milton Lilbourne without a word about its manor house. It stands on the same side of the street as the church but nearer the other end of the village, and is most attractively seen from the grass-field opposite. Later English Renaissance in style, there is nothing in its symmetrical formality to disguise its English origin, which is why it takes its place with natural composure among the thatched and timber-framed cottages that neighbour it.

Easton, about a mile farther away from Pewsey, is the last place in this direction that can truly be called a Vale village. It is often named Easton Royal, of which the only explanation I have been able to discover is—to quote *The Place-Names of Wiltshire*—"probably because the east half of the parish was in the King's forest of Savernake". I wonder, though, if it was ever called "Royal" before the sixteenth century, when, at the dissolution of the monasteries, the lands of a priory which used to be at Easton were taken by the King and then given to the Seymour family, who had succeeded the Esturmeys as Hereditary Wardens of Savernake Forest. They lived at the now vanished Wolf Hall about a mile on the other side of Burbage. A brief history of the priory hangs in Easton church. It was founded in the thirteenth century when Stephen, son of Sir Adam of Easton, granted his house and all appertaining to it to the Order of the Holy Trinity for the purpose of establishing a priory or hospital or hostel at Easton. The brothers were to provide free hospitality for poor travellers, and from their resources and the alms they received contribute towards the payment of ransoms for Christians captured by the enemy during the Crusades. In 1493 the priory buildings were much damaged by fire, and the brothers were permitted by Henry VII to beg for alms throughout the kingdom in aid of their restoration. The original parish church was pulled down in the fourteenth century, the priory church being used by the villagers instead. In 1536 Henry VIII's commissioners, preparing the way for the dissolution of the monasteries, reported that the church as well as the house and outbuildings of the priory were in great disrepair, and soon afterwards the priory lands were given to Sir Edward Seymour to help him sustain the honours of being made Viscount Beauchamp. In 1590 the priory church, almost in ruins, was demolished and a

The Pewsey White Horse

new one built, this, after much nineteenth-century restoration, being the one we see at Easton today. A flint-and-stone building with a tower against the east end of the south wall, the interior is even simpler in form than the church at Wootton Rivers, consisting only of a hall-like nave in which the altar is close behind a rail at the end. The foundations of the priory buildings probably lie under two mounds near the church.

The Seymour who, as Viscount Beauchamp, was given the lands of Easton Priory, later became Earl of Hertford and then Duke of Somerset, and after the death of Henry VIII was chosen to be Protector of the Realm during the minority of his sister's son, Edward VI. Four years later he was charged with treason and felony, condemned to death, and on the 22nd January, 1552, beheaded on Tower Hill. A century later treasonable plotting against the ruling power was discovered in the peace and quiet of Easton itself. In 1655 a troop of Cromwell's men rode from Marlborough and arrested Major John Wildman in the act of writing a declaration on behalf of the "people of England now in arms against the tyrant Oliver Cromwell". He being more fortunate than Protector Somerset, his life was spared.

Easton is like Milton in beginning at the Pewsey road and being narrowly strung out for nearly half a mile along each side of a single street, but is unlike Milton in having its downland end almost at the foot of the Plain. Easton village street is also a little more sinuous and sunken in its dip towards the downs. For much of the way it is bordered with grassy banks that deepen head-high at the middle of the village but shallow into flatter verges at each end. They keep the cottage and house walls, the gardens, and the several farmyards and fields from pressing in upon the street closely enough to make it seem shut away from the downland spaciousness to which it leads. Easton always feels an open place, an impression that its garden trees and an elm here and there do not weaken. Most of its cottages and houses are of brick, either plain-walled or timber-framed, a few of the latter kind revealing their age in the silvery grey of the fissured posts and beams shaping the panels of lichened brickwork. Some of each kind are white or cream washed. Few have the hard angularity of tiled or slated roofs to break the varied sequence of weathered thatch which runs from end to end of the village and includes not only house-thatch but that of farm-buildings such as the timbered cart-lodge of seven bays in a farmyard beside the church. Below the church and this farmyard a line of three or four cottages on the opposite side brings the street almost to the pond from which the stream I have mentioned flows past Milton Lilbourne and Fyfield to join the Avon at Pewsey—whenever there is enough water in it. There is only a cattle-pasture between the pond and the foot of the dome-like swell of down called Easton Hill. As a smooth way the street ends at the pond but branches widely to right and left into tracks which, in skirting the pasture and then deeply grooving the scarp-slope of the Plain, come to the crest of the downs at each end of Easton Hill. Together they make a horse-shoe curve containing the pasture and the bare hillside, whilst the rounded summit and its clump of beeches make a skyline across the open end. Easton Clump, isolated there, is a landmark to the whole Vale.

Chapter XVI

WHITE HORSES

WILTSHIRE has more white horses than any other county—I mean, of course, those very much larger than life-size figures that have been shaped in the whiteness of chalk on the sides of downs by cutting away the turf. Of the eight turf-cut horses visible to-day on the Wiltshire Downs two are on the chalk scarps edging the Vale of Pewsey, five are dotted at mile-or-two intervals about the Marlborough Downs north of the Vale, and one lies within ten miles west of the Vale, on the scarp of Salisbury Plain between Bratton and Westbury. The northern half of the Wiltshire downland is definitely the county's white horse region, and is its racehorse region too, for training gallops ribbon some of the downs not far from the white horses.

No Wiltshire white horse is as ancient by many a century as the most famous turf-cut horse in the land, Berkshire's White Horse of Uffington, which lies extended on the edge of the downs about three miles east of the Wiltshire border. This strangely and rhythmically simplified horse takes us back to Celtic Britain, and has made its hill White Horse Hill and the valley it overlooks the Vale of White Horse. Wiltshire's oldest is the present Westbury horse, cut in 1778 to replace an earlier one which, as described and illustrated by Mr Morris Marples in his excellent book *White Horses and Other Hill Figures*, published in 1949, must have been an odd-looking animal indeed. With its long, up-curving, crescent-tipped tail, its dachshund-like body and its pop-eye too close to the base of one ear, it seemed so odd as to be offensive to the man who, as it were, rubbed it out and did it again. Mr Marples explains that "A certain Mr Gee, steward to Lord Abingdon, and evidently a connoisseur in horseflesh, took exception to the grotesque creature while surveying his employer's estates in the parish of Westbury, and undertook the duty of remodelling it on more conventional lines. This he did, no doubt to his own

satisfaction, though the opinion of posterity has been different."
Wiltshire's youngest white horse is one of the two in the Vale of
Pewsey, the Pewsey horse on Pewsey Hill at the edge of the Plain
about a mile south of the Vale's name-place. This also was cut to
replace an earlier horse, though not because Pewsey folk objected
to a shape which, by then, had almost faded into the hillside turf,
but to commemorate the crowning of a king. The year was 1937.

So I come to the Pewsey Vale white horses and must continue
to draw upon Mr Marples' book for dates and other information
about their history. It is such a full, authoritative and fascinating
book that I hope my few gleanings from it will send to its pages
those of my readers who have not yet enjoyed them and wish to
know more about what Mr Marples, with a twinkle in his eye,
suggests might be called "leucippotomy", or the cutting of white
horses, and "gigantotomy" or the cutting of giants in hillside turf.
First the Alton Barnes horse, cut in 1812 for Mr Robert Pile, an
Alton Barnes farmer, on the Vale's northern chalk escarpment and
in the sweep of the wide, shallow concavity between Walker's
Hill and Milk Hill above the villages of Alton Barnes and Stanton
St Bernard. Mr Pile, it seems, was unfortunate in the man he first
chose to set out and cut the horse, a journeyman painter known as
Jack the Painter, who then happened to be working at the farm.
For £20, paid in advance, Jack agreed to excavate to the depth of
a foot and fill up with chalk, but engaged a villager from Stanton
St Bernard to labour at the digging and filling. Before the horse
was finished Jack had disappeared and the £20 with him. To round
off the story, it is recorded that some time later he was hanged, but
we are left guessing whether it was for this bit of swindling or
another crime. In those days men were still being hanged for
theft.

Mr Marples gives the dimensions of the Alton Barnes horse
today as approximately 166 feet high and 160 feet long. The
height of these hillside figures has to be exaggerated to counteract
the effect of foreshortening caused by the slope: the slighter the
slope the taller the figures should be made to make them look in
proportion from a distance, which is, of course, how they were
meant to be seen. The aeroplane has turned them into landmarks
seen at very different angles from those which their earth-bound

designers would have thought possible, landmarks too easily picked out from the air to be left exposed under the eyes of enemy airmen. During the recent war the white horses and other hillside figures were either covered with turf or brushwood or else painted green, and were not exposed again until after 1945.

Rock as soft and porous as chalk soon begins to split and crumble when it is exposed to the weather. Its turf of many different plants is a protective carpet. Strip away the turf with the inch or two of dark brown humus under it and frost gets to work at the destruction which, in the end, reduces chalk to the powder that whitens every runnel of rainwater where it is exposed. For Time "hath an art to make dust of all things", as Sir Thomas Browne phrased it. The Vale itself was once a great arch of chalk and is the result of such weathering and water-flow. Reduced to the scale of chalk-pits and other hillside scars this surface erosion is always going on. A white horse is simply a shaped chalk-scar on a slope of down: it weathers like any other exposed place. This, unless the slope is too steep, leads to the encroachment of the turf outlining it—a very mixed community of plants—and to the patching of its whiteness with green where seeds have lodged and germinated. So, at intervals of about seven years, it must be scoured to keep it from fading into the hillside, its surface of chalk renewed, the crispness of its outline restored. Because of the writings of Thomas Hughes the Uffington scouring is the most widely known, but this was not the only place where the scouring of a white horse used to be a festival, a local holiday with games and merrymaking and with plenty of cakes and ale for others besides the spade-and-barrow men. It may be that these festivities were much more ancient in origin than the oldest of the turf-cut figures around which they were enjoyed. The experts in these matters relate them to prehistoric religious rites intended as appeals to the gods of fertility for plentiful crops and increase among flocks and herds, and think it likely that in these festive renewals of white horses the revellers were, without knowing it, preserving vestiges of the oldest of all regions.

Scourings of the Alton Barnes horse are recorded and appear to have been all work and no public play, except, perhaps, for the 1935 scouring, which was done as part of that year's Jubilee celebrations. We are told that two of its scourings before 1868 cost about a guinea each, the money being raised by public subscription. The second of these was carried out in 1866. To save time and labour the men who did the work got the fresh chalk they needed by opening a pit just above the horse and scarred the turf with an extra patch of white that persisted in remaining bare year after year. Only in 1952, eighty-six years later, has it become almost green again, though the rank growth and dark tone of its new herbage mark the place in another way.

The Pewsey white horse is on the other side of the Vale a little less than six miles southeast of the Alton Barnes horse and about a mile from Pewsey. Its slope of down is the part of the Plain's escarpment called Pewsey Hill, with Milton Hill to the east and a hip of down, Denny Sutton Hipend, to the west. The hill-crest isolates a small plantation of conifers above the horse, and the road from Pewsey to Everleigh slants past it in rising from the Vale to Salisbury Plain. The present figure, as I have already stated, is Pewsey Hill's second, cut in 1937 to replace an older almost vanished horse dating back to 1785, or perhaps a year or two earlier, for which the Robert Pile who had the Alton Barnes horse cut in 1812 was responsible; though because of the gap of about thirty years between these two horses—Pewsey I and Alton Barnes—Mr Marples wonders whether they were cut by successive Robert Piles from Alton Barnes, father and son. Whether they were or not, the first Pewsey white horse must, through neglect, have soon begun to fade out. It was last scoured in 1789, a cleaning-up that may have been both first and last. The owner of its site was strongly against revelry at the scouring, and evidently Pewsey folk were as firmly against a scouring with no revels. No wonder, then, that the horse disappeared. Its position was a little below and to the right of the new horse, and from the faint traces of it that Mr Marples was able to make out in 1940 he put its length at about 43 feet.

There are no uncertainties about today's Pewsey horse. It was the work of Mr Marples' father, the late George Marples, of Sway, Hampshire, who had gone to Pewsey in the spring of 1937 for the purpose of determining the position of the first horse. A committee had been formed to discuss means of commemorating the

Coronation of George VI. The restoration of the old horse or else the cutting of a new one was suggested as a fitting memorial. Mr George Marples, an authority on white horses and other hill-figures, was asked for advice and help. He made and submitted three designs for a new horse, one of which was chosen. It was pegged out on the hillside by its designer, the cutting and filling being done by volunteers from the Pewsey Fire Brigade in the latter half of that 1937 April. The horse is 66 feet long and 45 feet high. As one way of recording the date of the work the hillside displays the year in six-foot figures boldly cut above the horse's back. During the war both of the Pewsey Vale white horses were monuments—to quote Sir Thomas Browne again—"scarce below the roots of some vegetables". Now they are in the sun again.

Of the two it is the Alton Barnes horse that I catch sight of the more frequently in going about the Vale. Anywhere west of Pewsey I am always expecting a gap in the elms or a swell of open ground to reveal it, while east of Pewsey, in the much smaller part of the Vale, the Pewsey horse is so unobtrusive that its presence is often forgotten. As well as being on a higher slope of down the Alton Barnes horse is more than twice as long and three times as tall as the other, its higher elevation making it more widely visible, its greater size keeping it a recognisable shape at distances that reduce the Pewsey horse to a chalky patch of no particular shape. One clear sunny day on Knap Hill above the Alton villages I was asked, "Where's the white horse? Can it be seen from here?" I explained that the Alton Barnes horse lay out of sight behind Walker's Hill, the down peaked by the long barrow called Adam's Grave a few hundred yards to the west, but that the Pewsey horse was visible on the far side of the Vale. I pointed it out, yet binoculars were needed to convince the questioner that the distant gleam of white on the green side of Salisbury Plain really had the shape of a horse. A day or two later, in the same kind of weather, when I was in the marshy fields in the valley bottom between Etchilhampton and Wedhampton, a gap in their many elms exposed the Alton Barnes horse at about the same distance as we had seen the Pewsey horse from Knap Hill. Every curve and feature stood out so clearly that the eye needed no aid in recognising it for this horse and no other.

These white horses of the downs certainly came to life in their making, and by that have one quality, at least, of a work of art. They all have it, whether shaped to the attenuated simplicity of the Uffington horse, which may be called primitive but never artless, or to the more normal lines of the Pewsey horse, which is perhaps as natural a representation as the technique of cutting them permits. There are viewpoints from which the Alton Barnes horse looks a curiously angular animal, a creature of spirit, with a sort of gawky lightness in the action of its long, spindly legs. With head up, eye startled, ears pricked, and stumpy tail stiffly at half-cock, it looks as if it had just shied into a skittering dance. Seen from the road under the downs between Alton Barnes and Stanton St Bernard it is far enough away to be centred in the bare spaciousness of its setting, yet close enough for the details of its drawing and action to be revealed. It lies high on the insweeping curve of slopes by which the escarpment is here widely embayed between two massive shoulders of down, Milk Hill to the left and Walker's Hill to the right. On the skyline there is a solitary tumulus immediately above the horse, a small group of trees a little to the left of the tumulus, and a straggle of thorns along the top of Milk Hill. They seem very remote on crests from which the steeps of the escarpment fall away to the broad band of cornland below, there shelving quickly to a smoothness of lateral undulation, always gentle and irregular, along an equally gentle downward tilt to the road and then to the canal at the edge of the chalk about a mile within the valley. The slopes between the horse and Walker's Hill are vertically grooved with lesser hollows, but the inward side of Milk Hill is much less unevenly contoured—almost under the horse's feet it eases to a gradient stepped by shallow lynchets that prove it was not too steep for a Celtic ploughman to terrace it with little cornfields. These green relics of ancient ploughing are so small that they seem no more than garden plots beside the many-acred rectangles which today lie in downland openness between them and the elm-darkened interior of the Vale.

Southeast, now, across the Vale to the Pewsey white horse. For viewing it as good a place as any is the wide drove leading straight to its hillside from the southern outskirts of Pewsey where the main road to Salisbury and Devizes, having crossed the Avon, turns aside from the downs, its line towards them being continued by the drove. (A drove is an old green way along which cattle and sheep used to be taken to and from pastures, markets and fairs.) Here again the turf-steeps of the valley-side—this time the escarpment of Salisbury Plain—are separated from the elmy inward parts of the Vale by a mile-wide band of fields, all large, on a downland rather than a valley scale. It is a more level spread of fields than that under the Alton Barnes horse, perhaps with more meadow and pasture breaking up the sweep of ploughland; but here also, between Pewsey and the Plain's edge, there are few bushes and trees along the field divisions under the downs except where the drove, towards its middle point, has on one side a group of ashes by a cart-shed, and on the opposite side a short line of elms and ashes behind which the smallest pasture there is enclosed by thorn hedges and more elms. From this outlying island of tree-shade the straightness of the drove lies open again across the half-mile to the foot of the scarp and a solitary elm exactly under the white horse. The downs flanking this side of the Vale have neither as deep nor as steep a fall as those on the northern side. Their bluffs and shoulders do not stand out as boldly, their flow of skyline is gentler in rhythm. In spirit they give the impression of being less withdrawn from the valley world, so maybe it is fitting that their white horse should not be like what always seems to me the more spirited and wayward animal across the valley. The Pewsey horse is the more naturalistic but the less real. Not that it lacks life, but it does seem to me to lack that touch of individual eccentricity which keeps the Alton Barnes horse so much the more vivid in memory. The difference comes out as a contrast between a romantic piece of work, a capricious courser, and one that is undisturbingly academic, an easily controllable steed. Nevertheless, with head and neck outstretched and tail curving behind, the Pewsey white horse is a mover and has grace in its lines.

My place for seeing this one is just clear of the trees along the drove. It lies on the upper half of its hillside, Pewsey Hill, and not quite central in the sweep of the shallow arc into which the scarp is hollowed from Denny Sutton Hipend on the right to Milton Hill on the left. The sweep of the arc is given variety by the interplay of lesser fold and hollow along it under a skyline swelling into a summit curve above the horse and then dipping away very gradually on each side and as gradually rising again to reach the summits of the flanking hills. It is highest on Milton Hill and lowest on Denny Sutton Hipend, a smooth flow everywhere, with no abrupt changes. How these downland skylines hold the eye! Here and there a cornfield from the Plain lips over the crest. The top of a small plantation of conifers shows above it a little to the left of the horse; away beyond that it carries a cluster of beeches from which a thin line of ragged conifers leads away, and then the long, low mound of the Giant's Grave rising to a blunt east end, and lastly the beech clump on Milton Hill. Westward from the conifer plantation there is only the bare skyline. The slopes above the horse and those on each side are stepped into flights of strip-lynchets, those massive terraces of ancient farming which, despite their size, conform so fluently to the contours of the hillsides. Shepherds' Steeps they were once called, maybe a name they were given when the downland turf had covered them after their last ploughing.

CHAPTER XVII

MARTINSELL

MARTINSELL, the massive bluff of down overlooking the Vale between Oare and Wootton Rivers, is a presence and a personality. In *The Place-Names of Wiltshire* its name is traced back from the *Martinshall hill* of 1549 through *Mattelshora* and *Matlesore* to the *Mattelesore* of 1257, which, it is suggested, links it to *Mætelemesburg*, the Saxon name of the camp on the hilltop, and *ora* meaning a bank or a slope of a hill; so that to the Pewsey Vale Saxons the hill we call Martinsell was *Mætelmesora*. It is one of those hills that take possession of the imagination from the start, one of the high places that all sorts of people like to visit and revisit or look for in the distance and recognise with pleasurable feelings that may not be easy to put into words, for they spring, I think, from a deeper impulse than that which simply sends us to a hilltop to enjoy the exhilaration of height and a spacious view. We cannot forget the hill.

Wherever there are walkable hillslopes and skylines one shape among them will have this power of attraction that seems in every way to make it more real than the others and draws us to it as if by the gently insistent magic of a spell. I think of one or two I know in other parts of the country: Shropshire's Wrekin at the side of the Severn, Gloucestershire's Uley Hill where the south Cotswold scarp stands above another reach of the Severn, and Berkshire's Uffington Hill at the downland edge of the Vale of White Horse. There are plenty of others, more than I realised I knew until I began to remember and name them, though many are not well known outside their localities. An interesting thing about them is that they are usually hills whose contours have not been altogether natural since prehistoric times, but were modified to human needs by the people who lived there in early ages and shaped the curving banks of the earthwork enclosures, the mounds of the tombs and, on some of the slopes, the great steps of cultivation terraces that now seem to belong to these hills so naturally

188

that if they were all to be suddenly erased the hills would look not only unfamiliar but empty. Another interesting thing is the number that are places where, until almost within living memory, people have congregated to enjoy various sports and pastimes, often at Easter and Whitsun, the springing and green time of the year. There were, for example, the games and festivities held on Uffington Hill at the scouring of our oldest and perhaps prehistoric white horse, including a headlong race after a cheese, later a wheel, sent rolling down the precipitous side of the Manger, the deep coomb below that strange white symbol cut in the turf. On Martinsell, A. G. Bradley tells us in *Round about Wiltshire* published in 1907, there were great sports in the eighteenth and early nineteenth centuries. Cheese-rolling was not one of the events here, but instead there was sliding down the face of the hill on the jaw-bones of horses, the slope being no shorter and no farther from the vertical than the side of the Manger on Uffington Hill. In dry summer weather I occasionally see children sliding down the shaggy grass-covered steeps of a coomb behind their village at the northern edge of the Wiltshire downs. They sit on the discarded paper bags that held chemical fertiliser.

The hill-games are thought originally to have been something more significant than the pastimes of a country holiday, although they became this long before they died out. It is probable that they were as old as the earthworks on the hilltops and were just as much the remains of the people who made the earthworks, that in the beginning the games were, in fact, festivals of a pagan religion in which the fertility of cultivated earth and domesticated animals was set above all else. This fertility was then, as it is in no lesser degree today, a matter of life and death to men who had become farmers and herdsmen. If such were the origin of these games it would help us to understand why we still feel the attraction of hills like Martinsell, for there must yet be at least a trace of prehistoric blood in our veins and vestiges of ancient thought deep in our minds. The games have gone, but Martinsell remains, a place for picnics or a walk along the top, with the Vale of Pewsey open below and many a mile of downland receding beyond the Vale, except to the west, where the distant ridges are those of limestone hills beyond the chalk, the farthest being the limestone of Mendip.

I have seldom been on Martinsell and seen no one else there, though I have seen more people on Uffington Hill in one afternoon than on Martinsell in a year.

It is the last commanding height eastward along the Vale's northern flank of downs. With build proportioned to the full scale of downland amplitude it comes as a closure and a massive buttress to the highest and boldest reaches of the chalk escarpment beginning at Tan Hill about five miles to the west. Tan Hill swings into Milk Hill, both topping 950 feet, and then, at a little below 900 feet, the separate summits of Walker's Hill and Knap Hill follow in succession, leading on to a more even flow that carries the scarp-crest along Golden Ball, Draycott, Huish and Oare Hills, the latter the prelude to Martinsell and the last rise of the scarp to over 900 feet before it falls and dwindles to an unimpressive division between the edge of Savernake Forest and the east end of the Vale. In shape the main part of Martinsell is roughly a rectangular, round-angled bluff, about half a mile long and a little more than a quarter of a mile across, thrust into the Vale from the upward tilt of Oare Hill and Clench Common. The tilt is gentle to the foot of the inward edge of the hill and then steepens into a very short rise to the camp's ditch and bank, beyond which the summit extends to an outward edge that is the crest of the hill-front's precipitous fall to the valley floor. The summit is an undulating plateau of which the eastern and slightly higher part, something less than half the whole, is enclosed within the single bank and ditch of the camp. At the hill's eastern end the slopes return to the diminishing scarp with a more shelving fall. West of the camp the plateau is elongated into a narrow spur that lengthens the hill-front by nearly half a mile and terminates as a headland high above the village of Oare, whilst behind the spur the deep hollow of Rainscombe sweeps back through its great horseshoe curve to Oare Hill. The end part of the headland is banked off by the Giant's Grave, a mound across its width, but as the mound has not yet been excavated we do not know whether it is a long barrow, as the name would suggest, or is simply a cross bank shutting in the promontory. In fact very little seems to be known about anything but the appearance of the various prehistoric earthworks on Martinsell. Beneath the Giant's Grave the lower slopes facing the valley are stepped with the terraces of strip-lynchets, and—to go back along the mile of the hill's turf steeps—there is a cluster of between twenty and thirty pit-hollows dimpling the somewhat gentler fall of turf from the beeches just outside the Clench Common angle of the camp. Here again systematic excavation is needed for the discovery of clues to their period of origin and their purpose; yet the way they lie together facing the morning sun, and the presence on the hill of the other remains that take us back into downland prehistory, is temptation enough to let the imagination cover them with thatched roofs, whether the pits under the thatch are sunken dwellings or places for storing grain. Should we be tempted we should note that the archæologists of the Ordnance Survey have had second thoughts about these pits, for on recent editions of the One-Inch map there is a blank where earlier editions marked them "pit dwellings" in the Gothic lettering used for antiquities.

Martinsell lies between the forking of two roads into the Vale. The main road from Marlborough to Pewsey and Upavon passes its west end by following the lip of Rainscombe in descending Oare Hill, going down under beeches through which, on the left, the bottom of that immense hollow is seen to contain a large house with parkland and fields deep within the wooded steeps curving to an outward end in the bare turf of the Giant's Grave headland. About threequarters of a mile behind Martinsell this road, coming to Overton Heath, bends into a kink from which a byway leads across Clench Common and then, at the hill's east end, wavers down the diminished scarp to Wootton Rivers. Today most of Clench Common is enclosed as arable and pasture, all the part between the road and the hill. The only part that keeps its original character is the thickety strip of gorse and bramble, bracken and heather, hawthorn and blackthorn to which the north margin of the road is still open. The downs here, including the Martinsell plateau, are capped with the layer of clay-with-flints that makes such a noticeable difference to the vegetation and the appearance of ploughed earth wherever it overlies the chalk. The few extensive downland oak-woods are found on it. If you would find bluebell, primrose and anemone woods on the downs you must seek them in the places where the colour of newly-sown

fields is a reddish brown closely speckled with the grey of in-
numerable flints. Martinsell and the downs behind it are within
the formerly much more wooded area that includes Savernake
Forest, and it is because of the presence of trees as well as the difference in height that so little of the open hilltop is seen from the
road on the common. Except where, in front of the camp, the
gently rising fields steepen quickly into the bare embankment, and
the bank-top is against the sky, this side of the hill has a varied
skyline of trees. Immediately to the right of the camp there is a
dense wood, whilst at the other end of the embankment the dome
of the beech-clump at the corner of the camp stands up behind the
beginning of a narrow plantation of ash trees that, in its leafless
seasons, edges the common with a sky-revealed frieze of trunks.
It is continued by a fringe of oak, ash and beech, with a backing of
tall broom, to where the road comes to the brow of the scarp at
the east end of the hill. This tree-fringe, but without the broom,
follows the scarp-crest for several hundred yards beyond the road,
and until the road has passed through it the only indication of the
sheer front that Martinsell presents to the Vale is a glimpse of
steep turf where the uppermost hillside bends down the sky behind the part of the frieze of ash trunks nearest the beeches.

The road across Clench Common brings me to my favourite
approach to the hilltop as soon as it has cut the trees screening the
common from the Vale and the hill's east end. On the valley side
of the trees it also cuts a track called Martinsell Ride that comes
along the scarp-crest from Hat Gate near the south corner of
Savernake Forest. This track is the approach, for it continues up the
hillside, which is there the end-slope shelving to die away on the
scarp, and passes along the back of the hill with the camp embankment between it and the summit. From the roadside it leads up to
the Martinsell clump of beeches on the slope under the nearest
angle of the camp, a broad green way margined by trees and
broom on the right, but open on the left to turf-slopes falling
away to the valley, gradually at first, then steepening as they
deepen in a forward swing that hollows this reach of the hillside
into the curve of a wide bay lipped by the camp's east-facing bank.
The massed beech-tops are rounded against the sky ahead, the
pit-hollows dimple the slope of turf in front of the beech trunks,

The Vale towards Martinsell

and the embankment, though its middle part is obscured by bushes and a few lesser beeches growing in the ditch, is a rampart along the curve of the hillcrest away from the beech-clump to a scraggy tuft of three or four weather-scarred conifers sky-caught above the convex profile of a steep that seems to reach down from the sky to the valley fields. No more than what I always think of as the hill's morning end is revealed, yet in it the hill-shape is plainly growing into the presence that is Martinsell and no other.

I fancy that those three or four trees, like other landmarks of their kind, are a magnet to all who come this way to the hill whether newcomers or not. Their lofty and always breezy-looking silhouette makes their skyline seem more distant than it is. They hold the eye and draw the feet, so that in walking up the track by the broom we find ourselves veering towards the open slopes and skirting the lower edge of the beech-clump, or perhaps going among the smooth columns of its trunks, to reach the valley-fronting crest instead of letting the track lead us between the beeches and the ash plantation to the back of the hill. I do not think I am imagining the gently insistent attraction I have to resist when I want to go to the hilltop the other way.

It is in rounding this tree-tufted shoulder that the hillside swings west and fronts the Vale with the mile of turf-steeps which end so abruptly at the Giant's Grave headland. For the first quarter of the mile the south bank of the camp lies along the crest and then turns away to cross the width of the summit where it is the division between the thirty acres or so of ploughland enclosed by the banks and the cattle pastures reaching away from the camp to the Giant's Grave. But not quite all the camp is ploughed. Behind the east bank it is surprisingly edged with a band of willows growing among bracken, and behind the south bank with the gale-stricken wreckage of a conifer plantation of which the two or three isolated trees at the turn of the hill are outliers. There is only a thin straggle of trees standing now, most of them in the sapless, weather-greyed rigidity of death, a few barely alive. The rest are either standing as snapped-off trunks or else lying uprooted among the jungle of bracken and ferns, bramble, briar and elder that is submerging them. In the vale below, at the foot of the hillside under the camp, Bromsgrove Wood seems

13   193

comfortably safe from such winds as could do that. The embankment curves round the wreckage to cross the open summit, and as if to be a more concealing division has masked itself with blackthorn and hazel, under squat, flat-crowned oaks until, with one of Martinsell's two ponds in front of it and the flint-speckled brown of ploughed earth behind it, there is only a patching of gorse and a few thorns. And so we come to the gentle undulations of the summit pastures and ploughed ground between the camp and the tree-tops jutting above the rim of Rainscombe, except where, between the coomb and the Vale, the pastures taper into the ridge that is the way to the Giant's Grave and the other end of the hill.

A large barn, its gable-ends facing east and west, stands in the open not far from the hill-front. It is very solidly built of flint banded with lacing courses of brick ending in brick angles, and has a slated roof and eaves-high, wagon-wide entrances opposite each other at the middle of its length. No weaker structure of its size could have weathered for long the wind stresses, the driving rains and the disintegrating frosts of such an exposed place. Yet not many years ago there were two cottages behind the barn, one of them surviving until about 1911. Its last occupant was a shepherd who, as Mr H. C. Brentnall, writing in 1924, puts it in a paper on Martinsell, "enjoyed the distinction of occupying the highest house in Wiltshire", and quotes the shepherd's opinion that it was "as healthy a place to live in as you could wish". No doubt he got water from the old dew-pond near the barn as well as from his rainwater butt. When I saw the pond last, on a day at the beginning of April, it had plenty of open water to make the island of willows in the middle a safely moated nesting-place for a pair of mallard that flew away when I approached. There are several Scots pines, bare, red-tinged trunks rising to the spread of evergreen crowns, between the pond and the barn, and with them a larch. On that April day the slender straightness of the larch trunk tapered amid the droop of twigs misted with the new green of leaf-tufts and beaded with the rose-red of cone flowers.

The top of Martinsell is the place from which to see the Vale of Pewsey both as a valley under the hill and a division between the north part and the south part of the Wiltshire downs. We have only to walk inward from the crest and Martinsell changes from a steep hill-front overlooking the Vale to a broad summit that sends the eye ranging over mile after mile of downland to skylines far from the Vale. The longest view is southward across the twenty-one miles between the hilltop and Salisbury spire: but to me the northward view is the more exciting because, years ago now, it was from the edge of the downs in this direction that I first saw and then came to the hill. In those days I was often on the Ridge-way where it follows the curve of the chalk escarpment from Uffington Hill past Liddington Hill and Barbury to Avebury, the distance across the downs to Martinsell narrowing from Uffington Hill's sixteen miles to Barbury's eight. The highest southward skyline revealed by these hilltops and the higher ridges of down near the old road is the crest of the scarp along Pewsey Vale, with Martinsell and its trees standing up unmistakably in the flow of what is otherwise an almost bare ridge. Caught from this side the hill's gradual eastward lift to a steeply rounded fall shapes and orientates it as if it were a colossal long barrow. At first sight Martinsell was so clearly the presence my foreknowledge of the hill had made me imagine it to be that the map was only needed to make identification doubly sure. To me it is now like looking back along the years whenever I stand behind the Martinsell beeches and look towards the northern edge of the chalk to redis-cover—tracing them from west to east—Hackpen's broad ridge leading to the beech-clumps on the skyline where its farther end approaches Barbury, and to the right of Barbury the crest of Smeathe's Ridge with Four Mile Clump below it and the old coach road from Marlborough to Swindon climbing the down to pass the Clump, and then, distance increasing, the level summit of Liddington Hill and smooth crest-line of Bishopstone Downs with a thicket isolated on it, and lastly the camp headland of Uffington Hill, which is the farthest of all and is in Berkshire over-looking the Vale of White Horse.

I cannot remember a disappointing visit to Martinsell however brief the time spent there. Sometimes I have got no farther along the summit than the conifer tuft at the corner of the camp, once or twice no farther than the hillside below the beeches, and once not even as far as that but only to the gate at the end of the hill. It has depended on the season and the weather, particularly the weather; but there has been something each time to keep the occasion apart in memory as a Martinsell day. As examples I take three consecutive visits in a recent year, the first in May, the second in June and the third in July.

The May day ended a mid-month spell of almost cloudless sunny weather by bringing a hazily sunny morning with a growing murkiness in the northwest and a thundery heaviness burdening the air. By noon the weather signs could not have been plainer, and I reached Martinsell Ride just as the forefront of a great bank of thunder cloud, moving southeast, had begun to overhang and darken the hill and the sides of the valley along its foot, and already there were streaming curtains of rain before the sunny side of the valley and the downs of the Plain. So far the lightning and thunder had been away over the downs behind the hill, but they were soon very close and splitting the blue-black clouds above a deluge in which the grey of rain alternated with the white of hail. It was not long, though, before Martinsell and the Vale had the sun again whilst the Plain had the commotion and the steely grey murkiness of the storm. With this as a background the returning sunshine brightened the Martinsell hillside and the valley as if their maytime green were giving as much light as the sun and making no leaf-shade. On the lines and groups of elms along the valley there was sufficient depth of tone in the glow of green to be a contrast to the paler radiance of grass and corn. On the hillside the sunlit turf was like a smooth pelt of green plush in the way it revealed the undulations of the slopes and the shapes of the pit-hollows. The storm silenced the birds, yet as soon as the downpour began to dwindle and the sunlight to gleam behind it, but whilst the lightning was still forking and the thunder booming and rumbling above the Plain, a nightingale began to sing in bushes near the hill-gate. He had not stopped when, the thunder rain coming on again, I saw that this was not an afternoon for the open heights of Martinsell and went home.

The June day, nine short of Midsummer Eve, had a gusty but warm west breeze, clear air and a sky full of the continual drift and gleam of billowing clouds among which the sun found many a gap for shadowing their movement on the downs and the valley fields. This was a Martinsell day remembered for its flowers, especially those along the track to the beeches and on the hillside near the track. I have previously mentioned the line of broom behind the track's fringe of trees. It has grown to a height of six or seven feet and was then at its climax of flowering, with every sprig a straight spike of flowers and the spikes so crowded together that the whole line made a splash of bright golden yellow behind the tree-trunks and hawthorn bushes, whilst the foliage screening it from the sun was still too airily spread and translucently green to dim its brightness. Then there were the flowers of the hillside turf, no rare kinds, but each in its own way giving colour to the drift of sunshine and cloud-shadow along the green slopes. For white there was the meadow saxifrage, though these flowers were now thinning from the numbers in the season's earlier companies, and for yellow the buttercups outnumbering all the other flowers and colouring the hillside everywhere. These two were tall enough for the breeze to keep them nodding and quivering. In the turf-mat itself the first rock-roses had opened, but there were yet too few for their yellow to carry far. Another white was hidden in one of the pit-hollows—that of dropwort opening from clusters of pink-stained buds. For deepest blue there was milkwort, whose little flowers are so much a part of the turf and often so closely congregated as to seem colour without shape until we bend down to look at them; and for a more limpid blue there was germander speedwell among the milkwort between the track to the beeches and the fall of the hillside. Some of the milkwort plants had pale blue, some had magenta and some had pinkish flowers, these being common variations, and the speedwell here, as if to emulate the milkwort, was also varying its colour; for while many were the normal sky-blue, others were a paler, chalky blue, others had this chalky blue tinged faintly with pink and others deeply enough to make them mauve. I have never seen so much variation in germander speedwell anywhere else.

The July day, a week past mid-month, stays in memory because it contained so much of the essence of full summer. I spent some of its morning on the hill in a blaze of sunshine from a milky-blue sky in which the only clouds were a few rounded, wispy-edged shapes too softly white and remote to be anything but summer fleeces. They seemed becalmed, but the occasional very slow drift of a smudgy shadow on the hillside proved they were not. First I went up through the pool of shade under the beeches and then along the camp to the tuft of conifers to look at the morning from a place high in the sun before descending again to sit for a while in the shade of one of the oaks in front of the broom. It was the kind of summer day in which there seems only one place where the intensity of sunlight is a clear, colour-revealing radiance—the spot where you happen to be. Away from it the clarity is more and more misted by the sun-glow in the air until it is lost altogether in luminous haze. As long as I stood under the hilltop conifers and looked down at the sun-hazy valley fields among the heavy darkness of their elms this shoulder of the hill seemed the one place in the sun where a shadow, whilst tempering the sun's blaze, had the glow of too much reflected sunlight in it to be shade. Yet it was the same when I had descended to the trees in front of the broom. This was the brightest place in the sun then. It was also richer in colour than the hilltop, for though the broom was so far past its flowering that the seed-pods were popping open in the heat, its long whisks were vividly green behind the grey ash and oak trunks; but now there was other colour for the sun to display—the rosy purple of rosebay willow herb under the trees, and the clear yellow of ragwort edging the track in front of both. Nor do I forget the two white admiral butterflies that flickered about the trees.

CHAPTER XVIII

WOOTTON RIVERS

THE two miles of the diminished chalk scarp from Martinsell to Savernake Forest do not look like downland. This part of the Vale's edge, with its capping of clay-with-flints, has been too much cultivated for that. There are no bare upland skylines here: the slopes are gentler in their fall, more even and only very shallowly embayed in their lateral flow, and much more hedged and coppiced than those elsewhere along the Vale. This reach of the northern scarp could hardly be more different from the truly downland reaches west of Martinsell or from those of the edge of the Plain facing it on the south side of the valley. In fact it margins the one corner of the Vale of Pewsey where I seem to be losing touch with the downs and to be least aware of the Vale as a downland valley. Here I find myself with the feeling of being in a place that was once much more wooded than it is today. No doubt the closeness of Savernake Forest influences the impression, as also does the knowledge that this part of the Vale lies within the area originally under Norman forest law; but the corner has its village, Wootton Rivers, a name that in derivation makes me feel that my sensing of vanished woods is not fanciful. *Wootton*, the root of the name, is Saxon in derivation and signifies the wood-ton or farmstead by the wood, the *Rivers* being the family name of those who became lords of the manor in the thirteenth century.

No village in the Vale of Pewsey gains more seclusion than Wootton Rivers by being away from main roads. About half the two dozen or so places in the Vale are near either a main road or a frequently used lesser road and can be seen from it, only one or two of them being more than a quarter of a mile away. The main road nearest to Wootton Rivers, the one along the Vale from Pewsey to Burbage, misses it by at least a mile; and when the two highways that run southward from Marlborough to Salisbury are passing east and west of the village it is almost at the middle of the four miles separating them. Unless you leave these roads and seek it along byways that are usually winding, sometimes quick-turning and sometimes deeply banked lanes, Wootton Rivers will never be anything but a name on a signpost. The canal towpath will also lead you to it, either from the direction of Pewsey Wharf or of Burbage Wharf, for this disused canal passed the south end of the village, and nature has now transformed it into the least canal-like waterway and as attractive an approach as the lanes. The railway, side by side with the canal in this part of the Vale, has a halt at Wootton Rivers, but the booking-office is at the Royal Oak halfway up the long village street. Although it is a main line the railway along the valley is not an obtrusive feature, least of all on this side of Pewsey. The passing of trains is much more often heard than seen.

Perhaps because it passes so close to Martinsell my favourite way to Wootton Rivers is the byroad that runs level and straight across Clench Common and comes to the edge of the Vale at the east end of the hill, there changing to a twisty lane going down to the village about a mile to the southeast. For most of the way its windings are too deeply banked and hedged, or else too much screened or overshadowed by trees, to give, especially in the leafy seasons, revealing fore-glimpses of the village until it is within a stone's throw of entering the village street. But for the closeness of Martinsell, with almost the whole of its east side remaining magnificently in view for a third of the way and, at the brow of the descent, the downs of the Plain in view across the width of the Vale, the lane would seem to be stealing into a different valley from that to which, four miles west of Martinsell, the road from Walker's Hill to the Alton villages swings down so openly.

On a sunny morning in the first week of May, when the beech leaves were newly edged with their silken fringes of gossamery down and theirs was the freshest and coolest green in the sun, I came to the end of Martinsell on my way to Wootton Rivers. The day was one of those in the transition from blackthorn spring to hawthorn summer, all that was left of the earlier whiteness of blossom being brown-stained petals and tufts of stamens along the black of thinly greened twigs, and the white flowering that would soon be replacing it in the hedgerows was still shut within green buds clustered among hawthorn leaves. The wayfaring tree was making the connecting link of whiteness. It is more of a shrubby bush than a tree, less bountiful with its flowers than either of the thorns, and usually stands singly or in twos and threes a little in front of rather than in the hedge. Its white rounds, containing many small flowers, are like umbels with shallowly curving tops, each at the tip of a straight branch and raised clear of the broad, elliptical leaves.

Everywhere along the lane were many other signs of the transition. I saw that here the ash and the oak were leafing at the same time, the black buds of the ash breaking into a cold green that seemed to make the oak leaves the more amber in their unfolding. In one place a nightingale sang, in another a blackcap and in another a whitethroat, and I watched two swifts—my first for the season—skimming north over Martinsell. There were, too, the numerous drifts of greater stitchwort in the new growth rising from the old and dead tangles along the hedge-banks. The botanists were right in naming it *Stellaria*, for it spangles its banks with white stars whose snowy purity makes most other whites of its flowering-time appear dull or else creamy. And how perfect in concord are this whiteness of the flowers and the pale, glabrous green of the slender stems and narrow, grass-like leaves under it. Then, much more widespread along the banks than the stitchwort, there was the coarser but decoratively handsome dead-nettle we call white archangel, its erect stems tiered at diminishing intervals with whorls of lipped and hooded flowers immediately above pairs of opposite leaves. Here was a white that looked creamy beside that of the stitchwort stars, though one nearer to their purity had begun to appear where the jungles of feathery hedge-parsley, now between two and three feet high, were opening the first of the umbels that would soon be bordering this lane and many another with their lacily filigreed whiteness at the foot of hawthorn hedges foamed with blossom. It was the beginning of dandelion time as well. For a few May moments, at any rate, we should forget the dandelion as a troublesome weed and let the sun reveal it as a wonder of warm yellow equalled in richness only by the kingcups along the brooksides. The lane passed between two meadows covered with them, but the flowers had to be close, like those fringing the verges of the roadway under hedge-parsley, stitchwort and white archangel, for the deepening of yellow into orange at the middle of the many-rayed discs to be seen.

At the edge of Clench Common a short and steep descent sinks the lane into the valley. This, the fall of the scarp, is the lane's steepest part. It goes down aslant, with an old chalk-quarry, bushy and grass-grown, and a low, wire-fenced bank between the quarry and the Martinsell footslopes on the right, and on the left a deepening bank under scattered thorns and a wayfaring tree or two until these give place to the shadier cover of oaks and elms. This bank is the face of the scarp. Near the bottom the lane turns outward into the Vale to follow a gentler fall and curve between lines of elms to where a reverse curve takes it almost level past a tree-shaded pond on the Martinsell side. Its fields are now valley meadows and cattle pastures with elms standing in their hedges. After the pond the lane is deeply banked in rising to the swell of a low fold at the top of which it divides, sending off along the crest a left-hand branch to East Wick Farm and Wootton Rivers, whilst the other branch, keeping the banks and continuing the cross-valley line, soon dips out of sight beyond the fold.

The farmstead is within two hundred yards of the turning and set back a little from where the wayside is open to the fields of the shallow depression between this part of the lane and the Vale's northern scarp, with Martinsell still boldly in view above the tree-tops to the west. The nearest buildings are barns of the traditional downland type, great timber-framed structures with thatched roofs and weather-boarded sides. Facing west towards the barns and Martinsell, the farmhouse itself is large and comfortably solid under a tiled roof that is saved from a too severe plainness by the triangles of its half-hips leaning back to and shortening the ridge, and by the central spacing of the two brick chimney stacks rising from the ridge above a dormer window halfway down the slope dividing their bases. The part of the house-front farthest from the lane—about two-thirds of it—has a much weathered surface of brownish-grey plaster from ground to eaves. The remainder shows the wall to be a mixture of materials. To the height of the ground-floor window-heads it is flint and sarsen stone banded with several lacing courses of brick in which the bricks are used as headers. Above this there appears to be only brick. The leaded windows of the front—one on each side of a door within a plainly arched porch, and three close to the eaves—could hardly be bettered for shape, size and spacing. Tile and brick, flint, sarsen stone and plaster have all weathered into quiet harmony. As I saw the farmhouse from the lane on that May morning, amid the green of the valley and with its orchard full of apple blossom, it was as if the sun brightened its patina of weathering rather than the tones of colour the weathering had subdued.

Opposite the entrance to the farmyard the lane turns inward to the valley again and falls very gently between broad grass margins and wire-fenced meadows across which, to east and west, are the least interrupted glimpses along the Vale the lane gives—an eastward undulation of fields ending as a massing of trees about a mile away towards Savernake Forest, and the same to the west, in the Martinsell direction, though on that side the limiting press of trees is closer. Here the lane went between the two meadows with the hosts of dandelions yellowing their May green. This comparatively open furlong ends at a swing to the left round the gable of a block of three cottages roofed with tiles and with their brick walls chequered by the bluish-black headers in the bonding. The date 1883, cut in a square of stone set under the point of the gable, suggests that these cottages may still be as they were first built. After passing the cottages the lane is soon winding between banks again, low hedge-mounds at first, then dipping more and more deeply between the almost vertical sides of a cutting topped with blackthorn, hazel and young ash. I knew that Wootton Rivers was very close, but the only indication of this was the increase in the number of singing blackbirds, for there are always more blackbirds about a village than anywhere else. The first glimpse of the village comes rather suddenly. This lane from East Wick Farm joins another, and from a junction set about with a holly, a beech, an ash and one or two elms, all great trees of their kind, the first cottages are seen where, a hundred yards ahead, the lane emerges from its banks to enter the village street at a point nearer the top than the bottom and almost opposite the Royal Oak Inn, the village's only pub.

Wootton Rivers is another of the Pewsey Vale villages with the simple form of a single village street. It lies along a shallow, irregular hollow that leads south for a mile or more from the low scarp between Martinsell and Savernake Forest to the broad swell of a mid-valley fold roughly parallel to the scarp. The by-road which comes to the hollow from Leigh Hill, at the edge of the Forest, enters the village at the upper or north end and leaves it by crossing the canal and railway about half a mile lower down, then forking to reach Easton and Milton Lilbourne on the other side of the Vale. More secluded by the meadows and pastures shelving down to it than by any congestion of trees immediately about it, the village has an openness that may be surprisingly different from what is expected if it is first seen from the canal bridge. Manor Farm, with its lawn and garden-beds between its front and a slope of grass to the canal bank, is the nearest house and is most attractively in view; but behind it there is a clustering of elms and other tall trees among which the church's spired-belfry and its clock-face are glimpsed in a way suggesting that here is a place as tree-beset as the Manningford villages by the Avon on the other side of Pewsey. Yet it is not so, for this is only the beginning of the village, and excepting the fruit trees in the gardens there are few trees in the parts beyond to make it seem an embowered place.

As an example of the narrow, one-street village Wootton Rivers is, I think, more of a piece than any other of this type in the Vale. Along the quarter-mile or so from the south or church end, to the north or Wesleyan chapel end, it is ranged comfortably on each side of the street, making a varied succession of houses, cottages and the homes which are scarcely more than cots, set apart by their gardens. Most of them are raised a little above the roadway, some fronting it, whilst others, usually in pairs under one roof, turn an end towards it, and with few exceptions keep the harmony of brick and thatch, with here and there some timber-framing, that gives the village its mellow unity. The few slated roofs, a shed-roof or two of rusty corrugated iron in one place, and the recent though not obtrusively sited council houses are the inevitable small discords which remind us that in the economics of present-day building there is little room for traditional style and craftsmanship, and at the same time make us wonder what agricultural villages like Wootton Rivers, old-time places in the true, not merely picturesque sense of the term, will one day become. In these villages the time has gone when new building was so certain to be faithful to the local traditions that it would be in harmony with the older as soon as it was finished, and only the lack of weathering would proclaim its newness. Where, in the past, a house or a cottage has been enlarged it is seldom easy to tell at a glance which is the newer and which the older part. Sometimes one indication of the later part is the absence of timber-framing seen in the earlier walls. Another may be a difference in the size of bricks, as where at Wootton Rivers, for example, a cottage was enlarged at one end, and from the outside the only indication of this is that the older part is walled with the thinner bricks of an earlier day.

One cottage in Wootton Rivers draws the attention because it has a clock-face on its front wall. Standing back from and raised above the street, the cottage can be well seen as a whole behind its garden; and with its timber-framing on a foundation of brick, and the rectangles formed by the timbers colour-washed a brownish yellow, all under the high ridge of the steep thatch in which two windows are dormered, it is interesting enough as a piece of cottage architecture; but, as the clock-face on its front tells us in lettering used to mark the hours above and below the third and the ninth, it is also "Clock-House", where a locally famous amateur clock-maker, Jack Spratt, lived until his death in 1935. He was a countryman who, fascinated by the mechanism of clocks, taught himself to make them; and as well as filling his home with the clocks he made, including their carved oak cases and the musical parts of those that played tunes, he made the one which shows its face in the gable of the village chapel, and the other which is still ticking away the hours in the church and has three faces in the wooden belfry under the little spire, the south face, like that of the chapel clock, having the lettering GLORY BE TO GOD instead of the normal hour-numerals. His skill became such that he would, when necessary, find the materials for clock-parts in the oddest things, as was proved by the circumstances under which the church clock was constructed.

When it was proposed that Wootton Rivers should place a

clock in the church to commemorate the Coronation of King George V and, because of the cost, together with the rather luke-warm support of the villagers, it seemed that the proposal would be dropped, Jack Spratt offered to make the clock for nothing if the village would provide him with several hundredweight of scrap metal—iron, steel, brass and lead. This offer, as one news-paper account put it, "evoked considerable mirth". Nevertheless he soon found himself in possession of a heap of scrap that in-cluded "steel spindles, iron bars and wheels from disused reaping, mowing and threshing machines, drills, a chaff-cutter, separators, bicycles, bedsteads, perambulators, fire-irons, saws, brass weights, gunmetal, gas pipes, pieces of lead, and a variety of odds and ends". It is also told that a London firm, approached about supplying wheels and pinions, and being sent a description of the clock and the escapement required, did not deign to reply. So with the help of the village blacksmith and a firm at Pewsey the clock was com-pleted, and with a broomstick for pendulum has kept time for the village ever since.

The present church, restored in the nineteenth century, dates from the Decorated period. It is very simple in form, having nave and chancel, a south porch, and at the west end a timber belfry capped with a broached and shingled spire. It is also one of the Vale's flint-walled churches, the exterior showing courses of split flints very much interrupted by larger blocks of what look like sarsen stone, roughly squared, and giving an oddly patched ap-pearance to the walls. An occasional brick or tile is the third ingredient of a mixture completed by the stone of the quoins. In such walling, and even though shut off from it by the porch, the church's Decorated doorway is like an almost perfect lyric among plodding prose. I say almost perfect because the curves of a crum-bling niche resting on the crown of the arch, with their inner cusping, marginal leaf and flower ornament, and final point, do not spring and flow from those of the doorway but seem the re-sult of a wrong afterthought. The niche is the single note out of tune with the plain yet subtle rightness of this doorway which, in a broad but shallow splay, is one arch composed of many, all curving down from point to springing and continuing without break into the verticals that bring them to the ground. They make an alternation of slender, daylit rounds and shadowed hollows, the lights brighter, the darks deeper according to the slenderness and the relief of the moulding, in outward succession to the scroll of the hood-mould which turns into a plain stop at the springing. The doorway leads to an interior with no lack of light, the wide, lofty nave becoming a chancel under the same width and height of roof, the only definite division a waist-high wall of plain lime-stone. The recession of the roof-trusses, their oak greying with age, each with its king-post between braces cusped into a trefoil above a collar-beam, and with cusped braces arching from wall-posts below it, gives an overhead vista of tracery from end to end. This church has a semicircular pulpit of creamy limestone, and the plainness of its curve being no more than sufficiently relieved by aptly formalised ornamentation—a band of foliage round the top, the spacing of three moulded circles framing trefoiled open-ings in the stonework under it, and below these a band of square, four-petalled flowers near the moulded base—it goes well with the bright simplicity of its setting.

The churchyard lies back from the village street and is ap-proached by a walk that begins opposite the rectory and leads along the side of Manor Farm to the churchyard gate. I have men-tioned the trees which make the immediate surroundings of the church the leafiest part of the village. The largest is a horse-chestnut of magnificent stature and spread, a noble tree under which the churchyard gate seems very small. Its bole stands beside the gate like a great pier from which the limbs spring and radiate in a way suggesting the ribs of some massive piece of fan vaulting, though in summer they are soon lost among the dense foliage they carry, whilst the lowest reach out so far and droop their tips so low that the tree is like a green dome resting on the ground. The two large houses near the church—the rectory across the way, and the farmhouse in the open between churchyard and canal—could hardly be more different in style. The rectory, I feel, is too formal for its village setting, the farmhouse holds its ground with as much natural ease as any of the cottages along the village street. The rectory is brick-walled and severely four-square, with para-pets behind which the tiled roof appears as if merely accepted as an unavoidable necessity that should obtrude as little as possible.

It is the same with the gables, for both end-walls are taken up to parapet height and then topped with flatter triangles of brickwork finished off as pediments between flanking chimneys. A strictly balanced arrangement of white-framed windows emphasises the formal effect of the whole, yet the severity is tempered by the mellow tone of the dark-red brickwork and the white of the window-frames. The farmhouse is simply one of the timber-framed cottages of the village built large: in it the same kinds of material—the oak, the brick, and, in an end wall, the blocks of sarsen stone—are combined in the traditional way to shape a home under the long and deep thatch of a roof that is as visible a part of the structure as the walls. Inset below the cap of a brick chimney rising from the ridge is a stone on which the date 1680 is inscribed.

CHAPTER XIX

SOME ANTIQUITIES

THE Pewsey Vale farmers are still grazing cattle and growing corn where, on the valley's downland borders, some of Britain's earliest farmers did the same. It seems likely that we shall never know with certainty how and where the first animals came to be made dependent upon the care of the human beings who formerly hunted them, or how and where the first seeds came to be saved and sown and the growing plants tended so that the grain could be harvested. By 5000 B.C. these things had happened somewhere in the lands at the east end of the Mediterranean: we know that by 3000 B.C. there were cities along the valleys of Nile, Tigris and Euphrates, and that each existed on the corn and meat got from its fields and pastures in such quantities as to feed not only the farmers and herdsmen but a palace community, a priesthood, soldiers, scribes, traders and many kinds of craftsmen. To the people of these cities Britain, if known at all, would be a very remote land somewhere beyond the western edge of their world, perhaps occasionally brought in as the shadowy and strange background to the hearsay of a trader's tale. There was corn in Egypt then, but none, yet, in Britain; for it was not until five hundred years later, about 2500 B.C., that the colonising drift of Mediterranean people across and around Europe brought groups of Neolithic or New Stone Age settlers to Britain with cattle, sheep and seed-corn in their boats.

They were our first farmers. The Britain they came to did not differ in build from the land as we know it today: the last of its many great changes had been that which, after the Ice Age, islanded Britain in the narrow and shallow seas of Europe's Continental Shelf, a change which also gave the islands their rainy Atlantic climate and the vegetation such a climate favours. When the New Stone Age farmers began to arrive any differences between their Britain and ours were hardly more than surface deep, and not in the pattern of highland and lowland. In the lowland regions were wildernesses of forest trees and scrub through which the rivers ran uncontrolled, their waterlogged valleys full of marshes and fens. Here the best drained and most open areas were the limestone and chalk uplands, sometimes called the scarplands, that are ranged below a line from the mouth of the Tees to the mouth of the Exe. First there is the long outer formation of oolitic limestone reaching from the Yorkshire coast to the Dorset coast, with the Cotswold scarp facing the northwest in the middle place, and behind this limestone the chalk hills radiating from the great hub of Wiltshire downland that is cut by the Vale of Pewsey from east to west. These pioneers of the farming way of life, having nothing more efficient for felling trees and clearing scrub than flint or stone axes, deer antler picks and the shoulder-blades of cattle for shovels, were forced to get their living from the open places on the hills. This is where we find the remains that are nowhere more numerous than on the downs enclosing the Vale of Pewsey. Each group of people must have been a self-supporting community of herdsmen and corn-growers, with, the evidence of excavation suggests, a greater dependence on cattle than on corn, for as tillers of the soil they had digging-sticks and flint hoes but no ploughs. Flint arrow-heads prove that the men were hunters still. Theirs was far too simple a way of life to require the building of cities: the nearest they came to it was in the shaping of the camps or earthwork enclosures that can still be traced on a downland hilltop here and there in the southern counties. These are no more than villages and do not hold their places on downland skylines as impressively as the long mounds of the tombs the New Stone Age farmers raised as well.

Two roads from the Kennet valley to the Vale of Pewsey, the highway from Lockeridge and the green Ridgeway from East Kennett, converge to reach the Vale by way of a gap between separate summits of the chalk scarp above the Alton villages. From the middle length of the valley the two summits stand out as familiar northward landmarks, flat-topped Knap Hill on the right, Walker's Hill a more pointed shape on the left, the natural differences in shape being emphasised by the New Stone Age remains which crown them. On Walker's there is the long barrow

called Adam's Grave, and on Knap the camp which takes its name
from the hill. No one knows how old the Ridgeway is, but it may
be a green road so ancient that here its vestiges descend to the Vale
between landmarks left behind by the people who trod it into
existence.

Knap Hill Camp is a landmark in another sense, for until Mr
and Mrs B. H. Cunnington, the Wiltshire archæologists, examined it by excavation in 1908–9 no one knew with certainty
how to recognise New Stone Age camps. Like the earthwork enclosures of later prehistoric times they are usually hilltop places
surrounded by one or more banks and the ditches from which the
earth and rubble of the banks were dug. In the later camps, most
of which belong to the Early Iron Age, the ditches were made
wider and deeper, the banks higher and more massive, and there
was usually one original entrance; but except for these things and
the greater weathering away of the banks and the deeper silting
up of the ditches because of their very much greater age, there was
no definite characteristic by which New Stone Age camps could
be recognised from unexcavated appearance alone, although it had
been noticed that their very much worn-down ramparts were
frequently cut by gaps that were difficult to understand, as they
seemed too numerous to be a feature of the original design of such
works. The single ditch of the Knap Hill Camp was completely
silted up, and when sections of it were cleared the discovery was
made that it was not continuous, but that at intervals it had been
left undug, and that each of these causeways—as they are now
called—was opposite a gap in the embankment. There are seven
of them, each about 18 feet wide, though the length of ditch
dividing them varies from 42 feet to 122 feet. The relics of the
everyday life of its occupants—what the archæologists call occupation litter—came from the ditch, suggesting that this was where
their dwellings were, and that the enclosure itself was used as a
cattle pen. The "litter" consisted of fragments of the rudest kind
of hand-made pottery, badly baked, soft and friable, and with
large grains of flint in its paste; flint flakes, burnt flints and pieces
of sarsen stone; fragments of ox bones, one jaw bone of a pig and
fragments of red deer antlers. The only human bone unearthed
was a rather small jaw with worn teeth found at the depth of five

feet. So it was by their excavations on Knap Hill that Mr and Mrs Cunnington restored these causewayed camps to the New Stone Age farmers. Afterwards there was a thorough examination of a more elaborate one on Windmill Hill, a low swell of down a mile to the northwest of Avebury and only five miles from Knap Hill. This camp, with its three separate rings of interrupted banks and ditches, one within the other, was excavated by Mr Alexander Keiller from 1925 to 1929. Britain's earliest farmers, the New Stone Age people who made and inhabited this type of earthwork, are now known as Windmill Hill folk.

The Cunningtons then turned their attention from the old camp to an enclosure adjoining it on the east side and occupying the comparatively level ground which links Knap Hill to Golden Ball Hill, the next part of the main scarp. Their excavations revealed this to have been a settlement distinct from and considerably later in time than the causewayed camp, the pottery discovered there being all well-made, wheel-turned and well-baked, of a kind proving that the site was occupied during the Roman-British period. But one discovery suggested that the occupation came to a sudden and calamitous end. A fireplace cut in the chalk was uncovered. With its white sides looking abnormally burnt and blackened, it was full of charred wood and ashes among which was the lower stone of a quern, fragments of pottery and four large iron nails. The quern stone was so cracked and splintered by heat that it fell to pieces as soon as it was touched. In her account of these excavations in the *Wiltshire Archæological Magazine*, Vol. 37, Mrs Cunnington suggests that "The quern stone, the large building nails, and the several kinds of pottery are not likely to have got into the fireplace in the ordinary course of domestic events." The condition of the quern stone proved the fierceness of the heat, and the fact that the fireplace was never cleared out is "suggestive of a conflagration and the desertion of the site afterwards". A clue to what may have happened, and the date of it, was a sixth-century Saxon sword found 18 inches deep in surface accumulation within the enclosure. In the year 592 Saxon fought Saxon at a battle waged astride the Ridgeway in the gap between Knap Hill and Walker's Hill. Perhaps this British fireplace at the farther end of Knap Hill glowed for the last time on that day?

There is evidence, though, that this enclosure was lived in for a time a thousand years later. The excavators uncovered the foundations of a rectangular building 23 feet long and 13 feet 6 inches wide. They were roughly built of brick-shaped blocks of chalk irregular in size, and in them was an irregular spacing of postholes. No hearth or traces of flooring were seen. The remains of pottery found there belonged to the seventeenth century, but the date of occupation was much more definitely fixed by means of numerous clay tobacco-pipes unearthed with the pottery, as some were marked with the stamps of known seventeenth-century Bristol pipe-makers. It is not known what these seventeenth-century pipe-smokers were doing up there. "It seems a little curious," Mrs Cunnington wrote, "that they should have chosen such an exposed and waterless spot; they were perhaps squatters, or shepherds, who only came here for the summer months."

Back again, now, through almost four thousand years to the New Stone Age tomb on Walker's Hill at the other side of the gap. Today known as Adam's Grave, the Saxons named it Wodnesbeorg, which is Woden's Barrow. The sixth-century battle I mentioned in connection with the fireplace within the later earthwork on Knap Hill is named in Saxon annals as the battle of Wodnesbeorg. To these people the barrow's origin was a mystery, its scale too big for human work, so they attributed it to one of their gods. This was the Saxon way with these things, and is why the great entrenchment that runs for miles across the downs at the north edge of the Vale and passes within a mile of Walker's Hill is known to us today as Wansdyke. In the later times when people sought to explain the presence of these great earthworks and mounds in the land, and had discarded pagan gods and forgotten most of the Saxon names, the mysterious embankments became the devil's dykes and ditches, and the mounded tombs the graves of giants or sometimes of that fabulous man called Adam.

Long barrows were not usually raised to hold the remains of one person but were communal sepulchres. Because of the number of skeletons found together when they have been opened they have been likened to family or tribal vaults. Although when well preserved they all appear to be the same kind of mound, broadest and highest towards the east end, where the burials are usually discovered, and gradually narrowing and diminishing to the west, some contain burial chambers formed of massive stone slabs, but others do not. It is thought that the latter type, classed as unchambered, may originally have had burial places of timber which has rotted away. The other type, the chambered long barrows, may have one or several of the stone chambers, and when they are entered from a stone-formed central gallery or tunnel with the portal at the east end the barrow is known as a passage grave. Adam's Grave has a chamber near the east end. Dr Thurnam, that indefatigable nineteenth-century cracker of barrows, opened the chamber in 1860, but it had been disturbed by an earlier cracksman, and so he found nothing among the debris of its ruins but traces of human bones and a finely worked leaf-shaped arrowhead of flint.

When a long barrow has not become a man-mutilated ruin it is an impressive piece of work, and even in ruin does not lose this power. They are great in scale in a way that does not need the evidence of measurement to confirm it. I have paced out the length and breadth of the Adam's Grave mound and estimated its height, but I did not notice that the eighty paces one way, the thirty the other way, and a vertical rise to the highest part that must be at least 20 feet made the barrow seem any the greater when the scale of its downland setting does nothing to diminish it. It rests upon and completes the hilltop that elevates it to be a landmark above the Vale. Seen from the hilltop itself, across one of the broad, flat-bottomed ditches flanking the barrow—that on the south side—this turf-covered mound curves its back as if it were a crouching, bison-like monster, with head sunk down, for ever looking into the east. Under its pelt of turf it is not entirely a mound of chalk. Thurnam's account of it mentions the remains of a retaining wall then visible at the east end of the base and consisting of upright sarsen stones set at intervals, the spaces between them being filled with dry walling of oolitic stones. The sarsen stones, three of which are still partly showing above the turf, were got from the downs not far away, but the stone for the dry walling must have been brought from the limestone hills a few miles to the north and west of the downs.

A second long-barrow landmark, though not standing out in

the same kind of isolated prominence that Walker's Hill gives to Adam's Grave, is the unchambered Giant's Grave on the opposite side of the Vale where the edge of Salisbury Plain makes an almost bare skyline south of Fyfield and Milton to the east of Pewsey. From the right distance between the Burbage road and the foot of the Plain its long, low shape is often caught silhouetted on the flow of the scarp-crest from Pewsey Down to Milton Hill. It is 315 feet long but only about 7 feet high at the east end, and if its shape in silhouette did not look a little too formal in the gradual rise of its back from the west end to the bluntness of the east end it might seem a natural lift and dip in the contour of the downland crest. Again we have to consult Dr Thurnam's records to learn what it contained. He wrote:

"During the summer of 1865 I had an opportunity of opening a long barrow of great extent on Fyfield Hill, near Pewsey, Wiltshire, locally known as the 'Giant's Grave'. . . . A moderately wide trench runs along each side but is not continued round the ends of the barrow. On the natural level, near the east end, a heap of three or four skeletons was found, the only perfect skull from which is of a remarkably long and narrow form. . . . One of the other skulls had been forcibly cleft before burial. The only object of antiquity with the skeletons was a finely chipped arrow-head of flint, of a beautiful leaf-shape. The point of its more tapering extremity was broken off when found. It has measured 2 inches in length by 9/10 inch in breadth."

The arrowhead was similar to the one he had found five years earlier in the ruined chamber of Adam's Grave.

The time came when Bronze Age round barrows began to appear among New Stone Age long barrows, and in the end these smaller mounded tombs greatly outnumbered the others. Many of each kind have been obliterated from the countryside: it may be that the round barrows, being smaller, have suffered the most, the early excavators and other diggers beginning the destruction, the farmer's plough finishing it. Even so, in Wiltshire they still outnumber the long barrows by twenty to one, and are nowhere more numerous than on the downs north and south of the Vale of

Pewsey. Like the New Stone Age people, those of the Bronze Age had to be upland dwellers, getting their living by grazing cattle and growing corn on the open hills. You cannot go far along the Vale's downland edges without sighting a round barrow, sometimes a cluster or a line of three or four, and there are very few which do not show plainly by their sunken crowns and pitted sides that the diggers have been into them at some time or other. Each covers a one-body grave below the middle of the mound. Sometimes it contains a skeleton lying on its side in a crouching attitude, sometimes an urn with cremated bones, the practice of cremation becoming more frequent in the latter half of the Bronze Age. Now and again a second and later burial is discovered in another part of the mound. Such objects as beakers, food vessels, incense cups, weapons and personal ornaments are usually found in the graves, though there are fewer of these things when the burial followed cremation. The custom of equipping the dead for the next world has led to some surprising finds in these Bronze Age barrows. Dr Thurnam went barrow-digging where there were four on Tan Hill at the edge of the Vale, and records that in one of them, "at a depth of three feet and a half, were the burnt bones, apparently of a young female, and with them a small bead of bluish glass and three larger ones with a pendant, all of jet". The blue bead was the more surprising find. It is not a glass bead but one with a pottery-paste core covered with a blue glaze and is similar to Egyptian beads of 1600 B.C. to 1200 B.C. Mrs Cunnington states in her *Introduction to the Archæology of Wiltshire* that seventy-seven of these beads have been found in twenty-three Wiltshire barrows, and shows that this is eight more than have been found in the rest of Great Britain and western Europe. She also says: "It now seems fairly certain that those found in our Wiltshire barrows actually came from Egypt."

Britain's Bronze Age began to change into its Early Iron Age about five centuries before the Roman invasions. Most of the great ditched and banked enclosures on downland hilltops, including the one on Martinsell, were probably made by the iron-using people of those times during which Britain became a Celtic land. Sky-caught, these earthworks proclaim their presence with an emphasis that is often dramatic. Less clear on the shallowing slopes of turf surrounding them, the shapes of what were contemporary cornfields need a low sun to give the time-worn balks or lynchets dividing them the shadows which reveal their rectangles chequering the green. In the Vale of Pewsey many are visible where today's unploughed slopes of the escarpment shelve towards the valley bottom, and we now know that in at least one place at the foot of the northern downland flank there was a village in which the cultivators lived, though all that is to be seen on the site today is no more than could be seen before it was excavated—the surface of the arable field under which its remains lie. Since the uncovering of much of it by Mr and Mrs Cunnington in 1911 and 1920–22, after their attention had been drawn to it "by the unusual number of rough implements known as hammer stones that were strewn over the ploughed surface", and the publication of their account of it in 1923, the site has become famous in archæology as the Early Iron Age village at All Cannings Cross in Wiltshire.

It lies at the foot of the downs opposite the village of All Cannings and between the Devizes road and the part of the valley-side that is Tan Hill, from which a spur of down, Clifford's Hill, is thrust southward into the Vale and dies away at the roadside opposite All Cannings Cross Farm. The ground is a very gentle incline of cornland, some of it embayed by a shallow coomb in the west flank of Clifford's Hill, which rises steeply and shelters it from east winds, whilst the loftier steeps of Tan Hill, though farther away, screen it from northward weather. It is open to the full width of the Vale west of All Cannings. The last time I walked across the site in coming down the track which descends from the Tan Hill plateau to road and farm, the field was a stubble having its September ploughing and looked no different from any other harvested cornfield at the foot of these downs.

It was not possible to uncover all the village, but enough was uncovered to show that it must have been an irregular grouping of oblong dwellings of which, in the six laid bare, only the clay floors and their adjoining outside yards roughly paved with hard chalk mixed with a few flints and broken sarsen stones, or else only the paved yards, had survived. The largest floor was 16 feet by 10 feet, with a yard 27 feet by 18 feet. Light wattle-and-daub

THE VALE OF PEWSEY

construction was inferred from the absence of post-holes and the lack of any evidence of walling except a few fragments of clay, or mixed clay and chalk, partly hardened by fire, one or two showing the impression of sticks forming the wattle, and some finger marks; and from the fact that where a floor remained it was covered with a layer of burnt matter suggesting destruction of the walls by fire when the village was abandoned, and then the almost complete decay of the debris as the surface soil deepened above it. Round about the dwellings were many circular pits of various sizes. Seventy-five were found in the area excavated. Dug in the chalk, they ranged in size from a depth of several feet and diameter of 5 feet to shallow scoops only $1\frac{1}{2}$ feet across. A few of the smaller were basin-shaped, most of the others straight-sided and flat-bottomed. The excavators came to the conclusion that the largest were too small to have been used as dwellings, and that the pits were used for storing grain and other food, although some may have been rubbish pits. By Early Iron Age times the pit-granary was far from being a new thing. Storage pits in the open would, of course, need roofs, and whilst most had probably been thatched, it was discovered that some had been vaulted with domed roofs of clay. Two which had remained in an almost perfect condition showed that they were formed of a mixture of clay and broken chalk hardened by fire. The crown of the smooth upper surface of one dome had been inlaid with potsherds when the clay was wet, and that of another with small flat slabs of chalk. When a pit had this kind of roof it was entered from the side by means of a passage sloping down to the level of the bottom.

Much "habitation litter" was collected, classified and afterwards described in detail by Mrs Cunnington in her account of the excavations. Almost all the pottery appears to have been hand-shaped without the aid of a potter's wheel. Bone objects included one-piece knives made from rib bones, pointed implements, combs and needles. Among the stone objects were hammer stones, whetstones and mealing stones or saddle querns. There were spindle whorls of baked clay. The bronze objects included brooches, bracelets, tweezers, awls and a razor; the iron objects gouges, awls, knife blades, one blade of a pair of shears and ring-headed pins. The bones of domesticated animals found were identified as those of horse, ox, sheep, goat, pig and dog; and the bones of wild animals as those of red deer, fox and water-vole. The only human remains were thirty-two fragments of skull bones, not found together but scattered about among other bones and pottery that had accumulated as rubbish. One fragment of a temporal bone had been shaped into a roundel about the size of a penny and perforated so that it could be worn as a pendant. No graves were discovered; but if, as is not improbable, the dead were cremated and buried without mounds in the kind of Early Iron Age cemetery known as an urn field, the place is not likely to be a long way from the village. In her account of the settlement Mrs Cunnington reaches the conclusion that it may have been founded about 500 B.C., and says, "Judging from the accumulation of humus and debris of pottery, broken bones and the large number of pits and so on, it seems probable that the site was inhabited for some considerable time, perhaps not less than a couple of hundred years. . . . Why it should have been abandoned will probably always remain unknown." Speaking for myself now, I have sometimes wondered whether, Tan Hill being so close, the people of this lost village may have been the first to assemble on its summit to perform the pagan fire-rites that gave the hill its name.

It is along the inward or north edge of the Tan Hill summit that the great Wansdyke earthwork comes nearest to overlooking the Vale of Pewsey in the Wiltshire part of its sixty miles between the mouth of the Severn and Savernake Forest. Here its bank is the most massively broad-based and high, the ditch deepest and widest, their scale and sinuous flow matching the scale and flow of the downland undulations. Wansdyke's purpose is still very obscure, as was its date until, in 1889 and 1890, General Pitt-Rivers cut two sections through it on the downs north of Bishop's Cannings, one near Old Shepherd's shore, the other near New Shepherd's Shore. These are the names of gaps made in it by a derelict reach of the old Bath road and the present Devizes road. The presence of Roman pottery in and below the bank and the fact that a little to the west of Old Shepherd's Shore the Roman road to Bath lies under Wansdyke indicate that it can hardly be pre-Roman in date. But was it a boundary, a defence, or both? Its ditch lies along the north side, so this must have been the direction the work was intended to face, and if constructed as a massive line of defence, the direction from which the aggressor was expected to strike. Above the Vale of Pewsey, at any rate, it still looks too much of a barrier to have been only a boundary. In the words of the historian R. H. Hodgkin, "It is therefore thought to be either a late provincial-Roman or an early post-Roman work, perhaps the last great effort of the Britons to save the southwest of the island from Saxon barbarism." Wandsyke passes westward from Tan Hill to Milk Hill, and there, between it and the scarp-crest and ringed with a few hawthorns, is a dew-pond which the Saxons, in a survey of the bounds of Alton Priors in A.D. 825, named as Oxen Mere. The pond is thus known to be more than eleven centuries old.

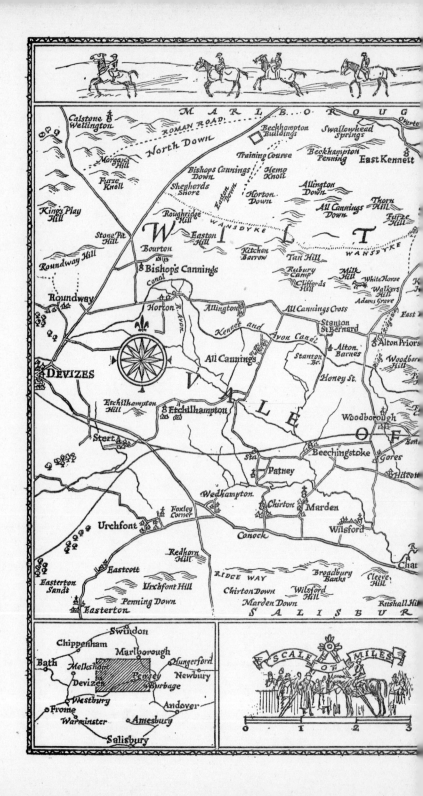

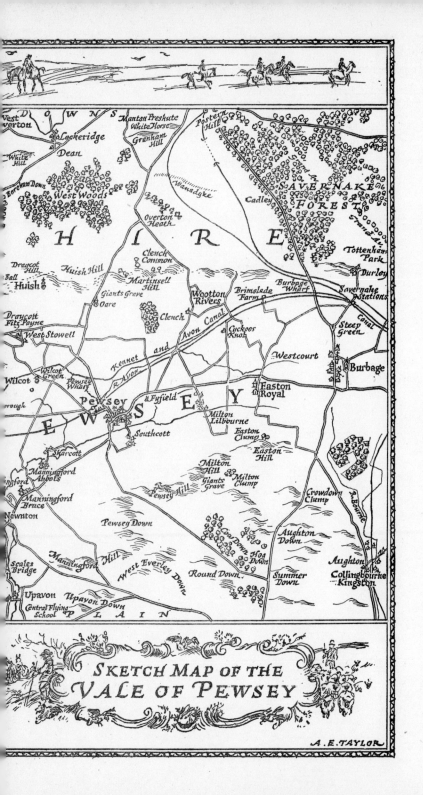

SKETCH MAP OF THE VALE OF PEWSEY

A.E. TAYLOR

INDEX

Acklea, 22

Adam's Grave, 8, 9, 18, 19, 102, 210, 213, 214

Alfred the Great, 21, 23, 168

All Cannings, 15, 35, 40, 43, 44, 138; bridge, 137, 138; church, 43, 44

— — Cross Farm, 40, 41, 217

Allington, 40, 41, 138

Alton Barnes, 8, 11, 12, 13, 19, 86, 87, 88; church, 89, 90, 96, 98

Alton Priors, 8, 15, 18, 19, 86, 87, 88; church, 87

Andrews & Dury, 19

Angelica, 51

Anglo-Saxon Chronicle, 22

Anne of Denmark, 38

Ashdown, battle of, 23

Ash tree, All Cannings churchyard, 46

Athelney, 21

Aubrey, John, 37, 38

Avebury, 6 18, 69, 76

Avon (Bristol), 3, 4

Avon (Salisbury), 2, 4, 12, 14, 15; east branch, 85, 165, 168; west branch, 14, 49–51, 53, 104, 122–124, 147

Avon gap (Salisbury Plain), 3, 14

A Wiltshire Childhood, 34, 54

Axe (Devonshire), 18

Azolla filiculoides, 143, 144

Barge Inn, 143, 144

Barrows, Bronze Age, 215, 216

Basing, battle of, 23

Bath, 3

Beads, Egyptian, 216

Beckhampton, 32

Beechingstoke, 121; parish boundary, 20

— Clump, 20, 115, 118, 119

Berkshire Downs, 23

Bishop's Cannings, 2, 6, 13, 14, 32, 34, 35; church, 35, 36, 39, 40, 96

Bottlesford, 20

Bourton, 2, 49

Bradley, A. G., 35, 189

Brentnall, H. C., 194

Brewose, William de, 80

Brickwork, 95, 124, 173

Bridges, canal, 139, 140, 141

Brimslade Farm, 138, 139, 140

Bristow Bridge, 135, 143

Broadbury Banks, 18, 19, 20

Broad Street, 19, 20

Bromsgrove Wood, 193

Building materials, 39, 44, 105, 106, 149, 163, 168, 172, 174, 176, 178, 194, 202–208

Bulb farm, Woodborough, 11

Burbage, 3, 13

— Wharf, 139

Butterflies, 75, 198

Butterfly orchid, lesser, 56

Calne, 13

Campion, red, 62

Candle-holders, 132

Cannings Marsh, 40, 59, 60

— Water, 60

Carduus tenuiflorus, 72

Caroline, Queen, 150, 151, 153

Carrel, 37
Celtic fields, 101, 185, 217
Charlton, 3, 14, 147, 148, 149; church, 149
Clatford, 6
Clay tobacco-pipes, 213
Cleeve Hill, 9, 126, 147
Clench Common, 190, 191, 202
Clifford's Hill, 6, 9, 41, 68
Clock, Wootton Rivers church, 206
Clock-House, 205
Coate, 6, 13, 32, 69
Cobbett, William, 4, 5, 6, 11, 91, 174, 175
Cob walls, 107–109, 130, 131
Cocklebury, 141, 142
Collett, Anthony, 115
Colt Hoare, Sir Richard, 111
Coombs, downland, 68, 175
Corn marigold, 115–118
Council houses, 44, 105, 106
Cunningham, T. S., 105
Cunnington, William, of Heytesbury, 111
—, Mrs B. H., 211, 212, 213, 216, 217, 218, 219
—, Mr B. H., 211, 212
Curlew, common, 61, 63–66
Cuttenham Farm, 19

Danes, 22, 23
Deane Water, 172
Development of English Building Construction, 108, 132
Devizes, 1, 6, 9, 13, 32, 35, 134
— Barracks, 11
Dewpond, 71, 220
Domesday Book, 21, 166
Dorset, 18
Dove-cote, Fyfield, 174
Draycott Hill, 9

Droves, 18, 186
Duck, Stephen, 93, 150–153, 157
Duck Feast, The, 156
Duck's Acre, 156

Early Iron Age village, All Cannings Cross, 217–219
East Anglia, 18, 22
East Kennett, 6, 86; long barrow, 6, 76
East Wick Farm, 202, 203
Easton Brook, 172
— Clump, 4, 30, 179
— Farm, 58
— Hill (Bourton) 9, 52, 54
— Hill (Easton Royal) 9
— Priory, 177, 178
— Royal, 4, 14, 177, 178, 179; church, 178
English Social History, 134
Ernle Memorial, 45
Etchilhampton, 3, 13, 32
— Hill, 1, 2, 3, 4, 9, 13, 32, 57
— Water, 60
Ethelred, 22, 23
Ethelwulf, 22

Ferraby, George, 37
Fireplace, Knap Hill, 212
Flowers, canalside, 145; marshland, 59; Martinsell, 197; riverside, 124, 125
Footpaths, 17, 18
Foxley Corner, 63
French Horn, The, 142, 143, 167
Frith Wood, 21, 27, 28, 80
Fyfield, 14, 172; mound, 174
— Manor, 173

Gandy, Ida, 34, 54
Gault, 2

Giant's Grave, Martinsell, 190, 193
— —, Milton Hill, 187, 215
Glaucous bulrush, 71
Golden Ball Hill, 9
Great Western Railway, 3, 134
Greensand, upper, 2
Grose, J. D., 72, 144
Gypsy camp, 17

Hackpen Hill, 6, 18, 76
Hare, Mrs Augustus W., 87, 92
—, Rev. Augustus W., 87, 90, 91
—, Augustus J. C., 91
Harmer, F. E., 22
Harvesting, 119, 120
Hatfield Barrow, 111
Herepath, 49, 58
Heron, 145, 146
Highways and Byways in Wiltshire, 81
Hill-games, 189
History of All Cannings, 77
Hodgkin, R. H., 220
Honey Street, 19
— — Farm, 19
Horse-trough, Pewsey, 167
Horse-ploughing, 41, 42
Horton, 2
— Bridge, 13
Housman, A. E., 31
Huish Hill, 9
Hungerford, 13
Hutton, Edward, 81

Icknield Way, 22
Imber, 18, 86
Inkpen Hill, 9
Innocent, C. F., 108, 132
Introduction to the Archæology of Wilt-shire, 216
Isle of Thanet, 22

Jack the Painter, 181
James I, 38
Jefferies, Richard, 17
Jones, Canon, 77

Keiller, Alexander, 212
Kennet and Avon Canal, 1, 3, 29, 52, 133–137, 140
Kennet River, 3; valley, 3, 6, 12, 18, 86
King-cups, 162, 163
Kitchen Barrow Hill, 68
Knap Hill, 6, 7, 9, 15, 16, 29
— — Camp, 7, 18, 211–213

Lady Bridge, Cocklebury, 135, 141, 142
Lockeridge, 6; road, 16
Locks, canal, 134, 139
Long barrow, East Kennett, 76
Long barrows, 213, 214
Lynchets, strip, 49, 126, 148, 187, 191

Macdonald, Archdeacon, 37
Machine-breakers, 91, 92
Manningford Abbots, 3, 12, 79
— Bohune, 3, 12, 79
— Bruce, 3, 12, 79, 81; church, 79–84, 96, 98
Marden, 3, 14, 23, 102–106; church, 109, 110; earthwork, 103, 111; manor-house, 106, 107
— Down, battle legend, 112
Marlborough, 12
— Downs, 1, 2
Marples, George, 183, 184
—, Morris, 180, 181, 183
Marsh orchids, 64, 65
Marten, 23
Martin, 23

Martinsell, 9, 12, 15, 67, 188, 190, 192–194; camp, 193; games, 189
— Ride, 192
Mason bees, 95, 109
Memoirs of the Parish of Bishop's Cannings, 37
Memorials of a Quiet Life, 91
Meretune, 23
Meyrick, O., 111
Milk Hill, 9, 15, 16, 67
Milton Hill, 4, 9; coomb, 175
Milton Lilbourne, 14, 174, 175, 176; church, 176; manor-house, 177
Mistle-thrush, 82
Moonraker legend, 47
Morgan's Hill, 32

Newbury, 3
Nicholas, Robert, 47, 48
North Newnton, 3, 12, 19; parish boundary, 20

Oare, 12, 13, 190
Oare Hill, 9, 12, 191
Old Sarum, 67, 76
Old Totterdown, 76
On Richmond Park and Royal Gardens, 154
Overton, 6
Oxen Mere, 220

Palmerston, Lord, 156, 157
Paradise Lost, 151
Patney, 3, 93
Pewsey, 3, 12, 13, 15, 18, 165, 166, 168, 169; mill, 166
— Feast, 169–172
— Hill, 9, 30
Phœnix Row, 169

Picked Hill, 2, 9, 13, 16, 29, 121
Pile, Robert, 181, 183
Pit-hollows, Martinsell, 191
Pitt-Rivers, General, 219
Place-Names of Wiltshire, 16, 19, 20, 59, 143, 166, 177, 188
Poems on Several Occasions, 150
Pond, All Cannings, 46
Puck Shipton, 20
Purging flax, 55

Ragwort, 72, 73
Rainscombe, 12, 13, 190, 191
— House, 12
Reading, 22, 23
Redhorn Hill, 63
Rennie, John, 134
Reredos, All Cannings, 45
Ridgeway, 6, 8, 15, 16, 18, 19, 20, 40, 86, 143, 195, 211
Rock-roses, 55
Roughridge Hill, 68
Round about Wiltshire, 35, 189
Roundway Hill, 9, 32, 50
Rural Rides, 4
Rushall, 2, 3, 14
— Hill, 9
Rybury Camp, 6, 68

St Anne's Day, 77
St Joan à Gores, 18
Salad burnet, 56
Salisbury Plain, 1, 2, 9, 11, 12, 14, 19, 30, 76
Salisbury spire, 67, 76
Sarum, See of, 35
Savernake Forest, 9, 15, 119
Scales Bridge, 2, 14, 133
Scirpus tabernæmontani, 74
Select English Historical Documents of 9th and 10th Centuries, 22

Seymour family, 177
Sharcott, 3, 18, 158, 163; bridge, 163, 164
— Barracks, 160–162
Sheep fair, Tan Hill, 70
Shepherd's Shore, New, 32, 49, 67, 219
— — Old, 38, 219
Shepherds' Steeps, 101, 187
Silbury Hill, 6, 69, 76
Skylarks, 32
Slender-flowered thistle, 72
Somerset, Duke of, 178
Southcott, 14
Spectator, 47, 151, 152
Speedwell, water, 52
Spence, J., 151
Spratt, Jack, 205, 206
Spring whitlow grass, 10
Stanley, Rev. Mr, 156
Stanton St Bernard, 138
Stellaria, 201
Stephen, King, 35
Stoats, 75
Stone curlew, 60, 61, 74, 75
Story-Maskelyne, T., 78
Stowell, 29
Studfold Hundred, 63
Sturt, 13
Swanborough Ashes, 21, 25
— Hundred, 21, 24
— Tump, 21, 23–26, 30, 80
Sword, Saxon, 212

Tan Hill, 9, 40, 41, 67–70, 113, 114, 219
— — Fair, 11, 70, 77, 78
Thames Gap, 18
Thatched roofs, 104, 105, 127, 129, 130, 149
The Poore's Arms, 147

The Thresher's Labour, 153–156
Thomas, Edward, 17, 79, 150, 153
Thorn Hill, 41
Thurnam, Dr, 214, 215, 216
Tomkins, Rev. H. G., 22
Topographical Map of Wiltshire, 19
Trevelyn, Sir G. M., 134, 174

Uffington Hill, 195; games, 189
Upavon, 12, 14
— Down, 30
— Hill, 9
Urchfont, 93
— Hill, 4, 9

Vale of Pewsey, from Walker's Hill, 9; geology and origin, 1, 2; location, 1; parishes, 15, 101, 102; shape and size, 3; streams and drainage, 2, 4

Wake, William, 47, 48
Walcway, 16
Walker, Clement, 19
Walker's Hill, 6, 7, 15, 16, 18, 19
Wansdyke, 6, 7, 15, 16, 18, 41, 67–69, 75, 76, 135, 213, 219, 220
Water speedwell, 52
Wayland's Smithy, 18
Wedhampton, 14, 32, 93
Weeds, 115
Welshway, 16, 19
— Hill, 19
Wessex, 21, 22
West Kennett long barrow, 69
West Saxon Council, 23
Wharves, canal, 136, 142, 143
Wheatears, 73, 74
White Horse, Alton Barnes, 63, 92, 102, 123, 181, 183–186

White Horse, Pewsey, 30, 169, 181, 183–187
— —, Uffington, 18, 23, 180, 185
— —, Westbury, 180
— — Vale, 76
White Horses and Other Hill Figures, 180
White Horses, scouring of, 182, 183
Wilcot, 13, 16, 29
— Manor, canal at, 142
Wildman, Major John, 178
Wilsford, 3, 14, 18, 19, 20, 122, 126–129; bridge 124; church, 131, 132
— Hill, 9
Wiltshire Archæological Magazine, 37, 77, 78, 111, 212

Wiltshire Notes and Queries, 16, 24, 105, 112
Wimborne, 23
Winchester, 22
Windmill Hill, Avebury, 212
Winterbourne, Easton Hill, 54
Wodnesbeorg, 213
Wolf Hall, 177
Woodborough, 12, 15, 19
— Hill, 2, 9, 13, 29, 121, 126
Wootton Rivers, 3, 15, 199, 200, 204; church, 206, 207; church clock, 206
— —, Manor Farm, 207, 208
— —, Rectory, 207, 208
Workway Drove, 15, 16, 18